A Buddhist Sensibility

STUDIES OF THE WEATHERHEAD EAST ASIAN INSTITUTE,
COLUMBIA UNIVERSITY

STUDIES OF THE WEATHERHEAD EAST ASIAN INSTITUTE,
COLUMBIA UNIVERSITY

The Studies of the Weatherhead East Asian Institute of Columbia University were inaugurated in 1962 to bring to a wider public the results of significant new research on modern and contemporary East Asia.

For a complete list of titles, see page 257.

A BUDDHIST SENSIBILITY

Aesthetic Education at Tibet's
Mindröling Monastery

DOMINIQUE TOWNSEND

COLUMBIA UNIVERSITY PRESS *NEW YORK*

Columbia University Press
Publishers Since 1893
New York   Chichester, West Sussex
cup.columbia.edu
Copyright © 2021 Columbia University Press
Library of Congress Cataloging-in-Publication Data
Names: Townsend, Dominique, author.
Title: A Buddhist sensibility : aesthetic education at Tibet's Mindröling
Monastery / Dominique Townsend.
Other titles: Materials of Buddhist culture
Description: New York : Columbia University Press, [2021] | Series: Studies of the
Weatherhead East Asian Institute, Columbia University | Revision of author's
thesis (doctoral)—Columbia University, 2012, titled Materials of Buddhist
culture : aesthetics and cosmopolitanism at Mindroling Monastery. |
Includes bibliographical references and index.
Identifiers: LCCN 2020028555 (print) | LCCN 2020028556 (ebook) | ISBN 9780231194860
(hardback) | ISBN 9780231194877 (trade paperback) | ISBN 9780231551052 (ebook)
Subjects: LCSH: Smin-grol-gling (Monastery : Tibet Autonomous Region, China) |
Aesthetics—Religious aspects—Buddhism. | Buddhism and art—China—Tibet
Autonomous Region. | Buddhist monasticism and religious orders—Education—
China—Tibet Autonomous Region.
Classification: LCC BQ6349.S59 T69 2021 (print) | LCC BQ6349.S59 (ebook) |
DDC 294.3/709515—dc23
LC record available at https://lccn.loc.gov/2020028555
LC ebook record available at https://lccn.loc.gov/2020028556

Columbia University Press books are printed on permanent and durable acid-free paper.
Printed in the United States of America
Cover image: Early eighteenth-century portrait of Terdak Lingpa, with his brother
Lochen Dharmaśrī (bottom left) and son Pema Gyurmé Gyatso (bottom right),
attended by monks handling material offerings.
Courtesy of Rubin Museum of Art

Contents

[v]

CONTENTS

Illustrations

Acknowledgments

Researching and writing this book has been a long and enriching process made possible by the generosity and guidance of many friends and colleagues. By a certain reckoning I started the project in 1997 as a college student traveling in India, Nepal, and Tibet, when I became interested in the history of women teachers at Mindröling. I soon learned about the tradition of laypeople studying there, which led me to the monastery's fame for Great Perfection, the literary arts, and medicine. This prompted me to investigate the history of training in the arts and ritual practices more broadly. My circuitous line of inquiry led me to become interested in the monastery's historical political connections, and from there I became interested in cultural and national identity. The framework of aesthetics occurred to me as one that could contain many aspects of Mindröling in a new and productive way. This ongoing process of discovery continues, as does my fascination with the phenomenon of Mindröling and my admiration for the people whose lives and work this book explores. As this brief summary suggests, Mindröling is a vast and complex subject—no single history can attend to its every aspect. I have been guided by my interests as well as by the serendipity of research findings, interpersonal relationships, and lacunae in the field of Tibetan Buddhist studies. Being interested in diverse topics required that I seek out the expertise of many people, only some of whom I can name here.

ACKNOWLEDGMENTS

I'm grateful to Gray Tuttle, who believed unwaveringly in the value of this project from the beginning of my graduate studies and provided a steady flow of insightful questions and historiographical guidance. Janet Gyatso's keen observations over the years pushed the research and sharpened the writing immeasurably. Discussing the ideas that fuel this project with them has been one of the greatest pleasures of my career thus far. I offer my deep thanks also to Bernard Faure, Michael Puett, and Chün-Fang Yü for their input through the process of this book's first life as my dissertation. Robert Thurman introduced me to Tibetan Buddhist studies as an undergraduate and read through the Dalai Lama's letters with me as a doctoral candidate. Reading and debating the Tibetan with him was a joy. Leonard van der Kuijp's comments on the early research papers that seeded the book helped me clarify the historical context. Tashi Tsering generously shared insights and materials with me. Hubert Decleer's love for Tibetan texts and his ethical commitments to scholarship sparked my excitement for developing my own research methodologies. Gene Smith's wondrous knowledge and endless enthusiasm fueled my interest in Mindröling, and his enticing clues and suggestions are still bearing fruit.

Over the years Pema Bhum has read countless Tibetan texts with me, shared references, and fielded my questions and theories with erudition, insight, curiosity, and humor. Lauran Hartley has provided structural support and resources at every turn. During the revision process, Riga Shakya provided valuable perspective on lay biographies in Tibetan literature. He also contributed some outstanding translations to the first part of chapter 5. Sean Price generously shared hard to find sources with me—I only wish I'd had more time to make use of them! Lama Gyurme shed light on the monastic curriculum and on the history of the murals and architecture of the temples in Tibet. He also told me illuminating stories about his life as a monk and artist at the monstery. Thanks to Berthe Jansen, who generously shared her knowledge of Mindröling's history with me, and whose expertise on monastic guidelines helped me understand Mindröling in sociological context. My thanks to Kunchog Tseten, whose expertise on Mindröling's medical tradition was a boon in my final stages of writing. I am also grateful for Chime Lama's feedback as a reader. Thanks to Sam Brawand for expert attention to the many details of preparing the manuscript for publication. Thanks also to everyone at TBRC/BDRC—Jann Ronis and Nawang Trinley, especially.

Many more scholars and friends have read and responded to drafts of chapters or related articles and conference papers and discussed the book's themes with me. I'm indebted to Julie Regan, Annabella Pitkin, and Ben Bogin, who all read advanced chapter drafts. Thanks too to Holly Gayley, Nicole Willock, Sarah Jacoby, Lama Jabb, Charlene Makley, Jake Dalton, Andy Quintman, Kurtis Schaeffer, Nancy Lin, Christie Kilby, Michael Sheehy, Joshua Shapiro, Alex Gardner, Benno Weiner, Michael Monhart, Peter Moran, Bryan Cuevas, and Douglas Duckworth. I'm grateful to the curators and staff at the Rubin Museum, who enhanced my appreciation for Mindröling's visual arts. I'm deeply grateful for the institutional and community support of Bard College. My brilliant colleagues there have helped me develop this book for an interdisciplinary readership.

The members of the Aesthetics of Religious Belonging workshop—Elizabeth Williams-Oerberg, Trine Brox, Erica Baffelli, Paulina Kolata, Jane Caple, Frederik Schröer, Johan Elverskog, and Levi McGlaughlin—make my obsession with Buddhist aesthetics seem perfectly ordinary. My thanks to them for buoying my spirits and helping me hone the critical terms for this study.

I've profited greatly over the years from discussing art and images with Jeff Watt of Himalayan Art Resources. I also thank those who shared photographs of Mindröling monastery in Tibet with me—Thomas Laird, Leigh Miller, Khandro Rinpoché, and Rob Linrothe, with whom I exchanged many stimulating e-mails about the Mindröling wall paintings and temple layout.

I'm very grateful to everyone who has worked on this book at Columbia University Press, especially my editor, Caelyn Cobb. Monique Briones has provided expert and energetic guidance on the technical details of preparing the manuscript. Leslie Kriesel's meticulous editing of the manuscript improved the final product immensely. They've made the publishing process a pleasure.

I express my sincere appreciation to the Schoff Fund at the University Seminars at Columbia University for their help in publication. Material in this work was presented to the University Seminar: Buddhist Studies. Thanks in particular to Zhaohua Yang for inviting me to participate in the seminar.

Above all, I extend my deepest admiration and gratitude to Jetsün Khandro Rinpoché and Jetsün Dechen Paldrön, who first inspired me to begin this research. I'm also indebted to all the monastic and lay members of the Mindröling community worldwide, who have fielded questions and guided my research over the years.

And at last, I extend my gratitude to my family and dear friends, especially Aaron and Sage William, who have been by my side every step of the way with brilliant questions, kind reminders, support, and love.

Thank you, all.

A Note on Translations and Transliterations

Unless otherwise noted, all translations are mine. Generally I phoneticize Tibetan names according to the Tibetan & Himalayan Library's phonetics guidelines, with some exceptions. The variation in English phoneticization of some names reflects my effort to use the spelling preferred by living people to whom I refer. Those spellings are different from THL's system. All Tibetan names and terms are listed in the index using the Wylie system of transliteration. Where appropriate, I include the Wylie in parantheses within the text.

I refer to three monastic "catalogues" (*dkar chag*). To distinguish them, I use English-language titles that are based on elements of the Tibetan original. In the case of the *Mirror of Memory Catalogue*, I adapt the poetic title. For the *Lamp of Teachings Catalogue* I adapt the editor's pen name. This publication includes seventeenth- and eighteenth-century documents, one of which is the third catalogue. This I refer to descriptively as the *Temple Wall Catalogue* because it was displayed in calligraphy on the walls of the monastery.

Introduction

Buddhist Aesthetics, the Cultivation of the Senses, and Beauty's Efficacy

We need see nothing wrong with the presence of objects, and even wealth, in religious practice. A small group of erudite monks within the Buddhist tradition has championed the idea that the highest spiritual goals can only be pursued in isolation from the material world. But *we* need not adopt this position. Nor did most Buddhists ever adopt a radical rejection of the material world.

—JOHN KIESCHNICK, *THE IMPACT OF BUDDHISM ON CHINESE MATERIAL CULTURE*

THE MAIN CHARACTERS of this story—the visionary Terdak Lingpa (1646–1714), the Fifth Dalai Lama, Ngawang Lobsang Gyatso (1617–1682), the regent, Desi Sangyé Gyatso (1653–1705), the scholar monk Lochen Dharmaśrī (1654–1717), and their inner circle—lived during the seventeenth and early eighteenth centuries in Central Tibet, in and around the city of Lhasa.

Mindröling, the monastic institution they established in 1676, became an influential center for Tibetan Buddhist practice and cultural production, crystallizing the characteristics of the Ancient or Nyingma (*rnying ma*) school.[1] The institution is still vibrant today with locations in Tibet, India, Mongolia, Taiwan, and the United States.

There are ways this history, which spans the first approximately fifty years of the monastery's existence, is particular and perhaps even unique to Mindröling's time and place in early modern Central Tibet.[2] At the same time, Mindröling stands out as one excellent example of how monastic institutions have served as civilizational centers for centuries across the Buddhist world. Like Samyé monastery in the eighth century,

Figure 0.1 Mindröling monastery courtyard, circa 2007.
Photograph by Leigh Miller

Mindröling was the product of a shared vision between temporal and religious authorities.

Lhasa: A Cosmopolitan Capital

At the time of Mindröling's founding, Lhasa was the heart of the Tibetan Buddhist world—a large area that spanned parts of what is now northern India, Nepal, Sikkim, Bhutan, Mongolia, and western China. Lhasa was a cosmopolitan crossroads[3] and a mecca for East and Inner Asian Buddhist pilgrims and traders, as well as missionaries and explorers. In Mindröling's early days, Lhasa was also the center of a new effort to unify the Tibetan polity under the rule of the Ganden Podrang (*dga' ldan pho brang*) government of the Dalai Lama and his Virtuous Way or Géluk (*dge lugs*) school. Founded in 1642, this government operated in fluctuating conflict and concert with various Tibetan, Nepali, Mongol, and Qing actors. The image of Tibet as extremely isolated is not accurate for the period this book concerns, and in fact Tibet was never truly isolated from its neighbors. This misperception reflects later Qing restrictions on travel from Tibet to India, as well as twentieth-century attempts of some Tibetans to resist imperialist influences through strategies of isolationism.[4]

An Early Modern Center for Tibetan Cultural Production

The founders, who were members of the aristocratic and illustrious Nyö (*gnyos*) clan and part of a lineage of Great Perfection (*rdzogs chen*) masters, established Mindröling near enough to Lhasa for its members to take part in this cosmopolitan milieu but far away enough to serve, ideally, as a retreat from the demands and distractions of the city. In keeping with this geographic situation between the court and the cave, Mindröling's influence reached beyond the scope of doctrinal Buddhist subjects, pervading worldly matters[5] and disseminating knowledge necessary for bureaucrats and literati as well as renunciants. Thus integrating the Buddhist and worldly spheres, Mindröling's founders helped materialize a Tibetan ideal of joining religion and society.

This is thanks largely to the fact that Mindröling was a center for training in *rikné* (*rig gnas*), which is often translated as "arts and sciences" and sometimes glossed as "culture," but which I translate more literally as "fields of knowledge" to convey the sense of disciplines of learning as "fields" in English. There are five major and five minor disciplines in this Classical Indian system, which was popularized in Tibet by Sakya Paṇḍita (1182–1251). The major fields are plastic arts, logic, grammar, medicine, and "inner science" or Dharma. The minor fields are synonyms, mathematics and astrology, drama, poetry, and composition.[6] In particular, Mindröling was known until the twentieth century for the literary arts, medicine, and astrology.

At the same time, and no less crucially, Mindröling was a paragon of monastic discipline, a model for ritual practice, textual compilation and redaction, the Tibetan Treasure or *terma* (*gter ma*) tradition, and a concerted effort to institutionalize the Buddhist ideal of an impartial worldview described by the Tibetan adjective *rimé* (*ris med*). Later this term became associated with nonsectarianism, but in Mindröling's early documents it

[3]

maintains the broader significance of an impartial, unprejudiced point of view that is not limited to sectarian matters but ideally encompasses all aspects of experience. Through their inclusive methods,[7] Mindröling's founders exemplified a Tibetan Buddhist, and specifically Nyingma, sensibility based in the philosophical views of the Great Perfection for which their family was already famous when the Fifth Dalai Lama sponsored the new monastery.[8]

Beyond literary arts, the monastery's influence extended into various other aesthetic spheres and artistic media—specifically music, dance, the making of mandalas, monastic sartorial styles, and incense making. In short, Mindröling's purview encompassed all the senses. The founders effectively established their institution as a center for ritual early on, in part by holding large-scale ritual performances such as an event in 1691 with hundreds of lamas from across Central and Eastern Tibet in attendance.[9] Activities like these put Mindröling on the map and helped spread its reputation for precision and excellence in ritual arts.

In these ways, Mindröling came to hold sway far beyond its monastery walls and the Lhasa region. As an educational hub, Mindröling became a civilizational center for the ritual and artistic media practices that shape and exemplify Tibetan Buddhist aesthetics.[10] Paying attention to its complex role in Tibetan history sheds light on the productive relationship between Buddhist institutions and cultural production more broadly and demonstrates how aesthetics can function as a connective tissue between Buddhist and worldly engagements.

An Educational Center with a Lasting Legacy

Once Mindröling's influence was established, one of the main means of maintaining it was through education. First and foremost, its students were monastics who learned a combination of reading and writing, deportment and memorization, ritual, the fields of knowledge, and meditative practices, depending on their interests and capacities. Lay students, mainly aristocrats, also studied at the monastery. Their role as sponsors and protectors was essential to Mindröling history, especially after Zungar Mongol troops destroyed the monastery in 1717.

Members of other Nyingma institutions also experienced violent persecution during this period, but the decades prior were extremely productive in terms of the establishment of formal monastic institutions in the Nyingma school. The six major Nyingma monasteries in Central and Eastern Tibet were founded and expanded between the mid seventeenth century and early eighteenth century.

From its early days until the mid-twentieth century, Mindröling was a model for other institutions, especially in its ritual traditions. It was also a locus of elite education for Central Tibetan aristocrats who would go on to become government officials, as well as monks, ritual experts, and meditators. Beyond the monastery proper, teachers who trained in literary arts at Mindröling went on to teach at Lhasa's most prestigious schools, where they prepared students for bureaucratic and diplomatic careers. Mindröling monks served as private tutors for young aristocrats being educated in their family homes. In short, it was the place for the cultivation of style and cosmopolitan aesthetics among the Tibetan literati and aristocracy as well as a model for both ritual and renunciation. The systematic, if implicit attention paid to aesthetics during its early days helped the monastery to become a place where Tibetan literati distilled and cultivated the tastes, skills, and sensibilities associated with cultural production.

As a result, practitioners from across the Tibetan Buddhist world traveled there to study and observe or take part in large-scale ritual performances. Moreover, according to a Mindröling monk I interviewed in 2016, the prestige of studying at Mindröling was so great that there were many stories of people who *had not* studied there claiming that they had. This anecdotal claim reflects an attitude I frequently encountered in my research in Central and Eastern Tibet, suggesting that Mindröling's aura of excellence was long lasting and highly valued across diverse geographical regions.

More Than One Way to Renounce

Mindröling's role as a civilizational center complicates the view that Buddhism is defined primarily by a radical rejection of worldly learning and materiality. But this is not to discount the fundamental importance of renunciation. Many Buddhist practitioners in general, and Mindröling figures in particular, demonstrate remarkable detachment from the material world, as well as even more significant detachment from objects of mental and emotional fixation. However, Mindröling's example reminds us that the ideal of renunciation is about uprooting attachment itself, not necessarily about rejecting materiality—certainly not when it comes to ritual. The problem is attachment, not the objects of attachment, be they material or otherwise.

Any idea that Buddhist institutions and cultural production are at odds is rooted in part in important Buddhist assertions about the ultimately illusory nature of reality, impermanence, and the liberating effects of nonattachment. This is especially important in regard to things that tend to elicit desire and fixation, such as high-quality objects made of precious materials. Why then are Tibetan Buddhist temples and shrines where practitioners gather to make offerings and conduct rituals full of such images? Clearly material objects can do more than elicit attachment. They can also support Buddhist practice.

Furthermore, Buddhist claims about the dangers and limits of engaging with the senses and their objects get confused with a modern Buddhist apologist perspective that suggests Buddhist practitioners and institutions are concerned not with the material, but only with the "spiritual." On the contrary, in Buddhist temples and shrines around the world, artistic and ritual media in the form of relics, texts, implements, and images are the physical embodiment and material support (rten) for Buddhist practice and devotion. Many teachings assert that after ritual consecration, images of Buddha actually embody the Buddha's presence rather than merely representing it.[11] The act of making material offerings to teachers, protectors, and enlightened beings is a mainstay of Buddhist practice. Therefore, with full acknowledgment of the importance of renunciation in Buddhism, in this book I take an interest in how Mindröling's founding members skillfully navigated the complex interplay among renunciation, the senses, and materiality.

In keeping with the Tibetan Buddhist theory that the Two Systems of Buddhist and worldly expertise (lugs gnyis) should be integrated, various overlapping factors converged to make Mindröling a center for both renunciation and cultural production. The founders were focused on the benefits of Buddhist practice for the ideal purpose of awakening and the utility of worldly knowledge, particularly relevant to bureaucrats, civil servants, and diplomats. At the same time, they were concerned with the reputation and longevity of Mindröling as a monastery, and with the well-being of their students and their descendants.

An Inclusive Approach to Institution Building

To build such an institution, Terdak Lingpa and those who helped him found Mindröling took an inclusive approach. They had to ensure that the monastery would thrive in a time when the Nyingma school was under threat and the general climate was marked by violent shifts in power. The dangers of forced conversion, annihilation, or reduced material support from lay patrons were very real concerns.

From the first generation of Mindröling, women held a remarkable position as prominent teachers. While the monastic guidelines (bca' yig) strictly forbid women in general from entering the areas where the monks lived, the existence of several outstanding female teachers and practitioners, beginning with Terdak Lingpa's mother and daughter and continuing up to the present day with Jetsün Khandro Rinpoché, is evidence of Mindröling's openness. All the most prominent examples were born within Terdak Lingpa's family and therefore had special status. Nevertheless, as I illustrate in the following chapters, Mindröling's founders were relatively inclusive of women beyond the family, as well.

Engagement with practitioners of all Tibetan schools, in a direct precursor to the celebration of nonsectarianism that emerged in Eastern Tibet in the nineteenth century, unequivocally is a feature of Mindröling's early identity. This is made abundantly clear through the lists of teachings received, collected works, and letters of the founders.

As a noncelibate tantric expert and Treasure revealer, Terdak Lingpa had an education and path distinct from that of his brother Lochen Dharmaśrī, who was a fully ordained monk. Beyond the leadership roles of these founding figures and their descendants, the paths of students at the monastery were also varied. Although aristocratic laypeople studied there, the institution was first and foremost a monastery, where most of the approximately three hundred and thirty students were monks.

Some of those monks excelled in the foundational education that included memorization of key texts, performance of rituals, Great Perfection meditation, and studying the worldly fields of knowledge. Other monks failed their basic exams and struggled to conduct the rituals that were the mainstay of community activity. Still other students were noncelibate religious experts, laypeople of the ruling class, and women. There were monks who came from less privileged backgrounds as well as members of the ruling class.[12] The institution was made up of a variety of people on a variety of Buddhist paths, and its success depended on each of them fulfilling their role in a way that would satisfy sponsors. Some students were in long-term retreat and some were experts in the artistic media necessary for Mindröling's high-profile ritual performances.

All these roles involved cultivating an attitude of relative renunciation, even for a young man studying at the monastery for a couple of years before returning to multiple lovers and a career in politics (as we will see in chapter 5). From the perspective of the founders, the vows and renunciation of a tantric practitioner such as Terdak Lingpa are more advanced and difficult to maintain than those of a celibate monk or nun. This is because the outer, physical signs of renunciation associated with monastic life are easier to observe and control than the subtle renunciation of a tantric master.[13] These roles all involved cultivating a degree of expertise in aesthetic activities, whether composing a diplomatic letter in verse or visualizing an elaborately adorned bodhisattva.

A Cosmopolitan Worldview Based in Buddhist Philosophy and Pragmatism

I use the term "cosmopolitanism" to characterize the mentality and style exemplified and cultivated at Mindröling.[14] To reflect on its suitability to a study of seventeenth-to-eighteenth century Tibet and its relevance to Mindröling in particular, I draw on this statement:

> The crux of the idea of moral cosmopolitanism is that each human being has equal moral worth and that equal moral worth generates certain moral responsibilities that have universal scope. Cosmopolitanism's force can well be explained by examining what the position excludes. For instance, cosmopolitanism rules out assigning ultimate (rather than derivative) value to collective entities such as nations or states, and it also rules out positions that assign no

moral value to some people, or that weigh the value that people have differentially according to characteristics like ethnicity, race or nationality.[15]

Applied to the context of Mindröling's early days, the term certainly does not signify what it means in a world made up of nation states. But the mentality expressed in many of the documents analyzed in this book does "rule out assigning ultimate (rather than derivative) value to collective entities." In the case of early modern Tibet, those were not nations but clans, religious groups, regional and institutional entities, and shifting imperial and military power bases. At Mindröling, the relative inclusion of women and the embrace of both religious and worldly learning are subtle expressions of this underlying view.

Moreover, cosmopolitanism here does not suggest the absence of a strong sense of identity.[16] I invoke a definition of cosmopolitanism not limited to any particular polity, but rather a more broadly encompassing worldview or mentality. In a time marked by violent sectarianism and major political power shifts, Mindröling's founders planted the seeds for a cosmopolitan institution by cultivating an institutional identity that was distinctively Nyingma but at the same time committed to an ethos of impartiality.

Aesthetics as an Implicit Category in Tibetan Sources

Such a range of activities, all focused on refining and training the senses, reminds us that beyond Mindröling, aesthetics has played a central role in Tibetan Buddhist experience. In particular, Mindröling's role within the fledgling Tibetan polity necessitated negotiating the potentials and pitfalls of worldly learning and the senses. For example, as a center for education in the literary arts, Mindröling trained teachers who went on to instruct members of the ruling class, some of whom also studied for a period of time at the monastery. This role was inherently political since writing skills, including rhetoric, composition, use of metaphors, and metrics were integral to positions of political authority.

However, these negotiations did not result in an explicit theory of aesthetics. Rather, Terdak Lingpa and his cohort expressed the significance of aesthetics discreetly, pervasively, and manifestly throughout their work.

The concern is evident in their attention to the details of how to conduct rituals properly and gracefully, the types and qualities of materials used in temples and images, the equation of beauty with nobility in biographic writing, the valorization of eloquence in writing and elegance in handwriting, and the cultivation of aesthetic skills. These are but a few of the implicit means by which the interest in aesthetics is apparent.

This is of course not the only important aspect of Mindröling, and it is a subtle but prevalent theme in the primary sources I employ, including biographies, letters, instructions for practice, monastic histories, curricula, and catalogues of materials offered to Buddhist masters and monasteries. Given the focus here, the style and formal qualities of these sources are as important as the content, although they are more difficult to evaluate and convey in translation. The textual sources are primarily from the seventeenth and eighteenth centuries, with some twentieth-century supplementary texts, all composed by people within or close to the Mindröling lineage. Different genres treat material culture in distinct ways.

For instance, biographies and monastic catalogues, two major genres of Tibetan literature, both pay attention to materiality and aesthetics, but they take very different tacks. Biographies tend to weave objects into life stories, illustrating the significance of events—such as encounters between important religious and temporal leaders—with material exchanges, consecrations, and ritual performances that are defined in part by the media being employed and the physical space being transformed. Monastic catalogues, by contrast, weave mythical and historical narratives about the monastery into the lists and descriptions of the materials the monastery comprises and contains.

Both genres pay close attention to objects such as paintings and sculptures; temple and stupa architecture; cloth and clothing; ritual objects such as horns, drums, bells, and vajras; relics from the cremated remains of previous teachers; jewels and fabrics donated, etc. Far from precluding a concurrent focus on topics such as philosophy and renunciation, which are also pervasive, attention to materiality and aesthetics are part of the same fabric of Buddhist cultural production. In short, both take for granted that materiality is part of Buddhist practice and experience. By approaching a spectrum of Tibetan genres with an eye toward materiality, we find a strong and pervasive concern with aesthetics.

The Power of Buddhist Aesthetics: Ritual Efficacy

What do I mean by Buddhist aesthetics? To begin, the standard scholarly definition of "aesthetics" to mean a developed theory of art and beauty, or the philosophy of art, is relevant here, but overly narrow. In popular usage the term sometimes is negatively associated with a focus on the superficial and an overvaluing of beauty at the expense of more profound and meaningful concerns. In contrast, I evoke the term's more foundational definition, "Of or pertaining to things perceptible to the senses, things material."[17] This definition eschews negative associations to focus on the objects of the senses and sensory perception, so central to Buddhist philosophy, ritual, and experience. I am also interested in the affective and emotional responses associated with sensory experience. This approach is in keeping with a turn in religious studies toward the study of materiality and the senses.[18]

There is no single classical Tibetan term that neatly translates as "aesthetics." There are, however, several modern ones. Since the 1980s a trend in Tibetan scholarship, in conversation with a trend in Chinese scholarship, has yielded a new field of study around Tibetan aesthetics. In China, the period just after the Cultural Revolution was characterized by "aesthetics fever."[19] In the modern Tibetan scholarly context the terms used for "aesthetics" are more specifically translated "skill or capacity in magic or illusion" or "art" (*sgyu rtsal*), "skill or capacity in beauty, elegance, and power" (*mdzes rtsal*), or less commonly "knowledge of things of beauty, elegance, and power" (*mdzes chos rig pa*). The latter is sometimes also translated as "fine arts."

In the late seventeenth and early eighteenth centuries, the founders of Mindröling frequently employed similar terms, particularly focused on advanced practitioners' mastery over illusory experience. In writing about topics such as temple construction, ritual music, and the history of the founding family, they also use phrases related to beauty and sensory pleasure, including "pleasant" (*snyan*), "beautiful" or "elegant" (*mdzes*), and "attractive" (*yid 'ong*) without designating a category of "aesthetics" per se.

In the same vein, the Fifth Dalai Lama writes this in praise of Terdak Lingpa: "renowned for engaging in whatever is suitable for the capacities and senses of your disciples, excellent or ordinary, the melody of your divine drum beautifies the hearing of all beings."[20] Here the author equates the mastery of aesthetics—"engaging in whatever is suitable for the capacities and senses"—with the ability to engage beneficially with others. The Dalai Lama thus implies that the affective responses elicited through Terdak Lingpa's aesthetic work are transformative for all beings, and he stresses the benefit for Tibetans in particular.

In another example, in a treatise on ritual music, Terdak Lingpa writes that music must be "melodious, appealing, beautiful, and pleasant."[21] All these qualities are associated with the efficacy of the ritual.[22] Working to please the senses not only is relevant in relating to other humans but also shapes considerations about how to relate to supernatural beings, buddhas, bodhisattvas, and other deities, and in turn supports successful practice.

Offerings and Aesthetics

This becomes paramount when making offerings. Whether to teachers, protectors, or enlightened beings, making offerings arguably is the most common type of Buddhist practice. As in ordinary gift-giving, in the context of ritual offering, the object should appeal to the tastes of the recipient. If the object does not adhere to the ritual specifications, for instance if it is flawed aesthetically according to the tastes of that particular deity, the offering will not do its intended ritual work. But how can one know the tastes of deities? This is perhaps a question without an answer, but one way to approach it is to rely on the visionary insights of people like Terdak Lingpa.

At Mindröling, the ritual music, dance, mandalas, etc., are designed and produced according to the pure visions (*dag snang*) of Terdak Lingpa. They are therefore considered authoritative. Ritual manuals based on his visions instruct practitioners to make offerings correctly, and beauty is not always an explicit concern. However, if an object is not pleasing to the recipient, it will not be effective. The offering need not be "beautiful" by standards other than those established within the framework of the ritual, but it must be correct, and to be correct it must fit the tastes of the intended recipient.

This is complex because Tibetan Buddhist practitioners make offerings to enlightened beings who personify both pacific and fierce characteristics.

They also make offerings to territorial deities, teachers, and political rulers. These rituals support both sublime and mundane aims, and like people, deities have widely varying tastes. For instance, fierce deities have a taste for blood, so in the ritual context of making offerings to them, blood would qualify as pleasing to *their* senses and therefore would be the correct offering.[23]

In monastic music, for instance, hitting one wrong note pollutes the efforts of all the musicians. The wrong note inhibits the effectiveness of the ritual since it will not be pleasing to the deity to whom it is offered; depending on the music, it might also sour the pleasure of the human audience. Likewise, a painting that does not adhere to prescribed specifications is not effective as a consecrated object of worship—and Buddhist ritual experts may refuse to consecrate an image that they see as incorrectly executed.

Distinct artistic media serve to facilitate a range of aesthetic experiences for humans as well as deities. The intended sound of Tibetan Buddhist liturgical music, the accurate proportions of a Buddha image, and the appropriate colors for a mandala have meaning beyond how they look to the maker and the viewer, and the sense of whether the work is good is closely related to whether it is executed correctly. The results have an effect on the human viewer as well as the formal recipient, since these artistic media are meant to elicit and support thoughts and feelings that further Buddhist aims.

Buddhism and Worldly Life

While aesthetics is an implicit theoretical category, the Tibetan concept of the proper integration of Buddhism and worldly life is explicit in the textual sources for this book. The concept of the "Two Laws" (*khrims gnyis*) or the related "Two Systems" (*lugs gnyis*) helps frame the range of subjects taught and practiced at Mindröling. These phrases are common in biographical materials describing Terdak Lingpa's family members, suggesting that they modeled the appropriate balance of Buddhist and worldly authority. These terms, which are by no means particular to authors associated with Mindröling, signify mastery of Buddhist philosophy and practice on the one hand, and worldly knowledge and authority on the other.[24] They are also effectively equivalent with the concept of the ideal integration of religion and politics (*chos srid zung 'brel*), which was central to the Fifth Dalai Lama and Desi Sangyé Gyatso's state-building project.[25]

The bridging of religion and politics is a familiar theme in writing on Tibet thanks to the institution of the Dalai Lama as Tibet's joint religious and political leader, a position that was consolidated during the Fifth's tenure. Over time, the individuals who held the position have had varying levels of political power—some have been extremely powerful and some have had only symbolic power. The Fifth Dalai Lama (and the Thirteenth Dalai Lama in the twentieth century) exercised considerably more political authority than any of the other men born into their incarnation line.[26] The Fifth Dalai Lama was not the first Tibetan monk to hold political power; this dynamic goes back to at least the eleventh century.

When faced with the demands of such a role, it becomes critical to ask, how are the Two Systems properly integrated? How can Buddhism be joined with worldly life without being corrupted? Aesthetics provides the connective tissue to join the two spheres.

The founders of Mindröling modeled the proper application of aesthetics through how they wrote and what they wrote about. Their oeuvres, the rituals they established, and the curricula they designed were sculpted for varied audiences in various contexts, in a way that was both appropriate for their moment and long lasting. Their efforts shaped Mindröling's impact on other Nyingma institutions, which has remained strong over the centuries. In short, Mindröling's special purview encompassed the Buddhist and the worldly through mastery over a particularly Tibetan Buddhist sensibility. By demonstrating how the two systems could be balanced, the institution embodied and imparted practices for being a cultured and authoritative member of Tibet's early modern society. This influence extended beyond Central Tibet through Mindröling's complex monastic network, the reliability of its ritual and textual corpus, and practitioners traveling there to study.

Mastery of the Two Systems required a carefully honed methodology and pedagogy. It is doubtful that Mindröling's founders could have achieved this balance if they had not been highly educated members of the upper class. They were privileged with outstanding training in both worldly and Buddhist subjects. Moreover, they had a well-established hereditary lineage on which to base the new institution.

[14]

In contrast to the Mindröling founders' embrace of the Two Systems, the Fifth Dalai Lama's Géluk school colleagues appear to have experienced significant ambivalence about the value of the worldly side of the equation. Is it a good use of one's time as a Buddhist to learn ornate poetry, astrology, medicine, or even philosophy? The answers are not obvious. On the one hand, it is essential that Buddhist teachers learn to be persuasive about the teachings of the Buddha, which involves rhetoric, a good sense of meter, eloquence. Moreover, omniscience means knowing *everything*. But on the other hand, life is short, and perhaps one ought to dedicate all one's energy to the Dharma alone. These questions have long histories in Indian and Tibetan Buddhist intellectual circles and were debated heatedly during the period of Mindröling's founding.

An Old Conundrum Becomes Urgent

In the very first pages of the Fifth Dalai Lama's autobiography, he expressed regret at not being educated thoroughly in the Two Systems, as were members of the hereditary lineage at Mindröling. He was aware of his need for expertise in both spheres, as a political and religious leader, and regretted that his training in worldly subjects was lacking.[27] This statement might be rhetorical, since clearly he was well versed in subjects such as ornate poetry. Perhaps he was responding to members of his school who expressed ambivalence about the proper place of the worldly part of the Two Systems. Some prominent Gelukpa scholars asserted that worldly learning is less valuable than religious learning.[28] Yet thanks to the nature of the Dalai Lama's new role, during the period when Mindröling was founded, it was urgent to establish institutions in which the Two Systems could be integrated. Mindröling's approach to education was one solution.

While some contemporaries of Terdak Lingpa and the Fifth Dalai Lama were suspicious about the value of worldly fields of learning, the founders of Mindröling appear to have been confident that the apparent tension between Buddhist learning and worldly learning could be negotiated. This can be explained in part by the fact that in their particular Buddhist philosophical framework, all seeming binaries should be understood as reflecting the nondual relationship of samsara (life as we know it) and nirvana (a state of liberation or enlightenment), or what are known in

Mahāyāna Buddhism as "the two truths" (*bden gnyis*) of ultimate and conventional reality. This is apparent in Terdak Lingpa's writing in the monastery's original catalogue, which was posted on the courtyard wall. Here he equates the physical structures of the monastery with expression of the two truths, especially for those who have trouble seeing the ultimate nature of things.[29]

That said, by the same logic, members of the Dalai Lama's Géluk school should not have been troubled by the apparent tension between Buddhism and worldly knowledge and authority. This difference in view highlights the special significance of Mindröling during its foundational period, which was also the seminal period of the Dalai Lama's new government. The religious and the secular somehow had to be reconciled, and the founders of Mindröling had the necessary expertise to reconcile them, systemically.

The Right Time and Place

In an interview with the late Gene E. Smith about Terdak Lingpa's Treasure collection, Smith said, "the Mindröling *terma* was just perfect in its construction. It was just the right *terma* for the particular time. If you look at the whole structure, it makes sense as a tradition."[30]

Although he and his family members were steeped in the various fields of classical learning, Terdak Lingpa's defining characteristic was not his monumental scholarship. Rather, he is known above all as a discoverer of concealed Treasures (*gter ma*).[31] Within his Treasure corpus are works focusing on the bodhisattva of compassion, the bodhisattva of wisdom, and the tradition of "Cutting Through" (*gcod*), among others. He stands as an example of a Great Treasure Revealer (*gter ston chen po*) since he discovered Treasures from all three major categories (relating to Padmasambhava, relating to Avalokiteśvara, and relating to Great Perfection) and the complete collection of his Treasures is understood to contain all that is needed to achieve enlightenment.[32]

Just as his Treasures appeared at the right time and place, so too were his family's expertise in the worldly fields of knowledge and their familiarity with the Two Systems well timed for his context. Moreover, the systematic

and inclusive approach he and his fellow founders took in institution building was in harmony with the efforts of the Dalai Lama and Sangyé Gyatso
to develop a reliable bureaucracy to unify and govern Tibet.

Aesthetics and Community Formation

This book is less concerned with the joining of Buddhism and politics than
with the intimately related dynamics of Buddhism and cultural production. That said, cultural capital and political authority are connected.[33]
Indeed, Mindröling played a vital role in the Fifth Dalai Lama's vision of a
centralized Tibetan polity, as a site of ritual activities, including ritual
warfare.[34] The Dalai Lama intended for Mindröling's rituals to unite
Tibetan regions and safeguard them from enemies. Terdak Lingpa appears
to have been less interested in political authority per se than in strategically aligning Mindröling so as to have the best possibility of success and
survival.

In this context, what is the connection between aesthetics and politics?
"Aesthetics can be taken as the space in which the limits of the political
itself are susceptible of being retraced or redrawn."[35] This was certainly the
case during the period when Mindröling was founded. How, then, did its
founders enact their role in the formation and cohesion of the broader
Tibetan Buddhist community? Through the aesthetic practices at the heart
of the monastery, Mindröling secured its place and contributed immeasurably to what we might call a "community of Tibetan Buddhist sense." As
Jacques Rancière puts it, "A community of sense is a certain cutting out of
space and time that binds together practices, forms of visibility, and pat-
terns of intelligibility."[36] In the early modern Tibetan context, the community forged by Mindröling generated a relatively cohesive sensibility across
time and space.

Mindröling as Perfect Buddhafield and a Complex Human Space

How should we categorize an institution—a school and a monastery—that
was a center for the ritual and Great Perfection system of philosophy and

practice; a haven for renunciants; a place to acquire pedigrees to teach and engage in esoteric practice; a school for aristocrats who would go on to be military generals, civil servants, and political rulers; the training ground for the literati (often the same individuals) who wrote highly erudite and sometimes erotic literary works, as well the author of the first Tibetan novel and the first Tibetan secular autobiography?[37] Simultaneously and inseparably, Mindröling was a place where renowned lamas came to study esoteric meditation techniques and the fields of arts and sciences critical in a Tibetan Buddhist context.

Even during its most influential periods, Mindröling remained relatively small, as designed by the founders. It was also prestigious, comparable in that regard to an Ivy League university or elite college. The cultural forms that were crystallized in Mindröling texts and practices generally were not framed as innovations, but as revivifications of ancient teachings that were perceived to have been corrupted. Examples include large-scale public rituals, literary forms such as grammar and poetics, handbooks for making art, incense, and musical liturgies. The founders intended that these reinvented traditions would be done more purely at Mindröling; to learn them at Mindröling was to learn them well.[38] And this training had an empowering effect, much like Buddhist ritual performances that supported rulers who were identified as bodhisattvas.

The tradition frames the monastery as the buddhafield of Akaniṣṭha, and in explicit ways, this designation corresponds to the reality of Mindröling as a center for Great Perfection practice. But considering the full range of engagements at the monastery and reading between the lines of documents such as the monastic guidelines, we find more complex, human challenges and concerns.

Conclusion: Aesthetics as a Bridge Between the Buddhist and the Worldly

Until the 1950s, laypeople studied at Mindröling or Mindröling-staffed schools in Lhasa. The students who held a Mindröling degree or trained under Mindröling masters were poised for positions of power in the government and society. Artistically, the writing they produced after studying at Mindröling was formally sophisticated, employing complex literary forms that could only be mastered with intensive training.

This book focuses on Buddhist aesthetic formations during the first fifty years of Mindröling's history. The monastery's many other aspects over the subsequent centuries speak out from the margins and help shape this account.

Today, many diverse groups all claim a long-standing and significant relationship with Mindröling: Buddhist nuns conducting long-life rituals and a community of tantric ritual experts in Amdo, Eastern Tibet; monks collecting offerings from pilgrims in a temple on the Barkor in Lhasa; exiled artists creating three-dimensional mandalas in Santa Fe; American psychotherapists on meditation retreat in the hills of Virginia; and to some extent, scholars and practitioners from all the Tibetan Buddhist schools, including the Fourteenth Dalai Lama. This diversity of purposes and audiences was already at play in Mindröling's early history in the seventeenth and eighteenth centuries. Still known for the elegance and precision of its ritual and artistic practices, Mindröling has survived periods of political chaos, violent persecution, the dawn of modernity, and geographic displacement.

During the time period this study concerns, Mindröling was, like other monasteries, an environment that was amenable to keeping monastic vows and conducting rituals. Less common was its function as a site of education in all the fields of Buddhist knowledge. Its founders sought to make it exemplary of these core functions of Buddhist monasteries, and at the same time of the specialties of their Nyingma school. In doing so, they magnified the potential for Buddhist institutions to engender cultural production and a community of aesthetics.

One of the most important ways Mindröling was different from other monasteries was its particular relationship to the Ganden Podrang government and the Fifth Dalai Lama's vision of a unified Tibetan polity. It also stood out for its ongoing role in educating members of the ruling class. By educating not only monastics but also a small contingent of powerful laypeople who went on to become Tibetan leaders, Mindröling played a distinct and crucial role in the relationship of Tibetan Buddhism, society, and the state.

This work takes part in a broader investigation of aesthetics and materiality in the field of religious studies. I offer interpretations of the foundational ties between Buddhist institutions and the ruling class, including royal courts, wealthy patrons, and modern governments, and suggest that these relationships have shaped the evolution of Buddhist aesthetics—the concern with art, taste, as well as the study of the senses more broadly.[39] I also argue that the necessity to offer pleasing objects to deities and teachers operates at the crux of the tension between the Buddhist and the worldly and has shaped Buddhist material culture and aesthetics. Further, I consider the secular, civil, or otherwise worldly applications of a Buddhist education and ask how Buddhist training relates to ethics, political theory, and the development of regional or national identities. In doing so, I probe the relationship between a cosmopolitan worldview and Buddhism's historical facility for adapting to new cultural milieus. These concerns, addressed though certainly not fully answered in the chapters that follow, all have bearing on Mindröling's history.

Chapter Overview

In chapter 1, I provide a historical overview of the factors that led to Mindröling's founding. The Nyö family group's long-standing political and religious authority prepared them to develop the institution. To demonstrate how this worked, I provide an introduction to the Nyö family and describe the events that led to the monastery's foundation in the late seventeenth century under the auspices of the Fifth Dalai Lama.

In chapter 2 I argue that Mindröling came into existence thanks to a combination of circumstances, rooted in the founding family's clan history. I explore key articulations of the founders' vision for the new monastery and continue the story of Mindröling's early blossoming. I also give a blueprint of Mindröling's monastic network, demonstrating the scope of its influence in the field of cultural production. The main relationship at play in this chapter is between Terdak Lingpa and the Fifth Dalai Lama, who was in the early phases of his fraught role as joint political and Buddhist ruler of a tenuously united Tibetan polity. The monastic histories that the founders posted on the monastery walls and more recently published as part of the monastic catalogue are my main sources. Although the monastery was small, from its early days Mindröling had affiliates and branches across the greater Tibetan area (*bod chen*). Such far-reaching monastic networks were and are a foundational element in Tibet's religious and cultural fabric. They affect trade routes, political liaisons, linguistic variations, and regional conflicts and are a crucial conduit for art practices and aesthetics. Through this institutional network, beyond the small elite monastery near Lhasa, the institution of Mindröling writ large stretched across the Tibetan Buddhist sphere, spreading its influence through its religious tradition (*chos lugs*), including formal liturgies and practices as well as its curriculum and more general sensibilities. The main role of the branches was to conduct rituals for the local populations (the most common task of tantric experts of the Nyingma school) based on Terdak Lingpa and Lochen Dharmaśrī's textual legacies. Some of the branches also replicated Mindröling's curriculum and instituted its educational practices to varying extents. Although the branches were many, oral accounts and biographies show that elite students from across Tibet sought to receive training at the main monastery, even if that required months of travel, due to its prestige and reputation for excellence. The fact that Mindröling became so widely influential despite the main monastery being so small attests to the significant cultural capital its founders possessed. In this chapter I develop the theme of Mindröling's special brand of cosmopolitanism, crystallized in the Great Perfection ideal of cultivating a radically unbiased worldview. In a time marked by various strains of cosmopolitan attitudes across the broader East and Inner Asian regions, I argue that the concept of being radically unbiased was a particularly Tibetan and even more specifically Nyingma expression of cosmopolitanism.

Continuing to explore the nature of the relationship between Terdak Lingpa and the Tibetan government, in chapter 3 I focus on the Tibetan epistolary genre and the Tibetan Buddhist theme of interconnected relationships (*ten 'brel*). I begin with letters written from the Fifth Dalai Lama to Terdak Lingpa on the occasion of his enthronement and his marriage. I also summarize letters written by Terdak Lingpa to the Fifth Dalai Lama's most powerful regent, Desi Sangyé Gyatso, and the Sixth Dalai Lama and present translations of two complete letters that exemplify Terdak Lingpa's epistolary style. Mindröling's prestigious place in the world of Tibetan education and governance is partly reflected in the letters Terdak Lingpa wrote to his students and donors. Many of the recipients were political figures in Lhasa or local leaders from across Tibet. Their correspondence with Terdak Lingpa shows that they looked to him for advice on how to bring together

Buddhist practice with their practical work in the world. They consulted him on topics as varied as the etymology and history of the Tibetan terms for "debate," how to govern justly, how to cope with stress and illness due to overworking, what to do in times of mourning, and of course instruction in Great Perfection practices, including ritual techniques and meditative practices. The responses show Terdak Lingpa's mastery of early Tibetan history as well as his attention to developments in other schools of Tibetan Buddhism. He was truly a man of letters. Because letter writing as a genre is both dialogical and to some extent particular to the relationship of sender and recipient, Terdak Lingpa's letters offer insight into the pedagogy applied at Mindröling and provide a partial cross-section of his most significant and formative relationships.

In chapter 4 I focus on the monastic curriculum at Mindröling, paying special attention to the themes of worldly fields of study in the arts and sciences, which Terdak Lingpa espouses as "the armor" that will protect monks in pursuing all their aims. Also key is the importance of cultivating expertise in the artistic media of Mindröling's large-scale rituals and the controversial allure of solitary meditation retreat among Great Perfection practitioners, potentially pulling them away from their duties within the monastic community or putting them at risk of indiscipline. A striking feature of the curriculum is the attention Terdak Lingpa, the document's main author, paid to the particular requirements and capacities of the individual student. While the primary course of study is laid out in some detail, there is a continual reiteration that the guiding logic of every individual's education should be his or her own particular strengths, weaknesses, and inclinations. In the brief three-page curriculum, Terdak Lingpa used a Tibetan phrase, *so so*, meaning "as appropriate to each," six times, and the term *rang rang*, meaning "of the individual," three times. This language suggests a flexible attitude in an atmosphere that catered to the individual. This dynamic is indicative of Mindröling's precarious position as a place that exemplified monastic discipline and virtue while also being a center for elite education of a relatively diverse population of lay aristocrats as well as lamas, yogins, monks, and nuns. These roles allowed Mindröling to span the demands and expectations of the Géluk school while exemplifying the particular strengths of the Nyingma school.

In chapter 5 I turn to the training of influential aristocrats and other exceptional students. I highlight the ways Mindröling's curriculum was unique and distinctly Nyingma in flavor, while also taking note of how the founders allied themselves with other monastic-scholastic traditions. My driving question is what made Mindröling the place for aristocrats to culti-vate the manners, tastes, and skills of the ruling upper class and at the same time, a center for the most respected Buddhist practices. I also address some of the seminal social and political alliances that stabilized Mindröling in its early period and allowed for its reconstruction after a devastating attack by Zungar Mongols in 1717. The link between Tibetan Buddhism and wider cultural production via training in the arts and sci-ences or *rikné* was a crucial element in establishing Mindröling's signifi-cance in the education of the ruling class. This rubric of *rikné*, adopted into Tibet from Classical Indian Buddhist tradition, explicitly includes the fields of knowledge that span artistic, scientific, and religious topics, thus evinc-ing the connection among Buddhism, culture, and aesthetics. To under-stand why Mindröling came to serve this particular role, it is necessary to consider more generally what the children of aristocrats needed to learn or acquire from school in order to be prepared for positions in the government and how Mindröling addressed those needs. Biographies, inscriptions, and portraits offer descriptions of noble people that reflect the ruling class aes-thetic and give a sense of what characteristics would have been considered most valuable. Beyond the refined tastes and cultural signs that mark the "noble" ruling classes, technical skills like reading, writing, and account-ing and an array of more subtly acquired characteristics helped boost an aristocrat's role in society and government. Further, Tibetan aristocrats benefited from persuasiveness, diplomacy, self-confidence, articulateness, political savvy, and military training. Biographies suggest a rudimentary knowledge of Tibetan medicine and astrology were also key, as were com-petitive sporting skills like archery and, perhaps above all else, language arts such as grammar and poetics. The characteristics that signal nobility were gained through a matrix of family life, schooling, and career experi-ence. In early modern Tibet, Mindröling became a hub for this training.

Several prominent authors who were affiliated with Mindröling during this period produced writing that was remarkably frank in addressing sex and romance. A key example is found in the life story of the Tibetan king Miwang Polhané. On his way to study at Mindröling, after saying an easy farewell to his wife, he had a more emotionally fraught experience leaving his favorite lover, with whom he spent one last passionate night making love and exchanging poetic love songs. Polhané's amorous encounters played an important role throughout his biography, not only in the section on Mindröling. Broadly, the erotic elements of the biography shed light on Tibetan aristocratic values and tastes, the significance of virility in portraits of Tibetan cultural heroes, and the place of erotic literature in Indian and Tibetan Buddhist high culture. More to the point here, they demonstrate the literary sensibilities inculcated in lay students at Mindröling. This topic is examined further in the epilogue, which considers the future of Mindröling and its cultural legacies. Although the roots of the trend of alumni composing erotic literature are not explicit in the curriculum or the following account of Polhané's course of study, the literary aesthetic cultivated at Mindröling clearly allowed for and encouraged that style of writing.

In the epilogue I focus on the alliance between Polhané and Terdak Lingpa's daughter Mingyur Peldrön, a renowned teacher in her own right whose position in the lineage was complicated by tensions between her vision for the monastery's future and the leadership decisions of other members of her family.[40] I explore the period just after Zungar troops destroyed Mindröling during a broader campaign to overthrow the Qoshot Mongols, led by Lazang Khan, and assert their control over the Tibetan area. The second generation of Mindröling hierarchs, supported by Polhané, rebuilt the monastery and reestablished its traditions, which have continued with remarkable success until the present, now extending to a global community of practitioners.

A Note on Scope and Methodology

In researching this book project, I have come across many faces of Mindröling. My focus on aesthetics as the connective tissue between the Buddhist and worldly activities of its founders and subsequent members is only one of many aspects I could have written about. No portrait could fully encompass Mindröling in all its rich complexity, and in writing this book I have tried to better understand a singular facet that previously was underdeveloped and undertheorized. I believe this approach adds to the scholarly and practical understanding of how Tibetan Buddhism was and continues to be experienced by people in the world.

In pursuing my interest in aesthetics as a theme in Mindröling's history, I found compelling resonances with religious and cultural institutions in other times and places. I came to think of Mindröling not only as a monastery or an institution, or even as a network of affiliated institutions, but as a cultural and social phenomenon. I developed my research methods with an eye toward the fullest possible picture of that phenomenon. Trained primarily as a textualist, and hindered by historical, political, and geographical factors from drawing more on the material cultural evidence I wished to include—such as a mandala made from Terdak Lingpa's mother's jewels after her death and a lifelike image of Terdak Lingpa made of incense—I focus on the diverse texts that document the material and cultural traces and help paint a picture of the phenomenon of Mindröling in its early years. In the following chapters, I engage historical, literary, and ethnographic methods to investigate how Mindröling came to be and how its members have continued to thrive, discreetly and steadfastly exemplifying Tibetan Buddhist cultural production.

ONE

Historical Background
Laying the Foundation for Mindröling

In the Tibetan region of Kharak the people had never before seen such an attractive and handsome figure. With strong healthy limbs, he was a pleasure to look at. The bridge of his nose was high, his forehead was broad, his eyebrows were long, and his features were distinguished. As for his skin, like the jasmine blossom, it was white and smooth, making him nectar for the eyes.

—LOCHEN DHARMAŚRĪ

AT THE HEART of the institution of Mindröling is a powerful Tibetan clan,[1] called Nyö (*gnyos* or *smyos rigs*).[2] For centuries before Mindröling's conception in 1676, members of the Nyö clan, as aristocrats and Buddhist masters, integrated worldly and religious authority in the Southern and Central Tibetan regions. According to Terdak Lingpa's outer biography, when the first Nyö ancestor arrived in Tibet in approximately the sixth century, his beauty made a vivid impression on the local population.[3] The above description draws attention to the aesthetics of this founding ancestor's attractive appearance. This handsome ancestor is illustrative of the mytho-historical backdrop against which Mindröling came into being. This is a mythos in which beauty is not skin-deep but is symbolic of virtue and power; a mastery of aesthetics is equivalent to the mastery of the sense perceptions and their objects, rather than a superficial concern with mere appearances. Thus, aesthetics connects Buddhist and worldly expertise and authority.

Figure 1.1 Thirteenth-century portrait of a lama from the Nyö clan.
Courtesy of Sotheby's Auction House

Buddhism, Cultural Production, and Power

In this chapter I demonstrate how Mindröling's founders drew on imperial models, reincarnation claims, education in *rikné,* the Great Perfection view of *rimé,* and clan status to build their new institution.

The intimate relationship among Buddhism, cultural production, and power has helped shape the diverse histories of India, Sri Lanka, China, Japan, Southeast Asia, and Mongolia, and other regions where Buddhism has been active. Likewise, in Tibetan Buddhist regions, Buddhism's tantric technologies for empowering and bolstering the perceived legitimacy and potency of rulers and its association with cosmopolitan knowledge and the markers of civilization made it especially appealing to the ruling class. This is true to such an extent that it is fair to say that when Mindröling was founded in 1676, Tibetan Buddhist knowledge and authority were mutually constitutive. The history of this dynamic can be traced back to at least the eighth century.

A clear example of this phenomenon emerged when Tibet's early imperial patrons of Buddhism worked in concert with monastics, tantric masters, and tantric consorts to shape the first major Tibetan Buddhist monastery, Samyé. Narratives of the emperor Tri Songdetsen, the monk Śāntarakṣita, and the tantric adepts Padmasambhava and Yeshé Tsogyel provided the template for later collaborations between political leaders and tantric masters. And during the Yuan dynasty, Tibetan lamas acted as imperial preceptors (Chinese: *di shi,* Tibetan: *ti shri*), instructing and empowering the imperial families in both religious and cultural knowledge, and thereby supporting their political authority.

Making direct reference to these historical examples, Terdak Lingpa and his family worked with members of the new Ganden Podrang government to found Mindröling. Together they imagined their collaborations with the Fifth Dalai Lama as a reenactment of the building of Samyé by making reincarnation claims that identified all the major actors with past masters. The Dalai Lama also appointed Terdak Lingpa as his imperial preceptor. By making the old new in these ways, and as a product of this early modern moment and an important element in the Dalai Lama's vision for a unified Tibetan polity, Mindröling would come to function as a civilizational center.

Laying the Ground for Mindröling

This section looks back to the people who laid the groundwork for the monastery over the centuries, beginning with accounts of the first recorded Nyö ancestor and moving through the Tibetan imperial period when Buddhism first took root, and through the second dissemination (*phyi dar*) or renaissance of Buddhism in the eleventh century,[4] with an eye toward the late seventeenth century when Mindröling was founded. Previous generations of the Nyö clan paved the way for the prominence of Mindröling. To set the stage for these individuals, I first briefly describe the climate in which the monastery came into being, recounting the history just prior to Mindröling's founding, when the Nyö family group's connections to the Fifth Dalai Lama and his Gelukpa coterie became instrumental.

I then highlight continuities in the lives and educations of key Nyö family members over time, as narrated in biographical works by members of this family that functioned to shore up their mythos. These include the integration of religious and worldly authority, mastery of the Great Perfection (*rdzogs chen*), expertise in the classical fields of knowledge known as rikné (*rig gnas*), the relatively high status of women, and the impartial mentality of rimé (*ris med*). In the process, I contextualize the Mindröling founders' efforts to update and systematize older heterogeneous Nyingma texts and practices.

The Seventeenth-Century Political Climate and the Need for New Educational Structures

When Terdak Lingpa was born in 1646, the Fifth Dalai Lama was in the complicated position of ruling a newly and ambiguously consolidated Tibet. With the military aid and support of the powerful Khoshot Mongol Gushri Khan (1582–1685), the Fifth Dalai Lama's Ganden Podrang government had been in control of Central Tibet since 1642. This was thanks to the khan's victory over various competing groups.[5] The large geographical region that came nominally within the Dalai Lama's purview was home to diverse groups of people, most of whom shared a strong connection to Buddhism and many of whom used Tibetan scripts and spoke Tibetan language, although from region to region, groups had distinctive cultural identities and some spoke mutually unintelligible dialects or altogether different languages. The strength of local identities and histories made the project of unifying a greater Tibetan polity a challenge, to say the least. The ongoing effort to consolidate power over the greater Tibetan area—long governed by local power bases—that began during this period took place on overlapping political, cultural, social, and religious fronts.[6]

In these efforts, the Dalai Lama and his supporters looked back to Tibet's imperial period, when Tibet's power extended throughout Central Asia and into China, for inspiration and legitimacy.[7] The Ganden Podrang's aim to form a cohesive Tibetan polity required a centralized bureaucracy. This was in contrast to the decentralized Pakmodru (*phag mo gru*) and Rinpungpa (*rin spungs pa*) periods that immediately preceded the rise of the Ganden Podrang. The period was also marked by a fascination with new technology, science, and empiricism.[8] The state building project, spearheaded by the Dalai Lama's regent, Sangyé Gyatso, required that the populace be drawn together as a community through the implementation of media such as regularly scheduled large-scale rituals, a unified calendar, and shared institutions.[9] A working and stable bureaucracy would regulate and negotiate these intersecting state functions.

The project demanded new educational structures as well, to cultivate members of the new bureaucracy and literati. Within the Dalai Lama's school, the three large Géluk monasteries of Ganden, Drépung, and Sera, close to the capital city of Lhasa, became the Central Tibetan centers for Géluk scholasticism. Monks from distant regions congregated to study in these centers. The institution of Mindröling soon would emerge to satisfy other ritual and educational needs.

Looking Back at Mindröling's Family Lineage: The Nyö Clan

In this context, what qualified someone to establish a prestigious educational institution? One factor was social status, which was partly determined by family and clan affiliations. As a member of the Nyö clan on his paternal side and a descendant of the imperial family on his maternal side, Terdak Lingpa' was well positioned for authority. This clan had been a powerful force in the southern part of Central Tibet for centuries. In addition to the founders of Mindröling, prominent Nyö clan members included the Treasure revealer Pema Lingpa (1450–1521), the Bhutanese royal family, and later, the Sixth Dalai Lama (1683–1706). Mindröling's history cannot be disentangled from the history of the Nyö clan and the Tibetan aristocracy more generally, starting with the origin myth of the handsome god and developing over the subsequent generations.

The Power of Beauty

The Nyö clan traces it roots in Tibet to the story of the beautiful figure we met in this chapter's epigraph. It is possible that the tale of the beautiful ancestor corresponds with the event of an actual person arriving in Tibet, perhaps from India, framed in mythological terms. This story is conveyed through oral tradition and recorded in the biographies of Terdak Lingpa and the Sixth Dalai Lama.[10] According to these sources, the ancestor was a god who was curious about some Tibetan nomads. He came down to earth from his divine home, known as the realm of luminous gods ('od gsal gyi lha'i gnas). The Tibetans were moved by his beauty and grace, since they had never come across someone with such an elegant appearance. The passage about the encounter in Terdak Lingpa's biography overflows with aesthetic terms—consider the use of "attractive," "handsome," "pleasure," "high," "broad," "long," "clear," and the phrases "skin like jasmine" and "nectar for the eyes." The passage aims to move and impress the reader with this sensuous description of the Nyö ancestor, whose beauty signals virtue and power. In fact, the most common Tibetan word for beauty (mdzes pa) also connotes elegance, power, and effectiveness.

Crazy Wisdom

The story as told by Dharmaśrī continues, recounting that his contact with humans contaminated the god, and therefore he was unable to return to his heavenly realm. He had to assimilate as best he could to his new environment. The Tibetans called him "Nyö" (smyos) which means "drunk" or "crazy." This is because interacting with humans had made him act as though intoxicated. As Terdak Lingpa's biographer states, "When the humans' defilements intoxicated him, they called him 'crazy,' and his family lineage was also known by that name."[11] Apparently he never shed his other-worldly, eccentric ways, and to this day the descendants of this handsome character carry the name Nyö. The name is not associated with shame or embarrassment, but with an aesthetic of freedom from conventions and mundane expectations.

The valorization of "craziness" is of course not unique to this family group. The characterization of yogis and lamas as exhibiting "crazy wisdom" is prevalent in Tibetan Buddhist societies.[12] Historically and today, there are practitioners whose charisma and insight manifest through the appearance of madness. The longer history of this phenomenon stretches back to the early days of tantric Buddhism in India, where poet-mystics such as Tilopa and Saraha paved the way for the tradition in Tibet.[13] Beloved exemplars of the Chinese Chan and Taoist traditions likewise display characteristics of unconventional and sometimes antinomian behavior, which supporters interpret as signs of insight and awakening.[14] The ideal of shocking antinomian behavior that defies expectation and rational interpretation carries a powerful rhetorical force.

Yet, despite the name, and unlike many of their relations from within the Nyö clan, the individuals who eventually founded Mindröling were the epitome of systematization and order.

Gods Made Human, Tibetans Made Noble

Like the Nyö, other aristocratic clans of Tibet traced their origins to deities who came down from the heavens to Tibet on ropes made of light (*dmu thag*). These families are known as divine clans (*lha rigs*). The story of the god who came down to earth marks Mindröling's family lineage as part of Tibet's highest social stratum.

A revealing comparison here is to the Khön family group (*'khon rigs*) of the Sakya (*sa skya*) school. The Khön family shares several traits with the Mindröling family, such as being headed by tantric experts who marry and have children rather than by celibate monks such as the Dalai Lama, and the relative prominence of renowned women scholars and practitioners.

Beyond these two examples, the members of "divine clans" are the main figures in many of Tibetan Buddhism's most powerful schools and lineages as well as powerful players in Tibetan political history.

A Cosmopolitan Setting

Although the handsome Nyö ancestor is said to have come from the sky, Dharmaśrī, the author of the biography in which the story is told, pays attention to the earthly cultural and geographic location of the event as well. He situates Kharak, Tibet, at the center of a collection of neighboring cultural centers, located in the four directions. Just before we meet the Nyö ancestor, the author orients us—to the south lies India (*rgya gar*); to the east, China (*rgya nag*); to the west, Kashmir (*kasmir*); and to the north, Mongolia (*hor*).[15] This orientation displays Dharmaśrī's attention to the distinctive societies and cultures surrounding seventeenth-century Tibet, which he describes as being cradled within a necklace of snowy mountains.

Dharmaśrī's attention to Tibet's geographic and cultural neighbors was not merely poetic. It reflected centuries of close contact, trade, and cultural exchange. Long before Mindröling was established, Tibet's noble families accumulated religious capital by sending their sons south to India and Nepal to study esoteric Buddhism and to retrieve texts and receive initiations and bring them back to Tibet. As those families became more prominent in the realm of Buddhism, religious capital and cultural capital came to overlap. By the time Mindröling was founded, the Nyö clan was rich in various types of capital.[16]

Religious, Cultural, and Political Capital

Crucially, the Nyö clan was instrumental in shaping what would become the dominant model of Tibetan rulership, known as *chösi zungdrel* (*chos srid zung 'brel*) or the integration of Buddhist and worldly spheres. Since the seventeenth century, this model has been epitomized in the joint religious and temporal institution of the Dalai Lama. But other lamas, particularly those who were *both* aristocrats *and* tantric experts, provided the precedent for the Dalai Lama to hold combined power. Per Sørensen writes, "It was through sheer authority accruing from bygone prerogatives or from records of yore delineating the heydays of their glorious past that clans and aristocratic families in Tibet often later would advance their hegemonic claims in an attempt to underpin political authority."[17]

To ascertain the Nyö clan's place in the development of this religio-political model more precisely, we have to look back to the eleventh century. The Nyö clan's influence in the Lhasa region extends back to the translator Nyö Lotsawa, who traveled to Nepal and India with the much younger Marpa Lotsawa.[18] (Marpa would go on to become the root teacher of Tibet's most famous and beloved yogin, Milarepa.[19]) The recorded history of the Nyö clan situates Nyö Lotsawa in the thirteenth generation of the clan's presence in Tibet, the first being that of the handsome fallen god.

In approximately 1028, Nyö Lotsawa traveled to India through Nepal for classical Buddhist training, receiving teachings in the Guhyasamāja, Krishna Yamāri, Cakrasaṃvara, Hevajra, Mahāmāyā, and Mañjuśrīnāmasaṃgīti tantras under the teacher Nakpo Zhapchung.[20] Like Marpa, when Nyö Lotsawa returned home he became a charismatic teacher and sought-after translator, since in addition to having received highly prized esoteric initiations, he was well versed in Sanskrit. In the Lhasa region members of the ruling class sought him out, particularly regarding the Guhyasamāja and Yamantaka cycles, which were in high demand due to Tibetans' rising interest in tantric Buddhism. Nyö Lotsawa transmitted three significant cycles of tantric teachings, generally referred to as the Tantra Trilogy of Nyö (*gnyos kyi rgyud gsum*) or the Father Tantra Trilogy (*pha rgyud skor gsum*).[21] These would later become an important part of the Mindröling tradition.

Wealthy Lhasa figures donated large swathes of land and significant amounts of gold to Nyö Lotsawa in material exchanges that would be repeated in the seventeenth century by the Fifth Dalai Lama in his sponsorship of Terdak Lingpa as a tantric master. Concerning this model of exchange, Sørensen observes, "The acquisition of original Indian esoteric teachings (often in the form of original Indian manuscripts from authoritative Indian masters) and cycles dearly purchased and remunerated with gold in India often exceeded the value of the latter and promised the holder considerable income and prestige back in Tibet."[22] In short, in this period of Tibetan history, members of Lhasa's ruling class valued expertise in tantra more than gold. In part due to Nyö Lotsawa's rise to fame, the Nyö clan became one of the most powerful in the Lhasa area.

Another major Nyö figure who helped lay the ground for Mindröling was Nyö Drakpa Pal (1106–1165/1182), "one of the first post-imperial rulers of Lhasa" and one of the "true precursors of the dual role characterizing the much later Dalai Lama institution."[23]

The histories of Nyö Lotsawa's influence and Nyö Drakpa Pal's subsequent rise to power illustrates a crucial shift in authority that started during the eleventh century, the dawn of an era often referred to as the second dissemination or renaissance of Buddhism in Tibet, when religious capital in the form of initiations and other modes of Buddhist knowledge came to equal and even surpass material wealth, social standing, and political alliances as the major factor determining authority. The Nyö clan's successful integration of power was the immediate precursor to that of Lama Zhang (1123–1193), who was a formative example for joint religious and secular authority in the Lhasa region.[24]

Nyö clan members continued to be prominent Buddhist teachers, ritual experts, and local rulers over the subsequent centuries. Most critically, the Nyö clan's lengthy history of influence came to a high point in the late seventeenth century, when Terdak Lingpa joined forces with the Fifth Dalai Lama to found Mindröling. The place of clans in Tibetan history is too extensive a subject to address in greater detail here; the main point is that clans were a crucial organizing element in Tibet's social and political hierarchies, and the Nyö clan formed the backbone of Mindröling.

How to practically integrate the Dharma with worldly life is one of the most consistent topics of Terdak Lingpa's discussions with persons in positions of power, as recorded in his collected letters, the focus of chapter 3. I propose that his perceived expertise in how to govern well while being a good Buddhist, as both a member of the Nyö clan and a visionary Treasure revealer, was an attractive attribute in drawing powerful disciples and patrons.

Mindröling's Institutional Precursor: The Mother Monastery of a Mother Monastery

In the sixteenth century Terdak Lingpa's ancestor Tulku Natsok Rangdröl (1494–1570) founded Dargyé Chöling monastery in the Dranang valley of the

Lhoka region. Dargyé Chöling became the major center for the esoteric philosophical and meditative system known as Great Perfection in Central and Southern Tibet until Mindröling took over that distinction.[25] The leaders at Dargyé Chöling were not monks but ritual specialists who had families while teaching and acting as heads of the religious institution. The highest leadership roles passed through family members, mainly father to son and uncle to nephew, as opposed to Buddhist institutions organized principally around teacher-to-student lineages or reincarnation lineages.

It seems that a relatively high level of education and authority for women characterized aristocratic family-based lineages like this. This may be because women were necessary for the perpetuation of the family and were therefore guaranteed a place in the lineage, even if that place was less authoritative than that of their male relations. More generally, the high quality of education among noblewomen compared to women of other social classes is of course not unique to Tibet. It can also be seen in the Chinese and Japanese cultures, for instance, where women of the ruling class have long had access to elite education.[26] Directly related to higher levels of education, aristocratic family lineages tend to have more women teachers and renowned practitioners than other lineages.[27] In this confluence of monastic and aristocratic models, every family member, male and female, played a role in the continuation of the bloodline as well as the Buddhist lineage. The monastic institution extended out from the central clan like a kingdom around its royal family. The family-based model that was in place at Dargyé Chöling would continue at Mindröling, where women family members had significant roles, beginning with Terdak Lingpa's mother, Lhadzin Yangchen Dolma.

Great Perfection: A Pinnacle of Tibetan Buddhist Theory and Practice

Great Perfection practice was the focus at Dargyé Chöling and would become central to Mindröling's identity. From a historical perspective, this system of philosophy and practice appears to have originated in Tibet. Great Perfection practice traces back to at least the eighth century and is documented as a tantric system in texts found in the Dunhuang cave complex, a major oasis on the Silk Route and a cosmopolitan center for Buddhist travelers and translators of many ilks during the Tibetan Empire.[28] The history of Great Perfection in Tibet is one of both suspicion and lionization. Tibetan Buddhist practitioners widely treat it as a potent and important system, though it is controversial in some circles.[29]

Adherents of Great Perfection situate it at the pinnacle of a nine-tiered hierarchy of Buddhist methods or "vehicles" (*theg pa rim pa dgu*). This schema has its roots in the *Gathering of Intentions Sutra* (*dgongs pa 'du pa'i mdo*).[30] This system, and particularly the rituals of its *Sutra Initiation*, were central to the formation of the Nyingma school's identity, thanks in part to the Mindröling ritual tradition.[31] Within this distinctive hierarchy of vehicles, all the methods have their merits, and each is appropriate for some practitioners. At the apex are the inner yogic vehicles, known in Sanskrit as *mahāyoga, anuyoga*, and *atiyoga*. Great Perfection is presented as the most advanced and efficacious method, at least for those who are suited and well prepared.

Great Perfection teachings valorize spontaneity and posit primordial enlightenment as the basic nature of the mind.[32] They also display a suspicion toward intellectualization and conceptualization, stressing the application of a nondualist view. Accordingly, Great Perfection sources can appear to call for an utter abandonment of all practices rather than an embrace of Buddhist practice per se. On this front, Great Perfection teachings are similar to the doctrine of emptiness, which is a means of approaching Mahāyāna teachings with the right view, despite the risk of seeming to negate the teachings themselves.[33] Great Perfection is both a philosophical view and a system of practice that seeks to apply nondual philosophy to transform the cognitive and emotional experience of the practitioner. Such a transformation ideally shapes every aspect of experience.[34]

According to exponents, the Great Perfection worldview is characterized by a lack of bias and prejudice, an ideal known as *rimé* (*ris med* or *phyogs ris med*). The *rimé* view does not originate with Great Perfection, but has roots in Madhyamaka and Mahāmudrā philosophies.[35] While today this term is most commonly associated with nonsectarianism, that is just one of its many (or infinite) expressions, as a commitment to holding no fixed perspective or position, to harboring no prejudice or bias. *Rimé* can refer to an individual yogin's utter detachment from worldly engagements, but it can also describe a diverse assembly of religious practitioners. My analysis of Mindröling sources has led me to understand that a *rimé* view can also manifest in inclusive social, intellectual, and aesthetic practices, for instance a relatively egalitarian perspective on men and women, an engagement with diverse philosophical perspectives, and an embrace of a range of formal literary styles. From a Great Perfection perspective, being *rimé* is equivalent to attaining enlightenment.

Superficially at least, part of the appeal of Great Perfection practice is its high status and mystique. This mystique, as made visible in the arresting murals depicting Great Perfection yogic practices in the Lukhang temple built by the regent Sangyé Gyatso for the Sixth Dalai Lama, pervaded the institutional phenomenon of Mindröling.[36] The Great Perfection is central to the Nyingma school, but Tibetan Buddhists from across all the major schools have practiced it. It is likewise important in the Bön tradition.[37] Proponents claim that these esoteric practices are suitable for only the most capable and advanced practitioners, contributing to the prestige of Great Perfection masters.

The focus on nonconceptual experience might suggest that Great Perfection is not a scholarly tradition. On the contrary, there is a great deal of sophisticated scholarship and research focused on Great Perfection within Tibetan Buddhist literature. The sensibility enculturated at Mindröling is shaped by this dynamic between the nonconceptual and the scholarly within the Great Perfection tradition. The legacy of Longchen Rabjampa (1308–1363) exemplifies this dynamic. He was among the most extraordinary scholars and practitioners of Great Perfection,[38] and his work was a vital element in Terdak Lingpa's education. He received Longchenpa's teachings as a direct inheritance from his father and root teacher, Trinlé Lhündrup (1611–1662), who was then the head of Dargyé Chöling. I turn now to a brief introduction to his life and work.

Terdak Lingpa's Father

The life stories of Terdak Lingpa's parents reveal that the themes of expertise in *rikné*, Great Perfection practice, and the integration of worldly and religious authority were integral parts of the family history. This will help set the stage for understanding Terdak Lingpa's particular strengths and interests, which shaped the institution of Mindröling. I will begin with Terdak Lingpa's father, Trinlé Lhündrup, whose father was a member of the

Nyö clan and whose mother was a member of the Gyal clan. Under his father's instruction, he could read and write by age five and received lay ordination at the age of eight. His education focused on Great Perfection teachings, grammar, and astrology. He is remembered as being particularly adept in the drawing and painting of mandalas and in ritual dances. He also had an excellent general education in both sūtra and tantra traditions. The particulars of his education and interests look a great deal like the curriculum that Terdak Linpga would formalize later at Mindröling, the focus of chapter 4.

Trinlé Lhündrup was recognized as the reincarnation of the ninth-century master Nub Sangyé Yeshé. This disciple of Padmasambhava was Tibet's first recorded expert in ritual warcraft, which he employed with the aim of defeating anti-Buddhist rivals and protecting Tibet's borders.[39] He played a crucial role in the establishment of these rites among subsequent Nyingma practitioners. Nub Sangyé Yeshé also authored an important early commentary on the *Gathering of Intentions*.

In short, when Terdak Lingpa was born, his father was the hierarch of Dargyé Chöling monastery, a member of the Nyö clan, a famous teacher of Great Perfection, and a reincarnation of a seminal Nyingma figure from the imperial period. Shaped by a commitment to an unbiased *rimé* perspective, Nyöshul Rinpoché writes, Trinlé Lhündrup came "to experience directly the enlightened intent of great perfection: the perception of awareness's naturally manifest appearances without bias."[40] The phrase "without bias" connotes a *rimé* view. His students included monastics, laypeople, and tantric masters. As an expert in all manner of ritual activity, he also used his skills to fulfill the needs of ordinary people, for instance averting illnesses and healing the sick. Trinlé Lhündrup died when Terdak Lingpa was about sixteen, before his first Treasure revelation. As his father's main student, Terdak Lingpa would take up his mantle of leadership. After his father died, Terdak Lingpa looked for guidance from his mother.

Terdak Lingpa's Mother

Terdak Lingpa's mother was Lhadzin Yangchen Dolma (1624–?). She outlived Trinlé Lhündrup by many years, and Terdak Lingpa's biographies portray her as a major influence and presence well into his adult life. These sources describe his mother as a female yogic practitioner (*rnal byor ma*) and they make it clear that her influence played a formative role in Terdak Lingpa's training and conditioning as a Nyingma master.[41] She is not depicted as merely a compassionate and nurturing mother, but as an authority in her own right, playing an integral role in Terdak Lingpa's intellectual and religious development. Mindröling sources refer to her by the unusual and poetic honorific Ma Rinpoché, joining her roles as a mother and a teacher in one affectionate title.[42]

Her family traced its genealogy directly to the Tibetan imperial family. Such a link to the Tibetan empire was extremely valued in Lhasa society, especially given the Fifth Dalai Lama's effort to re-create the imperial reach and reunite Tibetan regions under the Ganden Podrang. Since the Nyö clan did not rise to prominence till the eleventh century, his mother's link to the ancient Tibetan empire was an important element in Terdak Lingpa's pedigree.

Yangchen Dolma's father was Dumpopa Dondrub Wangyel (d.u.) an expert in mathematical astrology (*rtsis*) and a wealthy landholder. He and his ancestors were known for their mastery of the classical fields of learning known as *rikné*, for which Mindröling would become renowned. This Dumpo family line was based at a large estate in the Dra (*gra*) valley, near Dargyé Chöling and the eventual location of Mindröling. Her mother's family was also prominent. Her maternal uncle, with whom she was close as a child, was the Dalai Lama's chief chamberlain (*grub chen mgron gnyer chen mo*), a role that involved the significant duty of overseeing the state calendar.[43]

Yangchen Dolma was celebrated for her Buddhist learning and advanced meditation practice. Her stature as a great practitioner of royal ancestry is attested to by the fact that she is the subject of an extensive biography, a rarity among Tibetan women.[44] In oral histories, she is remembered for her mastery of dreams (*rmi lam*),[45] using a method of meditation that employs dream states to develop eventual control over one's state of mind in the moment of death. This is because dreams and death are understood to be similar transitional or *bardo* states. Dream-related practices have been a focus at Mindröling from its earliest period as part of Terdak Lingpa's Vajrasattva Treasure cycle (*rdo rje sems dpa' thugs kyi sgrub pa'i chos skor*), and Mindröling practitioners are known for mastery of lucid dreaming techniques, even today.

The biography, composed by Dharmaśrī, again reflects prominent themes in Terdak Lingpa's development, which in turn shaped the institution of Mindröling. Her life story does not describe her secular education in much detail, but recounts the many Buddhist teachings and empowerments she received. It also celebrates her character and suggests that her family recognized her as a special and capable child. The biography explains, "From a young age she symbolized the awakening potential of her clan—patience, love, compassion, and a virtuous heart of the very best kind. She was someone who possessed all the qualities of being beautiful to behold."[46] For much of her childhood, she traveled with elderly relatives and in the process was able to receive teachings and attend significant ritual events, such as those that took place at the Tenth Karmapa's encampment,[47] and received an empowerment from a disciple of the head of the Sakya school.[48] The list of tantric rituals and empowerments she received from lamas from diverse Tibetan schools is impressive indeed.

According to her biographer, who was also her son, Lhadzin Yangchen Dolma was a generous sponsor of religious activities. She donated large amounts of wealth for the construction of temples, and distributed food to people in need during a period of grave famine when she was a young woman.[49] Not long after the end of the famine, when she was in her early twenties, she married Trinlé Lhündrup. They had seven children, one of whom died at birth. Her remaining children received outstanding educations and rose to prominence in their respective spheres. Those who would be most prominent in their adulthood were Terdak Lingpa and his brother Dharmaśrī.

Her work as a sponsor in the local community drew admiration from many, but her biography also suggests her high profile elicited some envy and spite. One episode in particular recounts a period of vicious gossip directed against her. She appears to have taken this in stride, and her biographer frames it as having been caused by demonic rather than mere social forces.[50]

From the opening verses of the biography, which are composed in elegant ornate poetry, the author inscribes the subject in the mythos of Mindröling's history, describing her as a holy and fully enlightened figure, not born of human parents, who took the body of a human in order to give birth to countless bodhisattvas.[51] The author plays poetically with her name, which translates as the name of the goddess of learning and aesthetics, Sarasvatī. He intersperses the syllables across the verses to identify her with the qualities of awakening, using a delightful Tibetan poetic convention that is impossible to re-create in English.[52] Beyond the verses praising her as a mother to bodhisattvas and the list of her children's names and birth years, the biography focuses less on her role as a parent than on her stature as a practitioner and patron of Buddhist activities.

After Terdak Lingpa's father passed away, he and Yangchen Dolma traveled together extensively. During their travels Terdak Lingpa studied, taught, and conducted rituals and public teachings. She was present during many of the major events of his career, including visionary experiences in which he rediscovered Treasure teachings. She also offered her opinion on significant occasions, such as when Terdak Lingpa decided to take a consort after much deliberation and prodding from the Fifth Dalai Lama, an important episode addressed in chapter 3. Following her death, her children created a monument to her memory that exemplifies the marriage of the Buddhist and the worldly—a three-dimensional mandala constructed of her jewelry, including gold, silver, and gemstones.[53]

Beyond the value of this biography as a historical document, I suggest that Dharmaśrī deliberately and strategically portrayed Lhadzin Yangchen Dolma in powerful and eloquent terms as part of a wider institutional project at Mindröling. In particular, her example and accomplishments seem to have helped generate Mindröling's relative inclusivity toward women practitioners. Her high social status, prowess as a practitioner, and authority as a patron and sponsor, and the very existence of a thorough account of her life all augured well for the role women would play at Mindröling—the renown of several women teachers is one of the institution's lasting marks of distinction.

This brief history of the Nyö clan and the accomplishments and prestige of Lhadzin Yangchen Dolma are the immediate precursors for Terdak Lingpa's birth, early education, and upbringing, which I turn to now.

Terdak Lingpa's Childhood

Terdak Lingpa was born at Dargyé Chöling to these two esteemed parents, both from aristocratic families rich in cultural, religious, and political capital. In the outer and inner biographies, his biographer details numerous prophecies about his special birth and his position in a long line of visionaries. He received an extraordinarily rigorous education and training, practically from birth. As is the case with the biographies of other highly revered lamas, his life story recounts a childhood marked by miraculous occurrences, outstanding intellectual capacity, visions, and many signs of the blossoming of a deeply compassionate and ethical person. He was identified as the "speech emanation" of Vairocana, the great eighth-century Tibetan translator and student of Padmasambhava. He was also identified with the visionaries Dorjé Lingpa (1346–1405) and Ratna Lingpa (1403–1478), among many other previous masters. The legacy of Ratna Lingpa was especially significant in regard to Terdak Lingpa's work editing the *Nyingma Gyübum* (*rnying ma rgyud 'bum*), the collection of Nyingma tantras that were excluded from the Tibetan canonical collections known as the Kangyur (*bka' 'gyur*) and Tengyur (*bstan 'gyur*). Ratna Lingpa was responsible for compiling a previous version of the *Nyingma Gyübum*.

Terdak Lingpa's first ritual empowerment took place when he was four, under the direction of his father. The empowerment was on the *Eight Transmitted Precepts, the Consummation of Secrets,* a teaching on vows by the thirteenth-century Treasure revealer Guru Chowang. In regard to his day-to-day childhood activities, Terdak Lingpa's outer biography is not entirely flattering. There are numerous instances in which the child is portrayed as acting somewhat temperamental. These episodes reveal a familial affection and sense of humor on the part of the biographer, Lochen Dharmaśrī, even as he demonstrates a deep reverence for his subject. But the message is not simply that Terdak Lingpa was a humorously naughty child. Rather, the biographer's point seems to be that due to Terdak Lingpa's positive karma from previous lives, his childish anger was never destructive. His occasional tantrums worked, on the contrary, as a kind of playful demonstration of the illusory nature of reality. This is in keeping with characterizations of Terdak Lingpa later in life as a master of illusion, magic, or artfulness (*sgyu*), a characteristic central to his identity.[54]

In one example of an early exploit, while being carried piggy-back to a public teaching by an adult family friend, the child who would later be known as Terdak Lingpa became displeased for some reason and tugged at the friend's jewelry, angrily hurling a delicate and valuable turquoise earring on the ground. The biographer notes that despite the expectations of those present at the scene who were all sure the jewelry would be broken, the turquoise was unharmed.[55]

In a more extraordinary episode, when sitting in a monastic assembly the child became angry that the monk who was looking after him did not have his favorite teacup at hand. When the monk offered him a different teacup, he threw the full cup down the stone steps in front of the assembly hall. Not only did the teacup not shatter, but not a drop of tea was spilled. There are other similar stories in which he shows an unusual precocity, peppered with eccentricity.[56]

These cheerful anecdotes, in which the biographer seems to enjoy reminiscing about Terdak Lingpa's fiery temper and magical flair, foretell his fame as a master of illusory reality, keeping in mind that according to Buddhist teachings, all reality is illusory. On a more ordinary plane, to work with the senses and to master them is also to be a master of aesthetics.

For the most part Terdak Lingpa's childhood is characterized in the biographical sources by a quickness to learn and by reports of transformative visions, beginning at age ten. By that time, he is recorded as having achieved a high enough level of mastery of reading, writing, and ritual activities to act as regent for his father. In a pivotal development, when Terdak Lingpa was eleven, Trinlé Lhündrup took him to Lhasa to meet the Fifth Dalai Lama.

Family Connections to the Fifth Dalai Lama

The two of them went to Drépung monastery for this important meeting, which would mark the beginning of a lifelong connection. As one of the three main central Tibetan seats of the Géluk school, Drépung housed thousands of monks, and in 1650 it became the seat of the Dalai Lama's government.

During that visit, the Dalai Lama administered Terdak Lingpa's novice vows, ritually cutting a lock of the child's hair. Significantly, this rite corresponded with the delivery of a famous wooden statue of Avalokiteśvara, the bodhisattva of compassion, called the Kyirong Rangjung Pakba (*skyid grong rang byung 'phags pa*), to Lhasa. This statue was said to have been rediscovered as a Treasure by the emperor Songtsen Gampo, Tibet's first imperial patron of Buddhism. At the time of Terdak Lingpa's novice ordination, it was being shifted to Lhasa from the region of Kyirong, on Tibet's southeastern border, to keep it safe during a violent conflict with Nepal.[57] The Dalai Lama reportedly recognized this coincidence of Terdak Lingpa's visit and the statue's return as auspicious, since the statue was directly associated with the glory of Tibet's imperial period.

A second early meeting took place when Terdak Lingpa was seventeen years old and met the Dalai Lama at Samyé, Tibet's first Buddhist monastery, founded in the eighth century under the auspices of the tantric master Padmasambhava and the emperor Tri Songdetsen.[58] At that time, Terdak Lingpa had a vision in which the Dalai Lama appeared as Avalokiteśvara.[59] The official identification of a lama with the bodhisattva of compassion was contested at the time, since several people were simultaneously identified with this figure that was so central to the Tibetan Buddhist imagination. Terdak Lingpa's vision was important because it helped to vet the Dalai Lama as an authentic bearer of that identification.[60] Beyond this instance, Tibetan lamas' ability to identify rulers with enlightened bodhisattvas bore great weight, as demonstrated by identifications of Yuan, Ming, and Qing emperors with Mañjuśrī, the bodhisattva of wisdom. Terdak Lingpa's vision at Samyé was the first of numerous visions the two men experienced involving each other over the course of their lives.

Terdak Lingpa's Brother, Lochen Dharmaśrī

Another essential thread in this web of connections that led to the founding of Mindröling, Terdak Lingpa's younger brother, Lochen Dharmaśrī, had a lifelong relationship with the Fifth Dalai Lama, from whom he received vows when he was fifteen and full monastic ordination vows when he was twenty.[61] Although they played different roles, the brothers both had the privilege of being a member of the Nyö clan, and greatness was prophesied for both. It was prophesied that Dharmaśrī would contribute greatly to both religion and worldly life in Tibet.[62] As a scholar and artist, Dharmaśrī would play a significant role in generating Mindröling's renown as a center of Tibetan Buddhist knowledge and cultural production. A telling example of the depth of his connection with the Dalai Lama is that the Gelukpa ruler reportedly commissioned the young Dharmaśrī to paint an image of a fierce deity used as a support for his practice, just before the Dalai Lama's death in 1682.[63]

In short, although Terdak Lingpa and Dharmaśrī were children when the Dalai Lama's government was coming to power, they forged an early connection that lasted all their lives. From the time of their earliest encounters, the Fifth Dalai Lama took a keen interest in the brothers. One of the ways this manifested on a symbolic level was through the practice of identifying figures as the reincarnation of (often many) previous masters. For example, all the founding members of Mindröling were identified with figures from imperial times through reincarnation, which they often reasserted on each other's behalf. Terdak Lingpa, who was recognized as Vairocana,[64] would assert the Fifth Dalai Lama's identity as a reincarnation of Tri Songdetsen.[65] (Much more common was the claim that the Dalai Lama was connected to Songtsen Gampo.) Dharmaśrī was recognized as an emanation of Yudra Nyingpo, who was a disciple of Padmasambhava and Vairocana in the eighth century. As we will see, recontextualization of the old was a constant theme in the long-standing connection between Terdak Lingpa and the Dalai Lama.

The Fifth Dalai Lama's Wider Nyingma Ties

In the broader context in which these relationships developed, the Fifth Dalai Lama had relationships with many Nyingma masters, beyond this family. Although his official position tied him to the Géluk school and its particular political and ritual investments, he had family affiliations and strong personal interests in Nyingma teachings and practices. Over the course of his reign, the Dalai Lama studied esoteric philosophy, received ritual initiations, and took counsel with Nyingma lamas, sometimes prompting disapproval from his more orthodox Géluk colleagues. One important role that Nyingma lamas played for the Fifth Dalai Lama's government was as experts in ritual warcraft, performed to help the government fend off military enemies. The Dalai Lama's secret biography indicates that these rites caused him anxiety because they challenged Buddhist ethics. Nonetheless, such rites were part of his rise to power, and he recorded his own related visions.[66] The Dalai Lama's biography, composed by Sangyé Gyatso, also recounts that the prophesies of Ratna Lingpa and Dorjé Lingpa

Figure 1.2 Wall painting of Padmasambhava from Mindröling monastery.
Photograph by Leigh Miller

(previous incarnations of Terdak Lingpa, according to biographies and underscored in the Dalai Lama's letters) were instrumental in his identification as the rightful Dalai Lama. These examples are part of a wider pattern of mutual legitimation that would be vital in Mindröling's position as a civilizational center.

At the heart of the heterogeneous Nyingma tradition are Padmasambhava and Yeshé Tsogyel, the originators of the Tibetan tradition of rediscovering Treasure. In the founding of Samyé monastery, the emperor Tri Songdetsen released the queen Yeshé Tsogyel from their conventional marriage so she could become Padmasambhava's consort or tantric partner. At the same time, he provided Padmasambhava with royal patronage. This formative narrative reverberates throughout the life stories of countless men and women who take part in the Treasure tradition, which is still vibrant today.

In most cases, visionaries such as Terdak Lingpa discover teachings generated by Padmasambhava and concealed by Yeshé Tsogyel with the intention that the appropriate person at the appropriate time under the appropriate conditions will find them. A *tertön* (*gter ston*) is someone karmically tasked with rediscovering these *terma* texts, objects, and teachings, when people and places are ready to benefit from them.

The story of Padmasambhava, Yeshé Tsogyel, and Tri Songdetsen is directly funneled into the foundation of Mindröling, where Terdak Lingpa becomes the equivalent of Padmasambhava, his consort is equivalent to Yeshé Tsogyel, and the Fifth Dalai Lama is Tri Songdetsen. This mythos fueled and gave shape to the impetus for founding Mindröling.

The Start of Terdak Lingpa's Career as a Visionary

Terdak Lingpa's formal career as a Treasure revealer began when he was eighteen years old, in 1663. At his mother's urging, he traveled from Dargyé Chöling across the Tsangpo River to the valley of Yemalung, where he revealed *The Knowledge Holder's Heart Essence* (*rig 'dzin thugs thig*). He pulled the *terma* out of a crack he found in a rock-face cliff.[67]

When he was twenty-two, he revealed his second Treasure, *The Lord of Death Who Destroys Arrogance* (*gshin rje dregs 'joms*), at Yarlung Shedrak.[68]

Tulku Thondop Rinpoche translates a richly detailed account of the dream in which Terdak Lingpa receives the prophetic instructions for finding it. In the dream he encounters a *ḍākinī*

> in the form of a beautiful, smiling young lady attired in colorful silk with precious jewel ornaments. She began showing him the expression and indications of great bliss. By having union with her he was liberated into the expanse of freedom from elaborations, the nature of the experiences of exquisite great bliss. The *ḍākinī* said, "The wisdom of great bliss is nothing else than this. Now you have accomplished the auspicious circumstances." And she took off her precious ring and put it in his cup saying, "Keep it as a sign of accomplishment."[69]

The aesthetics of this passage are striking. Notice the sensory and physical aspects of the dream—colorful silk, precious jewels, exquisite great bliss—which results in Terdak Lingpa finding a Treasure scroll in his cup upon waking. The woman's beauty matters, as do her sumptuous clothes and ornaments. Their physical connection opens his potential to discover the Treasure. The account of the actual discovery is equally rich in imagery, emotion, and affective impact. Such material underscores how a sense of beauty and a mastery of the senses and expression are tied intimately to authority and effectiveness in this context.

When the time comes for him to reveal the Treasure, the account from Terdak Lingpa's inner biography is again rich with sensory imagery and force. In this passage, he has arrived at the rock described in the prophetic guide, when suddenly a massive chasm more than one hundred stories deep opens between him and the rock. At the height of about five stories over his head, rainbow lights appear in the shape of the symbol that was meant to mark the location of the Treasure. He feels terrified by the sheer drop of the chasm, sees no way of reaching the Treasure, and falls unconscious with fear. Then: "instantly he found himself on top of the rock. There he found a tent-like cave, with walls like crystal covered with bright frescoes. In that cave were a young and beautiful lady and a handsome man, both dressed in exquisite white clothing. . . . The lady gave him two scrolls and the man a three-cornered casket made of *se*."[70]

The vividness of the emotional state—his terror and anxiety—stands in an exciting contrast to the relief and pleasure of awaking in a crystal cave painted with vivid images on the walls. Physical beauty and exquisite clothing are the predominant characteristics of the figures in the cave. Here again, beauty matters—not for its own sake alone, but also because it seems to convey a sense of rightness and order, which undergird Terdak Lingpa's authority as a Treasure revealer perfectly suited to his time and place.

In sum, Terdak Lingpa discovered four major Treasures between the ages of eighteen and thirty-five.[71] Here I focus on how Terdak Lingpa's career as a visionary intersected with his relationship to the Fifth Dalai Lama. Take the example of the Treasure he discovered in public in 1680, called the *Doctrinal Cycle of the Great Compassionate One as the Gathering of all the Sugatas* (*thugs rje chen po bde gshegs kun 'dus kyi chos skor*), his fourth and last Treasure.[72] It included thirteen scrolls of yellow paper that contained the details of a new style of ritual dance.[73] The dance tradition developed at Mindröling, based on this Treasure, would become an important model for other monasteries, in another example of Mindröling's aesthetic influence and cultural network. The deity of focus in this ritual dance cycle is Avalokiteśvara, with whom the Fifth Dalai Lama was identified. It is significant also that this act of rediscovery took place in public. The visibility of the event reverberates with the Fifth Dalai Lama's efforts to communicate a particular message about Terdak Lingpa, and later Mindröling—as a site of special significance for the enrichment and protection of Tibet.

More generally, throughout Terdak Lingpa's biography, he appears in public, or literally in the "marketplace" (*khrom*), giving instructions, audiences, and initiations. The public nature of Terdak Lingpa's visionary activities and teachings helped establish him and Mindröling not just in the Lhasa region but across Tibetan Buddhist areas. The public aspect of Terdak Lingpa's work helped to strengthen his reputation and then build a platform on which to establish Mindröling, which had official ritual responsibilities to support the Tibetan government and became a place ordinary people knew about and diverse religious experts congregated during large-scale ritual gatherings. According to Terdak Lingpa's outer biography, the audiences of his public appearances often comprised people from across cultural Tibet, including the regions of Mon and Sikkim.[74]

Echoing the Beauty of the Nyö Ancestor

In a similar fashion, Terdak Lingpa's Nyö ancestor had made an appearance in the marketplace of Kharak, where he made such a strong impression on the local people. The focus on the physical beauty of the Nyö figure as an indication of his power and virtue are similar to descriptions of Terdak Lingpa, whose students described his physical presence and appearance in glowing terms. Consider this passage from the biography of Miwang Polhané (1689–1747), a lay aristocrat who studied at Mindröling in the early eighteenth century and who went on to rule Tibet. The author of the biography, Dokharwa (1697–1763), also studied at Mindröling. (I discuss their education at Mindröling in chapter 5.) The author recounts Polhané's arrival at the monastery and his first meeting with the famed Treasure revealer: "Having arrived at last, walking on foot, he could not be satisfied until he met with the Vidyādhara Terdak Lingpa in person. The precious teacher sat mountainlike and noble. The maṇḍala of his smiling face shone with the brilliance of a hundred thousand moons. His white moustache and beard were extremely beautiful, decorating his face with a mālā of moon rays. Endowed with great compassion, he pacified the senses of sentient beings."[75]

Terdak Lingpa's physical beauty, expressed here in luminous terms, had the effect of making the senses (*dbang po*) of those around him calm and peaceful. The author's attention to his facial hair is reiterated when he states that Terdak Lingpa's beard moved "like a white fly whisk," a symbol associated with both royalty and enlightened teaching.[76] His beauty was not only visual—it encompassed his speech and general presence as well. The passage continues to describe Terdak Lingpa's eloquence during this initial discussion with Polhané and his uncle, who was his chaperone on the journey to Mindröling: "The nectar of his pure speech caressed their ears and penetrated their hearts. Every word expressed a hundred thousand different tastes of pure meaning. He easily explained the path of liberation and omniscience in a relaxed and delightful manner, making its natural radiance lucidly clear."[77]

Terdak Lingpa's appearance—noble and beautiful—is coupled with verbal eloquence that makes him capable of conveying the Dharma effectively, "caressing" his students' ears and "penetrating" their hearts. His words even seem to taste good. His style is relaxed, easygoing, and delightful. The visual beauty and his powerful communication style go hand in hand. His aesthetic traits are valued by the author and presumably the intended audience; the implication is that these are not *mere* appearances but reflect a deeper mastery that is the basis for his efficacy as a teacher. In the accounts of the Nyö ancestor and Terdak Lingpa, as well as in the broader practice of depicting Buddhist masters in richly aesthetic terms, attractiveness is closely associated with merit, virtue, and power. For these figures, affective impact and the power to move us is part and parcel of their authority.

A Pleasure Grove for the Buddhist Senses

Mindröling Takes Root

Pillars of coral, beams of sapphire,
the most splendid colors, embellished with gold,
shine forth as much as is desired, with glittering flourishes.
The effect is like that of all the beautiful belongings of the demigods piled
up together.[1]

—TERDAK LINGPA, TEMPLE WALL CATALOGUE

DURING MINDRÖLING'S EARLY years, what was it like to enter the main
hall, described lavishly by Terdak Lingpa in this verse, which was written
in fine calligraphy on the monastery's wall? What impressions did the
architectural structures, colors, scents, lighting, and textures of the place
make? How did the two- and three-dimensional images of historical teachers and enlightened buddhas impact the senses of those making offerings
and supplications? What responses did practitioners have upon entering
the hall for ritual gatherings? And what feelings were evoked in the pilgrims arriving from across Tibetan Buddhist regions? How did the space
shape those who passed through, whether they were monks, workers, artists, village residents, sponsors, lay students, ritual experts, retreatants, or
visiting lamas? In sum, did the monastery's structure and design evoke the
Buddhist pure realm of Akaniṣṭha for which Mindröling monastery was
named, and if so, how?

In the previous chapter I analyzed the historical factors that led to the
creation of Mindröling. In this chapter, motivated in part by the questions
above, I give an account of the founding of the monastery, attending to its
physical structures, philosophical underpinnings, and cultural networks.
To do so, I examine the context in which Terdak Lingpa, the Fifth Dalai

Figure 2.1 Early eighteenth-century portrait of Terdak Lingpa, with his brother
Lochen Dharmaśrī (bottom left) and son Pema Gyurmé Gyatso (bottom right),
attended by monks handling material offerings.
Courtesy of Rubin Museum of Art

Lama, and their close associates at the Ganden Podrang court in Lhasa articulated and manifested their vision of Mindröling as a new civilizational center.

Mindröling was established within the Lhoka (*lho kha*) area, not far from Lhasa, in 1670. The location is adjacent to the valley where Terdak Lingpa's family had long been established at a practice center called Dargyé Choling. The new main temple was completed and Terdak Lingpa was enthroned in 1676, the year generally cited as the date of the monastery's official foundation.[2] The site was a relatively remote and secluded valley in a place well suited to undistracted study and practice, far enough from Lhasa to offer refuge from the business of the capital but close enough to the city for Mindröling lamas to be involved in the affairs of the court. Today, when approaching the monastery in South Central Tibet, one passes through a relatively arid and quiet valley. The monastery is concealed within the landscape until it becomes visible quite suddenly, tucked into the hillside.

Mindröling would remain a relatively small establishment, housing about 330 monks in the main monastery, about 30 nuns in an adjacent retreat center, and a number of visiting lay students. To varying degrees and in keeping with their individual interests and capacities, they would engage in Great Perfection philosophy and meditation, the arts and sciences, and the ritual techniques Mindröling's founders crystallized so effectively for their time and place.

A Cosmopolitan Structure and a Name Replete with Meaning

The main temple structure was designed to integrate three distinctive architectural styles—Tibetan, Chinese, and Indian—with woodwork details in Nepali style. This particular blend referenced the design of Tibet's first monastery, Samyé (*bsam yas*), which likewise has a tri-tiered structure representing the same Buddhist architectural styles. The visual and structural reference is significant and demonstrates a kind of historical echo in the establishment of Mindröling as a new Nyingma center for "taming" Tibet's landscape and inhabitants (human, animal, and supernatural) through the institutionalization of visionary insights and tantric practices. As the main sponsor, the Dalai Lama aimed for Mindröling to draw together and protect a unified Tibetan polity. As the head of the monastery, Terdak Lingpa aspired to invigorate, clarify, and safeguard the Nyingma school, which was previously diffuse and which he perceived to be marginalized, fractured, and threatened.[3] He had good reason to worry, as later events make clear.

The full name of the monastery is Akaniṣṭha Uddiyana, Isle of Ripening and Liberation, the Great Pleasure Grove of Ultimate Meaning (*'og min o rgyan smin grol gling nges pa don gyi dga' ba'i tshal chen po*). This name reflects a prophecy attributed to Padmasambhava, the mytho-historical Indian tantric master credited with establishing tantric Buddhism in Tibet in the eighth century, in part by safeguarding the construction of Samyé. Terdak Lingpa was directly connected to Padmasambhava as a Treasure revealer (*gter ston*) who was perceived to have special access to his hidden teachings. The name also identifies the monastery with the Buddhist pure realm, Akaniṣṭha, meaning "none higher." This is where the Guhyagharbha tantra, central to Mindröling's activities, traditionally is recorded to have been revealed.[4] The name marks Mindröling as an unparalleled ("none higher") site of tantric learning and practice. It also identifies the monastery as a haven for practices associated with Uḍḍiyāna, as the home of both Padmasambhava and Garap Dorjé, who is credited as the originator of Great Perfection, the system of philosophy and practice for which Mindröling became famous. So the monastery's name, assigned by Terdak Lingpa in keeping with the prophecy and in concert with the Fifth Dalai Lama, simultaneously reflected a prophetic link to the tantric master Padmasambhava and his home in Uḍḍiyāna, the highest Buddha realm of Akaniṣṭha, and the project of ripening (*smin*) and liberating (*grol*) the minds of practitioners in a garden of pleasure and meaning. All of these factors were critical to the role Mindröling would come to play.

A Family Lineage, Including Women

Beyond the physical walls of the monastery, the name Mindröling refers to a transmission lineage (*brgyud*) in which teachings and practices are passed from person to person in an ideally continuous relational sequence.[5] At Mindröling, this is a continuum of people who, over the generations, have received and in turn passed on a carefully cultivated collection of teachings and ritual methods conveyed through texts, oral instructions, or mind-to-mind transmissions. In Tibetan and Zen Buddhist contexts in particular, keeping track of teacher-to-student lineages is a fundamental organizing and legitimating principle.[6] And throughout the Buddhist world, establishing an unbroken lineage that traces back to the Buddha is a major priority; therefore, teacher-to-student connections are carefully accounted for and have at times become a source of dispute.

At Mindröling this lineage of people was and is centered around Terdak Lingpa's family, and extends to the many students and practitioners who receive teachings and initiations in the Mindröling tradition, whether at the main monastery or at an affiliated institution. Since Mindröling primarily is a family-based lineage (*gdung rgyud*), with the principal positions of authority passing from father to son and uncle to nephew, its history is interwoven with the genealogy of the Nyö family group, described in chapter 1.

An organization that centers on a biological family necessarily includes a significant place for women. To state the obvious, women play a fundamental part in family lineages since they bear the children. However, far beyond the work of giving birth, at least five women from the family lineage have emerged as major figures at Mindröling since the seventeenth century. This line of women masters began with Yumchen Lhadzin Yangchen Dolma and Mingyur Peldrön, who were Terdak Lingpa's mother and daughter, respectively.[7] The relative prominence of women at Mindröling is demonstrated by both textual and art historical sources, for instance biographies and painted portraits. In particular, wall paintings of lineage trees depict Mingyur Peldrön and the nineteenth-century Mindröling master Jetsün Trinlé Chödron as fully fledged transmitters of the Mindröling teachings. These visual depictions of members of the lineage are similar to family trees. Intact versions exist at the original Mindröling monastery in Tibet and at the monastery in Clementown, Dehradun, India, which was established in the mid-twentieth century. Lineage trees include only the most renowned and integral teachers, so the women's presence underscores the accomplishments of Mindröling's female lamas over the centuries. In addition to this visual demonstration of the importance of women teachers, today practitioners recite the women's names alongside their male counterparts' names in Mindröling liturgies.[8]

Further, Tibetan sources composed during Mindröling's early days record that Terdak Lingpa and his brother, Lochen Dharmaśrī, predicted that women, and Mingyur Peldrön in particular, would play an important role in the perpetuation of the Mindröling lineage.[9] Indeed, she helped save it from eradication in its second generation, mainly by transmitting her father's teachings after he had passed away and Zungar troops executed other members of the family in a brutal massacre focused on Nyingma institutions, which I address in the epilogue. Several other Mindröling women are the subjects of written biographies or play major roles as teachers and master practitioners in men's biographies. From the time period this work concerns, the biographies of Yangchen Dolma (Terdak Lingpa's mother) and Mingyur Peldrön depict women studying, practicing, teaching, and sponsoring meritorious Buddhist activities as the main work of their lives, as opposed to focusing on their roles as mothers or in supporting male practitioners, for instance as tantric consorts, although this is also important.[10]

I propose that the accomplishments and power of Terdak Lingpa's immediate female relatives and his support for their education and inclusion in the family lineage beyond their roles as consorts and mothers was rooted in his cultivation of an unbiased or rimé (ris med) worldview. This engendered a relatively inclusive atmosphere for women members of Terdak Lingpa's family and inclined him to engage deeply with women students, albeit constrained by historical and social contexts. This perspective is supported in his outer biography (which gives an account of his worldly activities as opposed to his introspective and religious experiences) and through his letters, which I analyze in chapter 3. In such documents, Terdak Lingpa demonstrates his openness to educating women students and corresponding with female disciples and patrons. Resonant with Dorothy Ko's findings on gender and class in seventeenth-century China and in particular her study of elite women's culture in seventeenth-century Jiangnan, my analysis shows that the women of Terdak Lingpa's family played a formative role as teachers and students at Mindröling, and likewise, women of the ruling class had access to the teachings, rituals, and correspondence of Mindröling's main teachers.[11]

Beyond Mindröling, Tibetan women in high-status families like the Nyö clan generally had access to more educational opportunities and social freedom than women of less prestigious and privileged families. Accordingly, a well-educated Tibetan woman might stand as a sign of the family's prestige. From this perspective it is likely that the prominence of women at

Mindröling was facilitated by the family's aristocratic status. This view is supported by the fact that women in other aristocratic families, such as the Khön clan of the Sakya lineage, were also gaining prominence at this time.[12] This suggests a more general societal shift allowing women relatively more freedom and access to education in the early eighteenth century, demonstrated by the density of biographies about women composed during that period.[13] In addition to reflecting a *rimé* perspective, which I expand on below, and perpetuating the practices of the lineage, Mindröling's educated and influential women stood as a reflection of the lineage's social and philosophical sophistication. Their status bolstered the high status of the Nyö clan and the Mindröling lineage more broadly.

As a noncelibate teacher and visionary Treasure revealer, Terdak Lingpa held the role of the first senior chair (*khri chen*), also known as the throne holder—the title for the head of the monastery. At Mindröling this position is passed from father to son, beginning with Terdak Lingpa's son Pema Gyurmé Gyatso (1686–1718), a brilliant scholar and poet who assumed the role for only a few years after his father's death.[14] (Tragically, he was murdered during the Zungar attack.)

The abbot (*mkhan chen*) is the second highest position of authority, held by the younger brother of the senior chair. If there is no living son available to take over the throne, the senior chair's daughter can either transmit the necessary teachings to a suitable successor, marry a qualified heir, or give birth to a son who can eventually be trained for the role, as was the case in the early twentieth century. Terdak Lingpa's younger brother Tenpay Nyima (1648–1674) was the first abbot. He was a renowned scholar of Buddhist ritual arts including dance, music, and visual arts.[15] This model of transmitting authority in the form of Buddhist teachings and cultural practices from one generation to the next made all family members crucial in the establishment of Mindröling. This was particularly true for the males who were in line to become senior chair and abbot, but also for women members of the lineage.

Envisioning Mindröling

Terdak Lingpa's illustrious family history combined with his charisma and skill as a visionary Treasure revealer, scholar, and skillful institution builder. These traits aligned with the Dalai Lama's aspirations for a unified greater Tibetan state modeled on Tibet's imperial period.[16] Terdak Lingpa's new monastery had the potential to fulfill functions that were outside the scope of the Dalai Lama's school's monasteries, such as education in subjects that were omitted from most monastic curricula.[17] At the same time, the Dalai Lama's support allowed Terdak Lingpa to cultivate a stable new center for the Nyingma school. Beyond the family's status, a web of interconnected prophecies, power relationships, religious commitments, personal connections, economic factors, and symbolic resonances all factored into the foundation of the monastery. Critically, the Dalai Lama envisioned Mindröling as an important component in his state-building project—its ritual activities and cultural influence as well as its integration of the priorities of various Tibetan Buddhist schools fulfilled crucial functions in his vision of the new Tibetan polity.

Terdak Lingpa was in his early thirties when the Dalai Lama sponsored the founding of Mindröling. The Dalai Lama provided several large grants of money, land, and labor for the construction of the new monastery. According to Terdak Lingpa's outer biography, the Dalai Lama reported dreams and visions related to the physical construction of the site and performed divination rites to ascertain the most favorable dates for important steps in the process of construction.

Contemporaneous Tibetan sources show that the Dalai Lama described his conception of Mindröling as an institution that would serve as a place of protection, benefit, nurturing, and cultivation for what he referred to as "greater Tibet" (bod chen). This is corroborated by letters the Dalai Lama composed and sent to Terdak Lingpa, in which he uses the same language to evoke a sense of Mindröling's power and significance for Tibet and its inhabitants. Once established, Mindröling replaced Dargyé Chöling, the family's previously established seat, as the principal center for Great Perfection practice in Central Tibet.[18] Through the founders' careful efforts, Mindröling's role would grow to be far more extensive than Dargyé Chöling's had been.

When construction of the new monastery was nearly complete and there was a question about the precise date when the work on the main temple should be finished and what materials should be used, Terdak Lingpa's biographer, his brother, Dharmaśrī, who appears to have been present during the conversation, reports that Terdak Lingpa requested guidance from the Dalai Lama.[19] The Dalai Lama did a divination and then recalled a dream in which he encountered "a woman with a purple complexion whose hair was tied back with a golden cord and who was wearing precious ornaments and a green silk dress" and a "giant black man" (*mi nag ngam bong che ba*).[20] These two figures subsequently were portrayed as overseeing the construction of the monastery.

In the Dalai Lama's dream, the woman revealed that the details and timing of the construction must be treated with care, and urged them to move ahead promptly. "If the construction takes place this year," she said, "there will be few obstacles and it will be accomplished easily." She continued, "If you are careful this will create conditions to benefit all of Tibet (*bod spyi*)." She promised that if the project went well, "Tibet's enemies will never strike and the well-being and prosperity of Tibet's subjects will increase."[21]

The "giant" in turn reported on more granular details, stating that "After statues of Amitāyus and the protectors, the consorts, and retinue are established in the main temple, if the approaching and accomplishing practices along with fulfillment and confession are practiced, the kings of Tibet will live long lives, encounter few obstacles, and their dominion will expand. Then all the Tibetan subjects' well-being certainly will increase."[22] Encouraged by the remarks of these dream interlocutors, the Dalai Lama determined to finalize the construction of the main temple immediately. He arranged for the necessary wood, materials, and workers to travel to the construction site. In the subsequent passage of Terdak Lingpa's outer biography, he is quoted as having stressed the importance of treating the construction workers well, carefully counseling Terdak Lingpa not to take advantage of or offend them. This presumably was meant to fend off negative gossip about the new monastery and any potential resentment of the family lineage on the part of the neighbors. Attention to the fair treatment of laborers is a notable theme in other Mindröling documents, for example the monastic constitution or guidelines (*bca' yig*) that Terdak Lingpa and Dharmaśrī wrote in 1689 to clarify the rules and regulations for monks' behavior.[23] (I return to this document in chapter 4.) The Dalai Lama's dream, conveyed through Terdak Lingpa's biography, established Mindröling's importance to the leaders and people of greater Tibet; according to his vision, the monastery had the potential to repel enemies, bring prosperity and well-being to the Tibetan people, and increase the lifespans and power of Tibetan rulers.

The Dalai Lama's dream of the elegantly dressed woman and the black giant who oversaw Mindröling's construction imbue the monastery's physical structures with increased signficance.[24] Beyond this illustrative instance, prophecy, dreams, and visions together constitute a prevalent theme in Mindröling literature and a formative force in its early history. While these are important elements across Tibetan Buddhist traditions, insights gained through visions and dreams are especially central to Mindröling, as the home of a Treasure revealer whose lineage was known for a Great Perfection practice of lucid dreaming as well.

Around the time of the completion of the main temple, in December 1676, almost ten years after his previous Treasure revelation, Terdak Lingpa discovered Treasures at Okar Drak. These were the Wrathful Guru (*gu ru grag po*) and Vajrasattva Atiyoga Cycle (*rdo sems a ti skor*).[25] This event did not directly impact the construction of the monastery as the Dalai Lama's dreams did, but the timing of the revelation so near to the completion of the main temple adds potency to this period of Terdak Lingpa's life and legacy. His revelations eventually were integrated in the curriculum of the monastery.

Offering Mindröling

In addition to serving these state functions, Mindröling was also conceived as a material offering from the Fifth Dalai Lama to Terdak Lingpa and his family. The *Lamp of Teachings Catalogue* states, "In 1675, the Great Fifth graciously bestowed ownership and complete authority of the entire area of Drachi, where Tharpaling monastery was previously located, and entrusted all the families as religious servants" to Terdak Lingpa.[26] In this regard, the establishment of Mindröling was a gesture of the older lama and statesman's respect and enthusiasm for the younger visionary, from whom he clearly expected a great deal. The *Lamp of Teachings Catalogue* records that in 1670, "The Great Fifth Dalai Lama assigned monks who were in permanent residence as well as providing an endowment for their complete material support" to live at Mindröling.[27] There were also monks and other students who came from branch or affiliate monasteries in other regions to study and practice at Mindröling for set periods of time.[28] (This explains why the monks assigned by the Dalai Lama are described here as "in permanent residence" at the monastery.) The Dalai Lama hand picked the first group of monks who went to live, study, and practice at Mindröling, further indicating his close involvement in the monastery's foundational period and his investment in its success.

Seventeenth-century documents corroborate the magnitude of the Dalai Lama's support. For instance, the *Yellow Beryl* (*Vaidurya Serpo*), composed by the regent, Sangyé Gyatso, includes a census documenting the monasteries of early modern Tibet. In the section about Mindröling, the regent provides a precise account of the grant Terdak Lingpa received to found it. His records are meticulous, including the details of the grant allotted to Terdak Linpga's wife or consort (*yum*): "twenty-two households along with their cultivated land and inhabitants, as well as five smaller households in and around the region of Dranang." These households would have had to provide the consort and her relatives with food and ongoing support. The expected (probably yearly) income from these landholdings was "2,988 bushels of barley."[29] This is a relatively minor amount from the perspective of the Dalai Lama's overall offering, but it is noteworthy that she was singled out in the grant.

The consort mentioned by the regent was most likely Ngödrup Pelzom, a relative of the Fifth Dalai Lama's mother who arrived at Mindröling around the time of Terdak Lingpa's official enthronement. There had been a string of deaths in Terdak Lingpa's extended family and community, and Terdak Lingpa's health was in decline. Her role as his tantric partner was to fend off obstacles to his career as a visionary caused by health issues. In the Tibetan Treasure tradition, visionaries like Terdak Lingpa engage with tantric consorts in order to successfully accomplish their work. The Dalai Lama insisted that Terdak Lingpa invite his relative, Ngödrup Pelzom, as a consort to Mindröling. This family connection parallels strategic marriage alliances between earlier Tibetan rulers. I will develop this point in the next chapter, but it bears mentioning in connection with the *Yellow Beryl*'s account of the grant.

Terdak Lingpa's outer biography makes several mentions of gifts particularly intended to support the construction and maintenance of the monastery. For instance, several successive grants of land and inhabitants[30] from the government are mentioned around the time of Terdak Lingpa's thirty-fifth birthday in 1680.[31] These are listed separately from the valuable items the Dalai Lama and his associates are recorded to have offered

Terdak Lingpa in recognition of his teachings, initiations, and empowerments. On the one hand, there were grants for the establishment of Mindröling, which provided ongoing income and support for the monastery, its
monks, and the family that governed it. Additionally, there was a flow of
material offerings granted to support the frequent ritual functions Terdak
Lingpa performed for the Dalai Lama, the regent, and the government.
These included excellent quality cloth, cymbals, statues, tea for the assembly of monks at Mindröling, fine horses and equestrian equipment, *thangka*
paintings, and so forth. The Tibetan records of both major and minor offerings demonstrate the significance of material culture and aesthetics for
the authors.

It is a common Tibetan biographical convention to list the specific materials given and received alongside teachings given and received. But the fact
that the lists are commonplace should not lead us to overlook them. In Terdak Lingpa's biography, as in many Tibetan biographies, many pages are
devoted to these lists of materials. As in other instances where Buddhist
authors pay attention to material culture, for instance the monastic catalogues I rely on in this chapter, this attention might be seen as problematic
because it seems to fly in the face of Buddhist ideals of asceticism and renunciation. Why do biographers dedicate pages and pages to listing material
offerings if their concern is the transmission of Buddhist knowledge and
insight? Authors attend to the details of the objects and their high quality.
This practice of recording offerings received underscores that materiality
and aesthetics have a central role in Buddhist societies, and the openness of
the practice of keeping records makes clear that this was not problematic.
The act of offering is considered beneficial to the giver, who gets to practice
generosity. What determines whether receiving offerings is in keeping with
Buddhist ideals is *how* the recipient manages the gifts. The standard narrative suggests that teachers used these offerings to support the activities of
the monastery. Case-by-case analysis reveals this was not always true, but
certainly the aim was for teachers like Terdak Lingpa to receive offerings and
do good with them by supporting the monastic assembly and its activities.[32]

To begin to address the complexity of the offerings the Dalai Lama made
to Terdak Lingpa, it will be helpful to consider the broad scope of the grant
given for Mindröling's founding. In the *Mirror of Memory Catalogue*, the
description of the grant suggests a more extensive gift than that recounted
in the *Lamp of Teachings* and described in the *Yellow Beryl*:

The supreme Great Fifth Dalai Lama bestowed an official government deed to assign land, tenants, and estates, confirming that the previous arrangement would continue as it was. Likewise, the three districts of upper Tibet, the four traditional regions of Ü and Tsang, the six ranges of Dokham, as well as the vast regions of Jar, Dakpo and Kongpo, together with Mon, Bhutan, Nepal, Khotan, Sikkim and so forth were offered. In short, it was said that from the stupa in Nepal, to Xining in Kokonor, with the border of the stone pillar in Inner Mongolia as the uppermost limit, the group of thirteen monastic centers and whatever sites are attached to those particular centers belong to Terdak Lingpa's father-to-son lineage. As for all the branches, they are too numerous to mention.[33]

This passage suggests that in the eyes of the twentieth-century Mindröling historians who wrote this catalogue, the Fifth Dalai Lama offered *all of Tibet*—here defined as a truly massive geographic area far beyond even the most expansive conventional definition of traditional Tibet—to Mindröling. By the same token, he bestowed Mindröling upon all of "Tibet," here indicating the areas where Tibetan Buddhism was practiced. Needless to say, the Dalai Lama did not literally give this vast area to Mindröling's hereditary lamas. Rather, he symbolically offered the Tibetan Buddhist world to the family lineage of Mindröling, and literally granted them particular temples and sites scattered across the vast area. In reality the accumulation and affiliation of sites took place over time, but here it is expressed as one grand bequeathal that took place in the seventeenth century. This implicitly called upon Mindröling's lamas to complete the exchange by exerting their potential to enrich, subdue, and protect Tibet, as the Dalai Lama explicitly entreated Terdak Lingpa to do in letters that are the focus of the next chapter.

In the central practice of making offerings to Buddhist teachers, masters, and institutions like Mindröling, ideally the donor's intention is what matters most in determining the effectiveness of the outcome. From that perspective, anything given with pure devotion would be transformed into a precious offering, and a visualized offering would be as valuable as a material one. But in fact the many careful records of offerings given and received in the Tibetan Buddhist context show that the actual material of the offering matters very much. This is especially true when the donors and recipients are powerful and well known, as in the case of the Fifth Dalai Lama and the founders of Mindröling. Biographies, letters, and monastic catalogues all provide careful records of objects the Dalai Lama and other major figures offered to Mindröling. In this way, the expression of generosity and devotion through offerings is interwoven with Buddhist concerns with aesthetics and material culture since the beauty, rarity, preciousness, or grandeur of a gift demonstrates the wealth and power of the donor as well as the worthiness of the recipient. All of this is at stake in many material offerings, including the gift of land and territory.

Like the visualized offerings practitioners give to buddhas and deities, the Dalai Lama's symbolic gift worked to demonstrate the devotion of the giver as well as the worthiness of the recipient. And in this case the *power* of the giver is also implied, since the extent of the offering assumes the Dalai Lama himself had authority over all the regions named. Several were never controlled by the Dalai Lama's central government. But Mindröling did have branches and affiliates in nearly all the regions named, suggesting that its eventual influence was even more far reaching than the Dalai Lama's political reach. Moreover, Mindröling had to be represented across the expanse of the Tibetan landscape in order to uphold the Dalai Lama's stated aim for the monastery to benefit Tibet, the Tibetan people, and Tibetan rulers. Surprisingly, I have not encountered evidence of resistance to Mindröling's broad influence, although surely its prominence came at the expense of other authorities.

With that in mind, what were the social ramifications of such a literal and symbolic offering? When the Dalai Lama officially offered the area of Drachi to Terdak Lingpa—including "land, tenants, and estates"—the people who lived there were designated as part of the gift. This meant they and their descendants would be obliged to offer the produce of their fields and labor to Mindröling, as well as to generally support the monks and other members of Terdak Lingpa's institution in perpetuity. At least from a contemporary standpoint, this fact complicates the ethical and socioeconomic dimensions of the gift beyond its symbolic significance. These were actual people whose lives were presumably changed by the Dalai Lama's gesture.

Indeed, it appears that not all the people of the Drachi valley were content with the arrangement. Some are recorded to have lashed out against the institution of Mindröling during the Zungar occupation from 1717 to 1720 (and again during the Cultural Revolution).[34] Although the available resources are discreet on this point, I speculate that the local people's involvement in damaging Mindröling property in the eighteenth century reflects some dissatisfaction with the arrangement established by the Dalai Lama's grant. To illustrate, the *Lamp of Teachings Catalogue* reports that after Zungar Mongol troops destroyed temples and monuments at Mindröling, the local people picked up where the troops left off and did a great deal more damage.[35] This is alluded to in Terdak Lingpa's daughter Mingyur Peldrön's biography, which asserts that the Drachi valley became extremely barren after the local people joined in the Zungar attack on Mindröling, in a kind of natural retribution for their destructive actions.[36] Another account sums up the aftermath in this way: "The religious books of Mindroling were piled up like an earthen hill, and people were caused to trample back and forth upon them."[37] The passive voice of this statement is provocative—who or what caused the people to trample on the texts that had been so painstakingly written, collected, and edited under Terdak Lingpa's direction? It may not be possible to answer definitively given the sources currently available. Beyond this particular context, the potential for monasteries to come under criticism by laypeople is a long-standing concern for Buddhist authors. Since Buddhism's foundation in India, "annoying" the laity has been a very real threat to the sustainability of monastic communities, which rely on the material support of laypeople. Various Mindröling sources reflect this worry, and chapter 4 demonstrates some of the ways Terdak Linpga sought to avoid displeasing the laity.[38] For now, suffice it to say the Dalai Lama's "gift" of the people of Drachi had long-term repercussions.

In sum, because Terdak Lingpa's family was part of one of Tibet's most prestigious clans, with a long history as landowners and leaders in the Lhasa region, Mindröling-as-offering functioned on multiple levels. In addition to being a religious offering from the Dalai Lama as a Buddhist patron, it was an official government grant of land and human resources to a powerful family group.

Locating Mindröling

The choice of geographical location for the new monastery was an important consideration, reflecting the concern with Tibet's imperial past, links to Padmasambhava, and a spirit of reviving and clarifying Nyingma textual and ritual traditions. The exact location was chosen based on a set of historically charged characteristics. A passage in the *Mirror of Memory*

Catalogue evokes an extremely significant and pleasant location: "between Uru and Yoru, near the southern bank of Yoru's Lohita river, at the birthplace of Minister Gar Tongtsen, is a place called Drachi, an extremely handsome location that blazes gloriously with positive qualities. In accordance with Padmasambhava's prophecy, the monastery is situated in that place."[39]

Significantly, the "extremely handsome" valley of Drachi was the birthplace of the powerful imperial Tibetan minister Gar Tongtsen, a major figure in the court of the eighth-century emperor Songtsen Gampo, who is credited with establishing the first Tibetan code of law, developing a written Tibetan script, and helping to establish Buddhism in Tibet.[40] Additionally, the monastery called Tharpaling (*thar pa gling*) had been situated in Drachi. Tharpaling was established by Lumé Tsultrim Sherab, famous as one of the "ten men from U and Tsang" (*dbus gtsang mi bcu*) who traveled to Eastern Tibet in the tenth century, received ordination and teachings on the Vinaya, and then returned to reestablish monastic Buddhism in Central Tibet, where it had fallen into decline.[41] When Terdak Lingpa set his sights on the Drachi valley, Tharpaling monastery had long since become dilapidated, but the site retained its aura of potent significance and beauty.[42]

The three key points here are that Mindröling's location was prophesied by Padmasambhava, associated with Tibet's imperial minister (who most famously developed a written script), and connected with the tenth-century revitalization of Buddhist monastic discipline in Central Tibet. The location also was characterized as attractive and ablaze with good signs. (Today it is quite dry.) These various threads from the past augured Mindröling's roles in Tibetan society—famous for the rediscovery of *terma*, education in writing and literary arts, and a model of monastic discipline within the revivified Nyingma school.

Decorating Mindröling

Once the location was established, the next step was to design and decorate the various spaces that would support and shelter the activities of the monastery. Tibetan sources from the seventeeth and twentieth centuries alike focus on the grandeur and the high quality of the materials and craftsmanship of the monastery's architecture as well as its cosmopolitan aesthetic.

This passage, excerpted from the *Mirror of Memory Catalogue*, is characteristic of the document as a whole (and like other Mindröling catalogues) in its attention to materiality and aesthetics. It gives a sense of the focus on high-quality and precious materials, artistry, and charisma at Mindröling:

> The main temple's upper and lower sections have one hundred twenty pillars combined. The assembly hall's innermost chamber, a Ü-Tsang style structure, has as its main image a three-and-a-half-story-high Buddha statue, extremely sacred and of the very best quality. He has a retinue of eight spiritual sons, each two stories high, and on either side there is a life-size statue of a gatekeeper. All this is in keeping [with a prophecy]. There is also a mural with a thousand Buddha images and wall-sized depictions of the two main disciples of Buddha, a Chinese bronze Buddha image with a golden color, a life-size statue of the goddess Tara, and a one-story-high stupa. In the sutra temple, there is a mural with a thousand images of the Buddha of Boundless Life painted in gold, a *thangka* depicting the one hundred acts of Buddha Gautama's life story, clay statues of the sixteen Arhats, and one-story-high statues of the four guardian kings made of the highest quality material. To the right of the assembly hall, in the large shrine room the main image is a one-story-high Buddha of Boundless Life in gilded copper. There is also an image that the Great Tertön [Terdak Lingpa] made in his likeness, with a face that actually resembles him; a one-story-high statue of Padmasambhava; magnificent clay statues of his eight manifestations, each one story high; and the one hundred and eight volumes of the Kangyur in especially fine quality calligraphy.[43]

Note the qualitative phrases: "of the very best quality," "Chinese bronze," "painted in gold," "of the highest quality material," "in gilded copper," "magnificent," and "especially finequality calligraphy." Observe the repetition of the terms "highest quality" as well as the specification of materials including bronze, gold, copper, and magnificent clay. The focus on the fine quality handwriting also reflects Mindröling's fame for written arts, including calligraphy.

In addition to the valuable materials and exquisite craftsmanship, the large size and grandeur of the images stand out, as does the work of Terdak Lingpa's own hand in designing the temple—represented by an image he made to look just like himself. The temple also includes figures from Buddhism's three main traditions of "Hīnayāna," Mahāyāna, and Vajrayana, elements of which are integrated into Tibetan Buddhism. The broader cosmopolitanism of Buddhist aesthetics is alluded to in the mentions of a Chinese bronze and a Central Tibetan architectural style. Although only these two distinctive styles are alluded to in this passage, the mention of differing styles reflects a broader attention to a range of architectural styles and aesthetic features in Buddhist temple construction.

A Material Manifestation of Emptiness

The Fifth Dalai Lama, Terdak Lingpa, and Lochen Dharmaśrī all contributed sections to a catalogue (*dkar chag*) of Mindröling that was displayed in fine calligraphy just outside the main assembly hall. For clarity, I refer to this as the *Temple Wall Catalogue*. No date is visible in the transcription I have, but the authors likely composed it shortly before or during the period

Figure 2.2 Calligraphy with decorative leaf-and-flower motif from pillar within Mindröling monastery, in seventeenth-century style (*'bru tsha zhabs ring ma*), possibly a section of the catalogue composed by the Fifth Dalai Lama, Terdak Lingpa, and Lochen Dharmaśrī.
Photograph by Pema Bhum

between 1676 (when Mindröling's main temple was completed) and 1682 (when the Dalai Lama died). The preserved and transcribed sections,which are incompletely preserved due to damage to the temple, are composed in skillful ornate poetry. Terdak Lingpa is described in this document not only as a Treasure revealer and tantric master but also as a master poet (*snyan ngag mkhan*), drawing attention to his literary skills.[44] In the section displayed on the southern wall, Terdak Lingpa expressed his intention for the architecture of Mindröling to materially manifest aspects of Buddhist insight and realization:

> To give our friends with wrong views access to the Two Truths,
> and to show them how to subdue, the veranda with twenty pillars,
> arranged in perfectly concentric squares, forms a vast palace
> for an ocean of the Victor's heirs, and at its very center—
>
> the Victor's grand inestimable mansion, a perfumed chamber.[45]
> Pillars of the four stages of miraculous ability are clustered and raised up.
> The thresholds are emptiness, signlessness, and absence of intention—
> these three kinds of liberation are opened wide.
>
> To the right and left, alcoves with latticed windows are constructed.
> In all, eighty-four great pillars are raised up.
> The three stories of the building are the three wheels.[46]
> The design is elegant, pleasing, marvelous—oceanic enjoyment!
>
> The great hall's foundation and all of its surfaces
> are plastered to be exceedingly smooth
> and will be anointed with sweet-smelling perfume—
> Pellucid as a jeweled mirror.[47]

This excerpt from the late seventeenth-century composition gives a sense of the splendor of the monastic space, albeit enriched for literary impact.[48] Terdak Lingpa composed the section posted on the southern wall, from which this passage is taken. Dharmaśrī composed a section written below that of his brother, and the Dalai Lama composed another section of the catalogue, which was posted on the northern wall of the monastery.[49] Who was the audience for this rich description in perfectly metered verse (which I unfortunately have not approximated in translation)? Who are those friends who misunderstand the Two Truths of ultimate and relative reality? And how was the space meant to do this enlightening work? What is most important is that Terdak Lingpa interweaves the materiality of the building with the philosophical tenets and practices he and his lineage are known for—the doorways are the Two Truths, the pillars are miraculous abilities, the thresholds are three kinds of liberation, and the building's stories are the three wheels of reading, hearing, and contemplation. All of this is perfumed, polished, and dazzlingly decorated. The worldly building is inextricable from the Dharma that the space is designed to protect and maintain.

Terdak Lingpa's section is also evidence of his skill in writing poetry. The rich sensory imagery offers a taste of how he conceptualized the integration of the material world with the accomplishments of Buddhist practice. The passage describes the main hall of the monastery as a delight for the senses, a panoramic and pervasive aesthetic experience inseparable from Buddhist realization of emptiness and selflessness. Through the lines of the poem, the physical foundation, walls, and decorations of the building materially support and protect the activities of Buddhist practice and learning. Implicit here is the claim that this focus on pleasure, beauty, and enjoyment need not be a distraction from the Buddhist content but rather is integral to it. The conventional (buildings) are the expression of the ultimate (emptiness). Therefore, to construct physical buildings and celebrate the materiality of the space need not distract from the Dharma. The text, displayed in a calligraphic style distinctive of Terdak Lingpa's day, demonstrates that the founders intended for the material structure of Mindröling to elevate and safeguard the practical activities of Buddhism that were inculcated through its curriculum of study and rituals.

The passage above is indicative of the entire document's brilliant interweaving of the Dharmic and the material. Every line marries an object or expression of the senses—sight, scent, touch, hearing—with a significant Buddhist philosophical or practical concept, such as the Two Truths (*bden gnyis*) and the miraculous abilities associated with tantric accomplishment. Since it is so difficult to realize these concepts, the first verse suggests, Terdak Lingpa built Mindröling. In this way the physical space is infused with the transcendent at a site thereby made appropriate for

Buddhist learning and transformation, even for those people who might otherwise misunderstand.

Setting an Unbiased Foundation

A principal philosophical tenet that motivated Mindröling's founders is the Buddhist ideal of an unbiased worldview, the historical roots of which I introduced in chapter 1.[50] Cultivating a *rimé* view is espoused throughout Indian and Tibetan Mahāyāna literature. The concept spans religious, political, and social distinctions. I argue that it crystallizes a particularly Tibetan Buddhist mode of philosophical and moral cosmopolitanism. Leading figures of what Gene Smith called Tibet's "nonsectarian movement,"[51] such as Jamgön Mipham Gyatso (1846–1912),[52] looked back in time to Mindröling's founders for inspiration and characterized the monastery's early days as marking a "golden age."[53] These nineteenth-century figures associated with nonsectarianism lauded Terdak Lingpa in part because he aimed to institutionalize the ideal of being impartial at Mindröling.

Scholars have productively critiqued the suitability of the term "nonsectarian movement" on a number of grounds, including that the leaders associated with the term were much too diverse in their activities and aims to comprise a "movement."[54] My objection to the translation of *rimé* as "nonsectarian" is that the Tibetan term is much more expansive than "nonsectarian" suggests. A genuinely *rimé* perspective is comparable to being enlightened, and that shapes all one's actions, not only those pertaining to sect. Translating the Tibetan adjective *rimé* into English therefore calls for an attentiveness to context—it can appropriately be translated as "unbiased," "impartial," "without prejudice," and even "boundaryless," or "directionless," among other more general possibilities such as "diverse" or "mixed," and this list is by no means exhaustive. To avoid the reduction of this term to merely "nonsectarian," it is important to keep its broader semantic scope in mind.

For example, Terdak Lingpa's biographer uses the term *rimé* to suggest that Terdak Lingpa, like other celebrated practitioners, came to embody this characteristic of the Great Perfection method. Terdak Lingpa's inner or religious biography (*gter bdag gling pa'i nang gi rnam thar*) consists of various materials compiled by Dharmaśrī and Terdak Lingpa himself. Dharmaśrī composed the following opening verses:

> Naturally arisen sun of knowledge, freed from the clouds of the two obscurations,
> your primordially pure, immutable, ultimate clear light ascends to the highest point of the sky's expanse.
> Light rays of well-being and happiness, *unbiased* toward beings, arise eternally as the union that resolves dualities in the indestructible dance.
> All-victorious transformation, I prostrate to you, great *tertön* and teacher.[55]

This passage, found in the opening pages of the biography, demonstrates that a *rimé* mentality (which I have translated as "unbiased") was a high priority. It is one of the main characteristics the author highlights when introducing Terdak Lingpa to the reader. Here the focus clearly is on Terdak Lingpa's enlightened qualities rather than on suggesting anything about his position on sect and sectarianism per se.

It is also of course true that someone who achieved and maintained a *rimé* perspective would not fall prey to sectarianism. And indeed, Terdak Lingpa forged connections with teachers, disciples, and donors across sectarian and regional boundaries, in a more external expression of the *rimé* worldview. This seems to have been both a savvy strategy to ensure Mindröling's stability and a genuine extension of the philosophical perspective he cultivated and propagated.

While I cannot prove that Terdak Lingpa perfectly embodied this ideal, it is clear that Mindröling was important to practitioners from across Tibetan Buddhist schools, while also modeling and even defining what it meant to be a quintessentially Nyingma institution. This dual aspect would at times serve Mindröling well, gaining it sponsors and students from across the Tibetan Buddhist world. At other times its strong Nyingma identity would make it vulnerable, as when Zungar troops sought to stamp out Mindröling and other Nyingma monasteries in 1717–1718.

This complex identity made Mindröling a site of great prestige that was also on the margins. This was because members of the Nyingma school, especially tantric adepts who also had families, had long had a complicated status in Tibetan Buddhist societies. For instance, after the fall of the

Tibetan empire and the termination of imperially sponsored Buddhist institutions, family-based communities of practice continued as the centers of teaching and ritual, largely under a thin veil of secrecy. These were the places where Tibetan practitioners carried on the work of being Buddhist, assimilating practices and teachings imported from India and fitting them to Tibetan specifications. When Buddhism was revived after a period of institutional quiet, critics vilified Nyingma practitioners for having let wither the foundations of celibate, monastic Buddhism and for engaging in violent ritual practices. At the same time, this marginality put them at the center of what it meant to be tantric. So while Mindröling was supported by the Dalai Lama and his government, at the center of political authority, it was also on the fringe of the Ganden Podrang establishment due to its strong Nyingma characteristics. This likely made it all the more important for Mindröling to reflect a *rimé* ideal.

For the authors associated with Mindröling during the period this book is concerned with, the term *rimé* seems to have had a primarily philosophical, soteriological connotation. The term developed through Great Perfection philosophy and practice, and refers to the impartiality and nondiscriminatory perspective of full awakening. The celebration of this ideal is demonstrated, for example, in the letters Terdak Lingpa wrote to disciples, where he uses a version of the term, *chok rimé,* to refer to himself as "the directionless vagabond" (*phyogs ris med pa'i rgyal khams pa*).[56] Here "directionless" signifies utter impartiality, celebrating his stature as a renunciant without direction, limits, or bias. This is a claim about the extent of his renunciation and the special quality of his perspective. In this way the adjective reflects the accomplishment of Great Perfection practices.

Terdak Lingpa also uses the term *rimé* when directing a student toward the highest goal of the mind of enlightenment—"generate the supreme mind of enlightenment for all beings without bias."[57] And in a letter to another disciple (possibly his sister), he writes:

> For the old mother beings of the six realms
> generate the benefit of impartial consideration.
> With emptiness and compassion, undivided,
> offer, meditate, praise, and practice.[58]

The term can also refer to people affiliated with diverse groups—men and women, old and young, members of different socioeconomic classes, people from different regions, different religious groups—gathered for a communal purpose.[59] For example, in the biography of Terdak Lingpa's mother, composed by Dharmaśrī, the author mentions such a gathering (*ris med pa'i dge 'dun*).[60] This usage also appears in *The Lamp of Teachings Catalogue*, where the Fifth Dalai Lama's funeral services are described in this way: "In the wood dog year 1694 on February 20, in honor of the Fifth Dalai Lama's funeral service, Desi Sangyé Gyatso renounced, meditated on awakening, and invited an assembly of diverse (*ris med pa'i*) sangha members to the Jokhang in Lhasa."[61]

So a *rimé* view transcends partiality without abandoning a particular perspective and subjectivity. The range of usages in sources associated with Mindröling's founding leads me to think that Terdak Lingpa and his collaborators used the ideal of an unbiased, impartial worldview as a guiding principle in building the institution of Mindröling. Another important way this manifested was in the inclusion of worldly subjects of learning as well as Dharma in the education offered at the monastery. This impartiality was a defining feature of Mindröling's identity and legacy from its earliest days.

Buddhist Arts and Sciences

The study of the arts and sciences or *rikné* (*rig gnas*), the traditional Buddhist fields of knowledge developed in India that included worldly and Buddhist subjects, was central in the education of monastic students and lay students alike at Mindröling. Dharmaśrī, himself a monk, not a layman, was a highly sought-after teacher of the arts and sciences, and as such drew students to Mindröling. As distinct from the study of Dharma per se, the other subjects of *rikné* are sometimes referred to as the "conventional fields" of learning (*tha snyad kyi gnas*).[62] The relationship between these fields and Buddhism is reflected in the Tibetan concept of properly balancing the Two Systems (*lugs gnyis*) of religious and worldly commitments and knowledge. The conventional fields of learning, which are distinct from but interwoven with the study of Buddhist doctrine, are directly engaged with cultural production and aesthetics. In brief, the

Figure 2.3 Early eighteenth-century portrait of Lochen Dharmaśrī.
Courtesy of Rubin Museum of Art

five major *rikné* are plastic arts (*bzo gnas rig pa*), medicine (*gso ba'i rig pa*), grammar (*sgra'i rig pa*), dialectics (*gtan tshigs kyi rig pa*), and religious doctrine (*nang gyi rig pa*). I discuss these fields in greater detail in the context of monastic education in chapter 4 and lay education in chapter 5; it is important to note here the central presence of these subjects in Mindröling's identity from its foundation.

The convergence of expertise in the arts and sciences (a rubric that also includes the study of Buddhism, but only as one of its five major fields) on the one hand, and esoteric meditative and philosophical practice on the other, would be key in shaping the particular role and authority of Mindröling, where training in *rikné* was a major purpose. Skill in these fields of knowledge was highly valuable to laypeople who came to the monastery as temporary students and went on to secular careers, but the monks at Mindröling also studied the subjects.

Circumstances combined to make Mindröling a principal location for the Dalai Lama to support the cultivation of *rikné* in Central Tibet.[63] In general in the Central Tibetan region, these fields of study were not as widely valued by members of the Dalai Lama's Géluk school as they were by members of the Nyingma school. (This was not the case in Eastern Tibet, particularly Amdo.) There seems to have been a concern that training in *rikné* in a monastic setting would put monks at risk of becoming overly involved in politics and administration. This anxiety led to a tendency for monastic curricula to support monks learning to read, but not to write.[64] And the main Géluk monasteries in Lhasa discouraged the study of *rikné* during the Fifth Dalai Lama's time. However, the Fifth Dalai Lama himself, as a consummate renaissance man with strong family ties to the Nyingma school, as well as his regent Sangyé Gyatso, highly valued the study of *rikné*. This is made clear through the style of their writing, which reflects a rigorous training in the literary fields of *rikné* with strong Indic influences. The Dalai Lama's new state-building project necessarily involved developing and consolidating Tibetan cultural production as well. Therefore he needed to assure the preservation and dissemination of *rikné* even as he discouraged monks at the main Lhasa Géluk monasteries from studying the more conventional and worldly subjects. Mindröling took up that task. In time, the Dalai Lama's main Géluk centers adopted some of the artistic practices connected to *rikné* from Mindröling, for example, the tradition's special form of monastic dance.[65]

Mindröling as the Center of a Buddhist Cultural Network

Today Mindröling is known as a "mother monastery" (ma dgon).[66] This indicates that adherents of the Nyingma school recognize it as a principal center for their traditions of practice and learning. There are six such monasteries in Central and Eastern Tibet.[67] Beyond the main monastery, many smaller affiliated monasteries, temples, and other communities of practice—such as the ritual centers for professional lay practitioners (sngags mang) that are common in Northeastern Tibet—follow various aspects of Mindröling's curriculum, ritual liturgy, or other aesthetic practices.[68] Such branches and affiliated institutions, which approximate or follow the Mindröling religious system (chos lugs), are found across the Tibetan Buddhist world. Some, such as Lumora monastery (klu mo ra) in the Eastern Tibetan region of Nyarong (nyag rong), took Mindröling as a direct model and adopted its monastic liturgies and curriculum. The shrine rooms still contain images of Terdak Lingpa and Dharmaśrī. Lumora and the main Mindröling monastery have been intimately related since the eighteenth century.[69] Likewise, the main Nyingma monasteries in Rebkong, a region in Northeastern Tibet famed for its literary and visual arts production, based their monastic organization and guidelines on those of Mindröling.[70] Other monasteries have more tenuous ties to Mindröling, but claim affiliation on some count. This network of interrelated institutions across the Tibetan plateau, Sikkim, Bhutan, Nepal, India, and more recently Europe and the United States is also in some sense invoked by the name Mindröling. The officially recognized branch monasteries are listed in the Lamp of Teachings Catalogue and added to the Mirror of Memory Catalogue. The institutional relationships between "mother monastery" and "son monasteries" (bu dgon) or branches (dgon lag) developed over the subsequent centuries as part of the Mindröling legacy that was initiated by the efforts of Terdak Lingpa and his immediate family.

Monastic networks have long been a critical element in Tibetan societies and have connected distant regions and peoples.[71] Through movement between monastic centers located across the Tibetan Buddhist area, aesthetic practices, sartorial conventions, artistic styles, ritual liturgies, economics, philosophical insights, political alliances, and more have spread and developed. From its earliest days, Mindröling's monastic network took part in this broader phenomenon, and while the main monastery was small by the standards of the largest Tibetan monasteries, it developed many significant affiliations through which its traditions spread.

Taking a closer look at Mindröling's monastic network, the *Lamp of Teachings Catalogue* lists places formally defined as "Minling branches" (*smin gling dgon lag*). The next list is of places that follow the Mindröling system but are not branches per se (*chos lugs gcig pa'i dgon lag*). First, the list of proper branches includes Dargyé Chöling, which was Terdak Lingpa's family seat and retreat site prior to Mindröling's founding; Zangtso, a hermitage founded by the fifteenth-century Ösal Longyang; Lhodrak Ling, near where Milarepa and Marpa formed their famous student-teacher bond; Chak Jangjub Ling, the birthplace of Terdak Lingpa's father, founded by a disciple of Bhutan's Buddhist hero Pema Lingpa; the retreat place of Go Gonpa; Chonggyé Mizhi Lhakang, near the birthplace of the Fifth Dalai Lama; Yarlung Négon, the home of Tibet's imperial line; Kongpo Dechen Tengon and Monteb Tsegon, both of which are situated in important border regions (to the southeast); and a site associated with the fourteenth-century master Longchenpa called Shang kyi Zabu lung.[72] According to the catalogue's editor, these monasteries were under the religious and temporal (*chos srid*) authority of Mindröling.[73] This suggests that in addition to adopting Mindröling's ritual cycles and curriculum, the other monasteries were governed by Mindröling's hierarchs to some extent. Moreover, when major events such as enthronement and consecration ceremonies or large-scale public rituals took place at the mother monastery, the branches were required to send representatives who delivered prescribed offerings to Mindröling.[74]

The second category of affiliates that follow the Mindröling system is looser and longer, since the definition of a monastery that follows this monastic system is left ambiguous. There are many ways to take part in the system, including adopting aspects of the curriculum, artistic practices, ritual liturgies, guidelines on monks' robes, and so forth. In the *Lamp of Teachings* this list includes the important Eastern Tibetan monastery of Degé Shechen, itself known as a mother monastery; and a monastery in Yardrok, where Terdak Lingpa's consort and the Fifth Dalai Lama's mother were both from. Of particular significance in regard to Mindröling's role vis-à-vis the Tibetan government and the impact that role had on the relationship between Buddhism and temporal rule in neighboring Sikkim, the

Sikkimese royal state monastery of Pemayangtsé is also mentioned as an affiliate.[75]

This Sikkimese connection is important. Mindröling's founders and their disciples helped secure Pemayangtsé's position as the state monastery of Sikkim and in the process influenced the selection of ritual cycles that came to dominate Sikkim's official engagement with Buddhist practice. Through the work of Terdak Lingpa's student Jikmé Pawo (d.u.), Mindröling played a formative role in the establishment of the Sikkimese state in the eighteenth century. Jikmé Pawo became the head of Pemayangtsé monastery after studying at Mindröling.[76] The institutional connection between Terdak Lingpa's family and the Sikkimese royal family was solidified through marriage. When Mindröling was sacked by the Zungar Mongol army in 1718, Terdak Lingpa's daughter Mingyur Peldrön and other surviving family members, including her mother and sister, took refuge in Sikkim, where Mingyur Peldrön's reputation as a master of Great Perfection teachings was established. Her younger sister married into the Sikkimese royal family during that time.[77]

In addition to the monasteries mentioned already, *The Mirror of Memory* claims locations as branches and affiliates that are not referred to in *The Lamp of Teachings*, perhaps reflecting a difference in the compilers' priorities. Examples of such different priorities might be the effort to draw attention to branches and affiliates in historically significant locations, politically strategic locations, or diverse regions covering a large geographic area. The additional monasteries listed in *Mirror of Memory* include Tsari Chözam Gon, near the important Central Tibetan pilgrimage site of Tsari; and Amdo Rebkong Nyin monastery and Rebkong Sib monastery, institutions on the "sunny" side (*nyin*) and "shady" side (*srib*) of the Amdo region of Rebkong.[78] Other sources suggest that in fact only the latter follows the Mindröling tradition.[79] *Mirror of Memory* further states that there are too many affiliated monasteries to possibly name them all, illustrating this point with the assertion that Lumora monastery has its own many "offspring" monasteries, the implication being that some Mindröling's branches are "mother monasteries" in their own right and that the accumulated institutional network therefore is immeasurable.[80] Most important, the branches and affiliates listed in both catalogues spread out over the entirety of the area of what was in the seventeenth century designated "greater Tibet" by the Fifth Dalai Lama and his regent, Sangyé Gyatso, with significant affiliates in Sikkim and Bhutan as well.[81]

Mindröling's far-reaching role in Tibetan cultural production is supported by its extended institutional network, so it is worth considering the characteristics of the list in general, and pointing out some of the more significant places. The network includes temples in the southern region of Lhodrak, where the famous yogin Milarepa studied with Marpa the translator. It also includes locations near Samyé, the first Tibetan Buddhist monastery and a model for the founding of Mindröling in its relation to the Dalai Lama's new state vision. A site in Chongyé is significant because that is where the Fifth Dalai Lama was born. A branch in the Yarlung valley, home of the Tibetan imperial family, signifies Mindröling's ties to notions of imperial authority. Other significant locations are the border regions of Kongpo and Mon. In sum, this network plants offshoots of Mindröling in border regions defining the perimeter of greater Tibet, in the valley associated with Tibet's imperial past, and in areas once ruled by strong local aristocratic families, some of whose power was threatened by the Dalai Lama's government in the seventeenth century.

Terdak Lingpa's Role as Imperial Preceptor

In 1682 the Fifth Dalai Lama, Terdak Lingpa's main sponsor, passed away. Shortly before dying, he named Terdak Lingpa as his imperial preceptor (*ti shri*).[82] This occurred just after Terdak Lingpa instructed the Dalai Lama on the *Nyingma Gyübum*, the *Collected Tantras of the Nyingma School*. This event is significant on a number of levels. First, the Dalai Lama's naming of an official imperial preceptor implies his own role as that of an emperor. Moreover, singling out Terdak Lingpa for this role helped solidify his place as a major figure in the work that would be continued by the regent, Sangyé Gyatso, who continued to look to Terdak Lingpa for guidance, advice, and counsel in the subsequent decades. Their relationship would also help establish Mindröling's role in the newly envisioned Tibetan polity, shaped on the model of the Tibetan empire that flourished in the seventh through ninth centuries.

The Dalai Lama's death came just six years after Terdak Lingpa took the throne at Mindröling in 1676. At a time when the relatively young Ganden Podrang government was in a tenuous balance with the Khoshot Oriat Mongols, who had established the Dalai Lama's religious and temporal authority, the regent, Sangyé Gyatso, concealed the Dalai Lama's death for fourteen years. Rather than revealing the truth and risking a loss of his power and a descent into political chaos, the regent selected a monk named Depa Trerap from Namgyal monastery who had a similar complexion to the Fifth Dalai Lama and was about the same age. For more than a decade, the regent and his small group of collaborators compelled the monk to pretend he was Tibet's religio-secular ruler. The monk lived virtually as a prisoner, making occasional appearances before Mongol officials when it could not be avoided and staying for long periods in supposed retreat.[83] This account is made more poignant by the fact that the young Sixth Dalai Lama was simultaneously held under virtual house arrest and would only be released and enthroned as a teenager.

Only a very few people were aware that the Fifth Dalai Lama had died. Terdak Lingpa was among them. As one of the regent's closest advisors during this fraught period, Terdak Lingpa provided instructions to the imposter to help him deliver a convincing performance in his role. According to Sangyé Gyatso's account of the period of almost fifteen years between the Fifth Dalai Lama's secret death and the official enthronement of the Sixth Dalai Lama, Terdak Lingpa continually advised and counseled the regent through the strife-ridden decisions involved in identifying the child who would be trained as the Dalai Lama's successor and keeping the death a secret.[84] Terdak Lingpa had also been instrumental in establishing Sangyé Gyatso's remarkable level of authority as regent in 1679.[85]

In short, Terdak Lingpa had a principal role in concealing the death of the Fifth Dalai Lama and advising the regent on both official and psychological levels. His involvement in such monumental decisions and historic events indicates his high level of influence at court. He, the Fifth Dalai Lama, and Sangyé Gyatso mutually supported and established one another's authority through symbolic and ritual means.[86] This is remarkable given Terdak Lingpa's responsibilities at Mindröling and the significant amount of time he spent in retreat.

Conclusion

At the newly founded Mindröling monastery, Terdak Lingpa and his family reinvigorated the Nyingma school through historical research as well as codifying ritual practices and aesthetic traditions that they traced back to Buddhism's roots in India. In contrast to the large Géluk monasteries that were the official centers of government at the time, Mindröling's founders set out to build a small and prestigious institution that would revitalize and preserve Tibetan Buddhist, and especially Nyingma, intellectual traditions and ritual and artistic practices across Tibetan regions. The monastery would never house more than 330 monks and about 30 nuns in an adjacent center. It became common for the children of Central Tibet's noble families to study at Mindröling before embarking on their careers in politics or becoming religious teachers.

Mindröling served a cultural purpose that none of the large Géluk monasteries could fulfill. From its early years, the monastery functioned as as a center of cultural production, ritual arts, and aristocratic education. The combination of ritual warfare (an important skill for Nyingma specialists), the arts, and high cultural production in an institution not overtly involved in politics resembles universities and colleges where weapons are developed in laboratories alongside poetry seminars, historical debates, graduation ceremonies, astronomy lessons, medical training, and social functions. The development of technologies for ritual warfare, medicine, or the shaping of an ethical individual or cultured person frequently happens within the same institutional walls. Mindröling, like an elite college, housed students engaged in various disciplines. The Nyö clan founders and the support of the Dalai Lama drew students from the most influential families, whose successes in the political, cultural, and social realms further strengthened Mindröling's status and appeal. It became a center of high art, education, and aesthetics, not just in a rarified sphere of Buddhism or monasticism, but in Tibetan societies at large. Through the establishment of satellite institutions, Mindröling's influence extended beyond Central Tibet, across and beyond the regions the Dalai Lama's government was striving so hard to govern.

Mindröling was established as an authoritative cultural center. In this regard it served a complementary purpose to the large political Géluk monasteries of Lhasa. It was an elite monastery that exemplified the values and standards of the Nyingma school while providing education and cultural resources for a diverse population. By maintaining a small, contained central community, the quality of the ritual and artistic practices at Mindröling could be controlled. The focus on esoteric, highly esteemed meditation practices contributed to the monastery's air of being exceptional. Likewise, all the fundamental ritual elements and artistic forms crucial to Nyingma practices, such as making mandalas, monastic music, and ritual dance, were transmitted meticulously to small groups of students and performed to great effect in large public gatherings.

In the next chapter, based on analysis of the content and style of the Fifth Dalai Lama and Terdak Lingpa's letters, I describe the mutually constitutive relationships that undergirded Mindröling, with a focus on the question of how to balance Buddhist priorities with worldly life.

THREE

Plucking the Strings

On Style, Letter Writing, and Relationships

Just as the progress of the sun and moon along the path of the twelve celestial houses is ceaseless, so should our discussion of the union of Dharma and worldly life continue like the sweet string of the *tambura* being plucked again and again.

—THE FIFTH DALAI LAMA IN A LETTER TO TERDAK LINGPA

WHAT WAS THE nature of the relationship between Terdak Lingpa and the Fifth Dalai Lama, as Mindröling's founding figures, and how did they communicate about their shared concerns? Their collected letters, which include formal correspondences as well as less formal instructions and advice addressed to a range of interlocutors, provide a rich literary source for understanding the religious, cultural, and sociopolitical forces at work in the making of Mindröling as a civilizational center.[1] These letters demonstrate the sensibilities of the writers in action as they discussed events and topics they considered meaningful, in the literary style that suited the particular motivation and recipient of each communication. Against that backdrop I investigate the mutually supportive and dialogical relationships of the Fifth Dalai Lama, Terdak Lingpa, and their contemporaries, through selected letters. These relationships were the driving force in creating and sustaining Mindröling in its early years and laid the groundwork for the role it played through the twentieth century, and to a certain extent today.

Given the prominence of the Fifth Dalai Lama and Terdak Lingpa, their letters serve as instructive examples of the predominant literary aesthetic of their day and as a who's who of early modern Tibetan literati. The Fifth Dalai Lama corresponded with Mongol and Qing figures as well as Tibetan leaders. As for Terdak Lingpa, thanks in part to the Dalai Lama's support

Figure 3.1 Wall painting at Mindröling monastery of Amitāyus flanked by the Fifth
Dalai Lama (left) and Terdak Lingpa (right) in high-quality seventeenth-century
painting style.
Photograph by Rob Linrothe

and in part to his rising fame as a visionary and scholar, many prominent leaders of all the Tibetan schools sought out his advice and instruction. He addresses his stylistically rich and diverse letters to influential political and religious leaders, both male and female.

In the first part of this chapter I analyze two letters from the Dalai Lama to Terdak Lingpa. At the time of their composition, Terdak Lingpa was in his thirties and Mindröling was newly established, while the Dalai Lama was in his sixties and had been in a position of power for at least three decades. Despite the gap in age and station, their relationship was that of mutual teacher and student. One letter from the Dalai Lama acknowledges Terdak Lingpa's enthronement as the senior chair of Mindröling, and the other celebrates Terdak Lingpa's connection with his wife or "secret consort" (gsang yum).

These letters reveal a worldview within which interdependent relationships constitute the person, and by extension, institutions and societies. The Dalai Lama not only is concerned with his own relationship to the younger lama but also invokes seminal visionaries and tantric masters from Tibetan history to frame his and Terdak Lingpa's activities. He celebrates Terdak Lingpa as the direct successor of past masters, proclaiming his special relevance in the current moment for Tibet. The Dalai Lama's focus on the marriage alliance as another crucial site of interdependence reveals the multiplicity of the relationships behind the founding of Mindröling.[2] For the Dalai Lama, the arrival of a new tantric consort at the monastery appears to have been at least as important as Terdak Lingpa's enthronement.

In both letters, the Dalai Lama situates Mindröling as a special site of benefit and enrichment for the people of the Snowland (gangs can). He emphasizes Eastern and Western as well as Central Tibet, collectively referring to these regions as Greater Tibet (bod chen).[3] This framing reflects the Dalai Lama's vision of Mindröling's significance throughout the Tibetan Buddhist world, not just in Central Tibet. It simultaneously signals his ambition to unify this massive area under his Ganden Podrang government's authority.

In the second part of the chapter I analyze letters addressed by Terdak Lingpa to various political leaders and lamas from across Tibetan regions and Buddhist schools. In both form and content, he plays skillfully with Indic and Tibetan poetics while demonstrating his knowledge of intellectual and cultural history, encouraging some students to be good Buddhists while maintaining their worldly aims and celebrating other students as radical renunciants. His stylistic range and the diversity of his correspondents reflect his work at Mindröling to institutionalize the ideal of an unbiased (ris med) approach, based in Great Perfection philosophy and practice.

Reflections on Tibetan Letters

Before turning to particular examples of writing by the Dalai Lama and Terdak Lingpa, it will be helpful to reflect on the nature of the documents under consideration. What I refer to here as the Dalai Lama and Terdak Lingpa's "letters" are categorized under the honorific Tibetan rubric of chap shok (chab shog) and sometimes called less formally tring yik (springs yig) or trin yik ('phrin yig). These various terms for "letters" can be translated as "epistle," "note," or "correspondence."

It is debatable whether letters in any language should be treated as a distinct genre, since they overlap so intimately with other kinds of writing. Suffice it to say that Tibetan letters occupy a porous category that intersects with poetry, song, religious instruction, biography, and more. When assessed in combination with documents such as monastic catalogues (dkar chag), guidelines (bca' yig), and biographies (rnam thar), letters add a vital dimension to the historical record and are particularly fruitful sources for considering the relationship between literary style and content and the dynamics of social and cultural bonds.

The letters I translate and analyze in this chapter have their own history as objects, whose materiality communicates the tastes, status, and interests of both the authors and the recipients. Unfortunately, the handwritten letters either are not extant or are not available. In the conversion from handwritten letter to printed book we lose invaluable information that would be conveyed by the seals, calligraphy, quality of paper and ink, layout of the parts of the letter, etc.[4] Nevertheless, even in their reduced form, the collected letters demonstrate the richness and complexity of the relationships at work in the foundation of Mindröling and illuminate the ideas and activities that led to its early flourishing.

Although the Fifth Dalai Lama and Terdak Lingpa's letters were composed before Tibetan letter-writing handbooks were popularized in the eighteenth and nineteenth centuries, the conventions outlined therein developed over many years and to some extent appear to have been in use when the Dalai Lama and Terdak Lingpa were writing. Later handbooks stipulate the exact placement of the address, the spacing of the content, the size of the handwriting, etc. Differences in the proportions used in laying out the document, the folding of the paper, and the arrangement of the writing on the page reflected the status of the recipient. In official circles, these formal details were carefully defined and regulated.[5] As formalized as letter writing between government officials and aristocrats was, there was room for intimate communication and individual expression.[6] The writings of these figures served as models for the later manuals and for subsequent Tibetan letter writers in both subtle and overt ways. This is especially evident in the influence of the Dalai Lama's ornate writing style.

The Dalai Lama's Letters to Terdak Lingpa

The published collected letters of the Fifth Dalai Lama contain two letters addressed to the "Dharma King Terdak Lingpa." I have not located corresponding letters from Terdak Lingpa to the Dalai Lama, although the Dalai Lama's letters suggest an exchange because he asks for a reply. I highlight two main themes in these letters. The first is mutually interdependent relationships or interconnections, known as *tendrel* (*rten 'brel*). The second is the pragmatic application of Buddhist teachings to life in the world, a theme exemplified by the Tibetan concepts of the integration of Buddhism and worldly life (*chos srid zung'brel*) and the proper balance of these Two Systems of religion and politics (*lugs gnyis* or *khrims gnyis*).

A Letter in Honor of Terdak Lingpa's Enthronement as Senior Chair of Mindröling

He sent the first letter, composed in rich and flowing prose, to Terdak Lingpa on the occasion of his enthronement at the newly constructed Mindröling in 1676. The letter indicates that the Dalai Lama also sent a message in verse for the occasion, but the verses are not included in the published collected letters.

Figure 3.2 Wall painting at Mindröling monastery of the Fifth Dalai Lama.
Photograph by Rob Linrothe

The outline of the letter is: (1) the formal greeting; (2) a brief explanation of the Dalai Lama's absence due to his meditation retreat; (3) a celebration of the enthronement, framed by commentary on Terdak Lingpa's previous incarnations and historical antecedents; (4) words of advice; and (5) an entreaty for a written response from Terdak Lingpa. As an extended "Dear sir," the Dalai Lama writes:

> Now, at the center of the swirling convergence of the ocean of the Nine Vehicles; at the pistil of the fully blossomed thousand-petaled lotus of deity, mantra, and wisdom; the performer of the amazing signs and marks; the very embodiment of the Padmakara, the second victorious Buddha; the field of glorious blazing brilliant light of the virtuous actions of the people of the Snowland; completely dispelling the two obscurations, you accomplish development and liberation in the indestructible Unexcelled Yoga whose profound meaning consists of Creation, Perfection, and Great Perfection; the eight major common siddhis and the activities of pacifying, increasing, magnetizing, and subjugating; renowned for engaging in whatever is suitable for the capacities and senses of your disciples, excellent or ordinary, the melody of your divine *dundubhi* drum[7] beautifies the hearing of all beings in general, and particularly those who live at the base of the great continent of Jambudvīpa. What else is there to say?[8]

The rhetorical query, "What else is there to say?" is apt here, since really there is not much more the Dalai Lama could say in Terdak Lingpa's favor. He addresses Terdak Lingpa as a teacher, a tantric master, and a Great Perfection practitioner. Further, he begins to stake out Terdak Lingpa's interdependent relationships with Padmasambhava (here called Padmakara), the eighth-century tantric hero of Buddhism's arrival in Tibet, as well as with the people of Tibet. In a cascade of praise, he asserts that Terdak Lingpa has achieved mastery of all tantric activities, engaging in actions to "pacify," "increase," "magnetize," and "subjugate." This indicates Terdak Lingpa's expertise in ritual arts, including wrathful rituals.[9] He summarizes Terdak Lingpa's skill as an enlightened teacher who attends to the sensory needs of his students in this way: "renowned for engaging in whatever is suitable for the capacities and senses of your disciples, excellent or ordinary." Here the Dalai Lama equates mastery of the senses with Terdak Lingpa's greatness as a teacher particularly suited to the needs of the Tibetan people.

Next the Dalai Lama explains his own situation, relating his experience in retreat to the enthronement event at Mindröling: "as for me, I gradually fulfilled the propitiation and service of the one with the five-knotted lock of hair, the bodhisattva Ākāśagarbha, showing himself in the perception of others merely as King Brahmā, the body-deity of the king who protects Tibet. I did not pass beyond the three doors for more than two weeks while focusing on a spacious sphere of experience."[10] The very existence of the letter suggests the Dalai Lama did not attend the enthronement, and this section explains why—he was in retreat doing a practice related to a deity who protects Tibet. In this sense the retreat is directly related to one of Mindröling's institutional purposes. Elsewhere the Dalai Lama expressed the aspiration that Mindröling would serve as a source of protection by repelling enemies from Tibet's borders.[11]

It might appear strange that the Dalai Lama did not attend Terdak Lingpa's ritual enthronement, but in fact the event appears to have been treated in an understated way by everyone involved. It is barely mentioned in Terdak Lingpa's outer biography, a running account that meticulously documents teachings given and received and material offerings exchanged over the years.

The next section of the letter turns to the actual occasion of Terdak Lingpa's enthronement as the first senior chair of Mindröling. The Dalai Lama sent this letter along with gifts and verses he composed personally to be recited by the monastic assembly at Mindröling. Concerning the actual celebration, the letter states: "you, the embodiment of the great family lineage holder, are established on the vajra throne like a naturally arisen *yung-drung*. This is because you fulfilled your inheritance, implementing your profound Treasure-discovering activities in keeping with the life story of the Buddha heir, the Great Visionary Dharma King Ratna Lingpa."[12]

This is followed by a section on Terdak Lingpa's career as a visionary Treasure revealer, which the Dalai Lama here presents as a continuation of the life story of the visionary Ratna Lingpa (1403–1478), compiler of an early collection of the Nyingma school's tantras, which for the most part had been omitted from the major canonical collections of translated Buddhist texts known as the Kangyur (*bka' 'gyur*) and Tengyur (*bstan 'gyur*). The Nyingma collection, of which various editions exist, is known as the *Collected Tantras of the Nyingma school* (*rnying ma rgyud 'bum*).[13] In keeping with this affiliation, Terdak Lingpa himself compiled an edition of the *Nyingma*

Gyübum, writing it out by hand in 1685.[14] This was just one of his efforts to consolidate, clarify, and reshape what it meant to be part of the Nyingma school, in part through textual production and redaction.

The mention of Ratna Lingpa begins a section that highlights Terdak Lingpa's relationships with previous masters and visionaries. Most fundamentally, the letter establishes Terdak Lingpa as a direct manifestation of the Indian tantric master Padmasambhava (here referred to as the Great Master from Uḍḍiyāna):

> The glorious Buddha of the three times, the Great Master from Uḍḍiyāna, willed with exceedingly loving kindness that the hundred thresholds of benefit and comfort for the beings in the future corrupt ages be opened. In the spontaneously accomplished auspicious connection, by the warm moist compassion of the three roots, the fruit of aspiration fully ripens.[15]

The inference here is that Terdak Lingpa's career is a result of Padmasambhava's intention and subsequent visionaries' work, leading up to the ideal time and place for Terdak Lingpa's own contributions to the Tibetan community through Treasure revelation and the founding of Mindröling. This leads to the other major relationships invoked in the letter.

The first is with Vairocana, Padmasambhava's close disciple and a principal figure in the history of Great Perfection in Tibet, who also compiled a collection of Nyingma tantras. The second is with the visionary Dorjé Lingpa (1346–1405). Both had Buddhist and Bön connections, and Dorjé Lingpa in his own time was identified with Vairocana, like Terdak Lingpa. In reference to these two previous figures, the Dalai Lama writes: "the great translator Vairocana and the Buddha heir bodhisattva Dorjé Lingpa and so forth, came in sequence as the kin of the people of Tibet, deliberately by the force of this wish."[16]

The relationships between Terdak Lingpa and a few key examples of his many previous incarnations (here Vairocana, Ratna Lingpa, and Dorjé Lingpa) are portrayed as mutually constitutive, not merely as a linear progression from past to present.[17] Although there is a sense of moving forward from the past through deliberate reincarnation, the letter also implies that Terdak Lingpa caused the arrival of the various figures, since he is identified with Padmasambhava, the first in the line chronologically, whose wish is claimed as the impetus for the subsequent masters' existence through his conscious intention to generate the Treasure tradition.

[94]

The next part of the letter draws more on Terdak Lingpa's defining connection with the people of Tibet: "the principal significance of this miraculous playful manifestation is that, in the shade of the white parasol of great billowing bodhisattva activities, in general the many beings who live in the era of corruption, and in particular all those who live here in this land, can happily take rest."[18] Here the Dalai Lama treats Terdak Lingpa's relationship to the Tibetan people as a combined result of his previous incarnations' activities and intentions and the good fortune of the Tibetans. The Dalai Lama reiterates that this relationship is the "principal significance" of Terdak Lingpa's present existence. He employs a standard Buddhist trope when he asserts that Terdak Lingpa benefits all sentient beings, but highlights his relationship to Tibetans in particular.

He closes the letter formally: "then please commit yourself, take this to heart, without merely pretending to dwell as the essence of Infinite Life. And respond unceasingly like the continuum of a river of auspicious chariots, I continually beseech you."[19] This closing statement identifies Terdak Lingpa with Amitāyus, the Buddha of Infinite Life, in an allusion to his mastery of rituals for extending lifespans and saving people from life-threatening illnesses. In the main temple of Mindröling, Terdak Lingpa and the Fifth Dalai Lama are depicted on either side of a beautiful image of Amitāyus in what appears to be a seventeenth-century wall painting, underscoring the connection the Dalai Lama expresses in this letter (figure 3.1).

It is curious that the Dalai Lama suggests Terdak Lingpa might be "pretending." His plea seems to suggest the danger of mere appearances, and calls for Terdak Lingpa to activate genuinely the potential the Dalai Lama perceives him to possess. This comment points to an important risk—that someone who has mastered the aesthetics of the sense perceptions and objects of the senses might pretend, persuasively, and thereby mislead others. I read the Dalai Lama's statement as rhetorical, but it resonates with debates over whether Treasure revealers are authentic and suspicions of Nyingma practitioners as being prone to corruption.

Throughout the letter, the interdependent relationships invoked overlap again and again, moving fluidly across time and through the Dalai Lama's multivalent allusions. While my focus here is on relationships between people, the term *tendrel* also signifies events. For instance, the Dalai Lama refers to the event of the enthronement by this term. Within the play of these interconnections, everyone's intentions are intertwined and subjectivities are mutually constitutive, with Terdak Lingpa at the center of the "swirling convergence."

A Letter Celebrating Terdak Lingpa's Secret Consort

With Terdak Lingpa established as the first throne holder of the newly founded Mindröling, the Dalai Lama anticipated that he would reveal further Treasure teachings. This was almost two decades after he discovered his first Treasure at the age of eighteen and his second at the age of twenty-two. However, an obstacle arose when Terdak Lingpa experienced poor health in the period just after his enthronement, according to his biographer, Dharmaśrī.[20] With the aim of repairing his health and supporting his visionary activities, he developed a relationship with a "secret consort" (gsang yum) with whom to practice sexual yoga. These aims, along with the pervasive Buddhist aim of enlightenment, are all reflected in the Dalai Lama's letter.[21] Upon her arrival at Mindröling, the Dalai Lama composed a second letter to Terdak Lingpa to celebrate their relationship.[22] This was likely in 1678 or 1679, two or three years after Mindröling was founded. The letter is written in ornate poetry (snyan ngag), a Tibetan system of poetics shaped by Sanskrit kāvya.[23] Both the Dalai Lama and Terdak Lingpa were connoisseurs of poetry, and thanks to their legacy Mindröling would become a major Central Tibetan hub for training in poetic composition and appreciation.

Throughout this letter, the Dalai Lama employs a variety of colorful terms for the young woman, demonstrating the multivalence of her role and treating the occasion as both a social event (a wedding) and a tantric ritual (the consecration of an enlightened yab-yum pair). The terms include "spouse" or "wife" (lcam), "female consort" (yum), "mistress" or "beloved" in a conventional romantic sense (mdza' na mo), and "secret consort" (gsang yum), the formal term for the tantric partner or wife of a visionary or lama.[24] The variety of terms and the informality of some of them might imply a degree of intimacy between the sender and recipient—recall that the Dalai Lama had known Terdak Lingpa since he was a boy. The diversity of terms certainly implies a complex social connection between the woman and Terdak Lingpa. Not only is she treated as his tantric ritual partner, but she is also presented as his spouse and lover.[25] The Dalai Lama does not state her name, but Terdak Lingpa's outer biography supplies more details, providing her name as Ngödrup Pelzom and identifying her family as the local leaders of the Yardrok region of Tibet.[26] Unfortunately, available sources do not give us access to her perspective on the relationship.

By drawing on the practically intertwining but theoretically distinct aspects of the relationship, treating it all the while as the object of veneration, the letter demonstrates the nuances of what these gendered terms signified in the seventeenth-century Central Tibetan context. The variety of terms further indicates the Dalai Lama's taste for poetic language, reflecting his effort to avoid repetition. It also reflects his training in Indian aesthetics and poetics, in which good writing necessarily includes an element of erotic feeling or *kama*. Moreover, poetry is said to teach "like a mistress in seducing,"[27] so the Dalai Lama's embrace of erotic allusions and inflections is characteristic of the form as well as indicative of the content of this letter about a romantic and ritual union.

As a further indication of the Dalai Lama's training in formal literary aesthetics, this letter is marked as belonging to a specific category of Sanskrit poetics, indicating the meter used.[28] Most of the Dalai Lama's collected letters are marked in this way, adding an explicit didactic element that serves to instruct the reader in poetic meter. The title page also includes multiple scripts to embellish and adorn the letter visually, further elevating the aesthetics of the poetic form. The introductory note reads: "when in accordance with the prophetic Treasure, Terdak Lingpa's consort from Yardrok approached the throne, a gift was sent out. The offering was made in the form of this letter called 'The union which is a bouquet of benefit and happiness' delivered by Lozang Yonten, a master of Phulung astrology."[29] The "union" of the letter's title doubly refers to the union of Terdak Lingpa and Ngödrup Pelzom on one level, and the theory of the integration of Buddhism and worldly life on another level. Worldly life here includes but is not limited to politics. The Dalai Lama played a key role in the decision to seek a consort for Terdak Lingpa, and he also had the final say in choosing Ngödrup Pelzom from among several possible candidates.[30] The main relationship addressed is that of Terdak Lingpa and Ngödrup Pelzom at Mindröling. Yet while her arrival and their potential as a tantric pair is the primary focus, there is also a strong undercurrent of the Dalai Lama's intentions for Mindröling's role in the Tibetan polity.

Significantly, the consort from Yardrok was related to the Fifth Dalai Lama's mother. And according to Terdak Lingpa's biography, it was the Dalai Lama who insisted Terdak Lingpa practice with a consort at this time, since his poor health threatened to prevent him from performing the prophesied visionary acts of rediscovery.[31] The fact that the woman chosen was a relative of the Dalai Lama suggests that this event was also a kind of marriage alliance between the Dalai Lama and Mindröling. This helps explain why the Dalai Lama refers to the match as an act of *chösi zungdrel*, in this case joining the Dharma of Mindröling and the worldly power of the Dalai Lama. This analysis is supported by the use of the term "get married" (*khab tu bzhes*) to describe the event in Terdak Lingpa's outer biography.[32] Furthermore, the extensive attention this event received in that biography, which focuses on Terdak Lingpa's worldly engagements and career as opposed to his "inner" spiritual life, demonstrates that this was a social and political union as well as a tantric, ritual union.[33]

In the opening verses of the letter, the Dalai Lama again praises Terdak Lingpa in the highest terms, replete with aesthetic imagery of beauty, mastery, and pervasiveness:

> Essence of the inexhaustible dharmadhātu, self-knowing, genuine
> Samantabhadra,
> unobstructed inherent radiance, rainbowlike beautiful pervasive master,
> glorious Vajrasattva,
> the hundred clans, the five clans, the three clans—the many dance as one.
> Extending more emanations than the particles of sand in the Ganga, you are
> the supreme venerable master.[34]

Next he introduces Terdak Lingpa's qualifications to engage in tantric practice:

> Having accomplished the invincible great transference in the vajra body,
> transcending many countable rosaries,
> whatever defiled body you manifest through magical means, you are the
> spring of teachings and beings.
> Resting like a *yung-drung*, your fame is soothing to the ear.

Notice the imagery—"rainbowlike," "beautiful," "dance," "sands in the Ganga," "the spring of teachings," and "fame that is soothing to the ear." The reader's senses are all invited to enjoy this celebration of Terdak Lingpa's qualities.

And again, similarly to the enthronement letter, this letter praises Terdak Lingpa as a teacher who has mastered the senses:

At the threshold of the infinitely subtle entryway of the nine vehicles,
your mind accords with the scope and senses of the ones to be trained.
As sentient beings are liberated by your guiding sixtyfold melody,
you remain in the realm of peace, like the other Conquerors.

The line "Your mind accords with the scope and senses of the ones to be trained" is an indication of Terdak Lingpa's work with aesthetics, not merely as a philosophy of art and beauty but as that which concerns training the senses.

Having established Terdak Lingpa's authority, the Dalai Lama was eager to depict him—and later in the letter, Ngödrup Pelzom as well—as thoroughly qualified to practice tantra, beyond the need for the austerity of celibacy, and essentially on the level of an enlightened buddha. He writes, "Arising in nakedness, you are free from the hindrances of the knowable world, / Since you know all that can be known."[35]

The Dalai Lama appears to express wholehearted support of this union. He also sings Terdak Lingpa's praises not only as a practitioner but also as a scholar, the "knower of the five fields of knowledge, the twice-born one who wears the Brahmin thread."[36] This reference to the thread worn by male members of the Indian Brahmin class is one of these two letters' many allusions to Indic cultures. The significance is ambiguous here, but one inference is that the Dalai Lama and Terdak Lingpa, as writer and recipient, share a common education and sensibility inspired by the high culture of Classical India and shaped by their Tibetan literati context. Further, since in some traditions, the number of threads worn changes based on age and marital status, another implication is that taking a new consort is a rite of passage for Terdak Lingpa, and that he is moving into a new phase of life. This possibility is further supported by the Dalai Lama's identification of Terdak Lingpa with the eighth-century translator Vairocana's childhood name (gan jag thang ta) later in the letter,[37] rather than his adult name, by which he is more commonly known.

The Dalai Lama frames his composition as an offering to this new couple, and at the same time, he asserts that the couple's relationship will benefit the people of Tibet:

> From the fierce spread of the sweet seed of bodhicitta,[38]
> the two accumulations are piled atop the root, tree, and foliage.
> In an unprecedented piling up of fruitional deeds,
> we take refuge in your grove of wish-fulfilling trees, in the center of the
>   Snowland's dense forest.

As his focus on the couple becomes more intense, the Dalai Lama highlights their capacity for enlightenment and their transcendence of conventional ascetic practices:

> Capable of binding thoughts with lotus threads,
> free from suffering, disciplined like an elephant drunk on barley beer,
> by one single step of practice, you progress to the level of buddhahood.
> You've finished with the fatigue of extreme asceticism.[39]

In the next stanza, the Dalai Lama turns his full attention to Ngödrup Pelzom:

> In the expanse of *Ae*, the female guide draws forth the wisdom of the four joys.
> The *Vam* syllable, communion of great joy! The mistress
> is unrivaled like the moon in the sky.
> Why else did Lady Kharchen's companion come from Uḍḍiyāna?[40]

In this provocative passage, the Dalai Lama incorporates technical language associated with tantric ritual practice (the syllables *ae* and *vam*) into the verse, and he suggests that celibacy is one of the types of discipline the practitioners have transcended. This is despite how important celibacy is to the Dalai Lama's Géluk school, to his own commitments as a fully ordained monk, and indeed to all Tibetan monastics. That did not prevent him from supporting such practices in the context of Terdak Lingpa and Ngödrup Pelzom's relationship, where sexual union was deemed appropriate and necessary.

The Dalai Lama praises Ngödrup Pelzom as an "unrivaled" practitioner, likening her to the Tibetan female exemplar Yeshé Tsogyel.[41] Remembered as Padmasambhava's tantric consort, Yeshé Tsogyel was married to the emperor Tri Songdetsen who was Padmasambhava's main sponsor. As is common in Tibetan literary depictions of tantric adepts, the Dalai Lama sets Terdak Lingpa and Ngödrup Pelzom on par with this prototypical Tibetan tantric couple. More remarkably here, the Dalai Lama suggests that Padmasambhava came to Tibet from Uḍḍiyāna to practice with Yeshé Tsogyel (referred to as Lady Kharchen).[42] This unconventional treatment of the foundational Tibetan narrative puts Yeshé Tsogyel at the center of the story. Rather than Padmasambhava coming to establish tantric Buddhism in Tibet, according to the Dalai Lama, he actually came to meet her. The implied parallel equates Terdak Lingpa directly with Padmasambhava and Ngödrup Pelzom with Yeshé Tsogyel. In this way, the couple's connection takes on historic and mythic proportions.

One reason for the Dalai Lama to take such a strong interest in the union is that the Treasure tradition asserts that some visionaries must perform tantric sexual practices (as opposed to practicing visualizations) in order to accomplish their revelatory work. The relationship with Ngödrup Pelzom was intended to ensure Terdak Lingpa's continued career as a visionary, in which the Dalai Lama was very invested. The Dalai Lama is explicit about this in his letter, where he writes:

Internally, the connection liberates
all the vast knots in the central channel.
Externally, your personal lot is now to open entirely the door of profound
    Treasure,
found by means of the ten million merits of the teachings and of sentient
    beings.[43]

This statement expressly demonstrates that the Dalai Lama saw Terdak Lingpa's relationship with his consort as essential to his work as a Treasure revealer.

The next section of the letter resembles a Buddhist consecration ritual (rab gnas), moving through all the formal steps of blessing the "father and mother" pair (yab yum), as if the living couple were an object of worship such as a painting or sculpture being prepared for its ritual use. The Dalai Lama goes so far as to assert the full awakening of the couple:

> As the one who spreads and gathers an ocean of countless mandalas,
> you are the pervasive master of the
> hundred clans of limitless peaceful and fierce buddhas.[44]
> On the arising of the union of father and mother, the flowers smile, aroused in
> their direction.

After employing this metaphor of blooming flowers, "aroused" by the couple, to convey a sexual connotation, he continues with the consecration imagery:

> The Sugatas, having lifted up the precious vase,
> perform the anointing while the gathering of knowledgeable women sing
> the melodious song.
> All the bodhisattvas give the benediction while the fierce deities
> frighten away the demons and the goddesses spread out a cloud of offerings—
> how marvelous![45]

By literarily consecrating the couple in this way, the letter again celebrates tantric sexual practices and extols these two practitioners. In this passage and throughout the letter, the Dalai Lama situates tantric practice at the center of Terdak Lingpa's identity as a visionary and implies that he would not be as beneficial to the Dalai Lama or to Tibet without this complex relationship with his partner. The letter continues:

> As the master of the Akaniṣṭha realm, in the form of the five certainties,
> you are the nature of enlightenment, like a grove of sala trees.
> Having trod upon the great stage of the thirteen vajras,
> dreams of pure and impure are one and the same.[46]

Having established the couple as a consecrated object worthy of veneration, the Dalai Lama invokes Mindröling, which is identified with the Akaniṣṭha realm where the Great Perfection teachings are said to have originated.

It is a common Tibetan Buddhist literary trope to compare one's lama to a tree, providing shade, fruit, and so forth. Here the Dalai Lama also suggests that Mindröling, as the home of Terdak Lingpa and his new consort, will be a place of nourishment and refuge, "like a grove of sala trees," for Tibetans. He suggests an expansive view of Tibet and claims a wide impact when he says the couple is "Creating a fortunate age for the people of greater Tibet (*bod chen*)."[47]

The letter closes with a reference to the Dalai Lama and Terdak Lingpa's ongoing discussion of the integration of Dharma and worldly life and presents a request for a response from Terdak Lingpa. It also mentions the messenger, whom the letter's notes identify as Lozang Yönten (d.u.), who arrived at Mindröling from Lhasa on horseback:

> Just as the progress of the sun and moon along the path of the twelve celestial houses is ceaseless,
> so should our discussion of the union of Dharma and worldly life continue like the sweet string of the *tambura* being plucked again and again as an ornament for the ear.
> Carrying a white scarf as an additional indication, riding a horse, having arrived at the vast Mindröling, the messenger presents this letter to you by hand.[48]

Notice the sensory resonance of the invitation to continue their conversation about Buddhism and life in the world, which is likened to the sound of a *tambura*, an Indian stringed instrument placed against a celestial backdrop.

This messenger appears to have been the same Lozang Yonten whom the Dalai Lama refers to frequently as the choirmaster (*dbu mdzad*) in his autobiography.[49] He was a close attendant to the Dalai Lama. Lozang Yonten and Terdak Lingpa were among the few people who knew of the Dalai Lama's death before the regent, Sangyé Gyatso, publicly announced it, almost fourteen years after he died. The choirmaster carried both letters from the Dalai Lama's residence in Lhasa to Terdak Lingpa.[50] The high status of the messenger underscores Terdak Lingpa and Mindröling's position in the Dalai Lama's court.

Ngödrup Pelzom's arrival at Mindröling marked an important moment in the life of a visionary whom the Dalai Lama calls the "womb-born Urgyen Khenpo," again identifying Terdak Lingpa with Padmasambhava.[51] For the Dalai Lama and others invested in the Tibetan visionary Treasure tradition, supporting the couple made sense since their union brought the possibility of further Treasure revelation. At the same time, given the Dalai Lama's family connection to the woman and his indication of the letter's subject as the union of Dharma and worldly existence, this union appears to have doubled as a marriage alliance between the Dalai Lama and Mindröling.

Equating the new couple with an enlightened couple works to rhetorically defend Terdak Lingpa from those who might criticize him and his partner for engaging in sexual yoga practices. Terdak Lingpa's vows did not require that he be celibate. On the contrary, engaging with a tantric partner was a crucial part of his practice, a point the Dalai Lama stressed when he argued that Terdak Lingpa should connect with a consort. Terdak Lingpa's biographer and brother Dharmaśrī quotes the Dalai Lama as asserting that previous Tibetan Treasure revealers failed to achieve the visionary revelations they ought to have because they refused to engage in sexual union with a female consort, or because they engaged with the wrong consort.[52] The implication is that Terdak Lingpa could similarly fail to fulfill his responsibilities as a visionary. In that case he would not live up to the aspirations ascribed to Padmasambhava and carried out by Vairocana, Dorjé Lingpa, and Ratna Lingpa, the previous incarnations mentioned in the letter sent on the occasion of the enthronement. Thus, the stakes for Terdak Lingpa and Ngödrup Pelzom were high. The Dalai Lama anticipated that their relationship would lead to the rediscovery of Treasures urgently relevant to their time and place in early modern Tibet.

Terdak Lingpa's Collected Letters

Turning now to Terdak Lingpa's letters, I will explore how his literary style compares to the Dalai Lama's and highlight the concerns and interests evident in his correspondence. To show how the style and content of Terdak Lingpa's writing demonstrate the sensibilities and worldview crystallized at Mindröling, I first present an overview of his collected letters and then analyze two examples.

Terdak Lingpa's letters are varied and diverse, giving a literary expression to the impartial or unbiased ideal for which he is often praised, and indeed for which he praises himself in a number of his letters.[53] His

Figure 3.3 Wall painting at Mindröling monastery of a young Terdak Lingpa.
Photograph by Rob Linrothe

compositions reflect his concern with Buddhist ideals of nonattachment, nondiscrimination, and equanimity, in relation to the practical demands and ethical quandaries of life in the world. Across the board, his letters reflect on how to be a good Buddhist practitioner while fulfilling social responsibilities, coping with complex emotional experiences, and dealing with the demands of life as someone with temporal authority. The content, style, and rhetoric of his letters mirror the complex aspects of the institution of Mindröling, where both monastics and laypeople were educated in religious and worldly subjects.

Compared to the Dalai Lama's letters, some of Terdak Lingpa's letters resonate with the ideal of spontaneous (*lhun gyi*) communication espoused in Great Perfection philosophy.[54] Some compositions end abruptly, as if he were interrupted by other business. The inclusion of such examples demonstrates that the compilers and editors of his letters considered even partial compositions worthwhile. Many letters show Terdak Lingpa's skill in formal composition and ornate poetry. He had the expertise to employ diverse conventions and a scope of metaphor, allusion, and poetic device comparable to the Dalai Lama's. He also shows a marked playfulness, virtuosity, and apparent enjoyment of his literary diversity and dexterity.

Examples of his more formal work include letters composed in the extremely difficult to execute "a-b-c" or acrostic form (*ka bshad* or *ka rtsom*); letters in the Tibetan *gur* style (*mgur*), which shares characteristics with but is sometimes treated as distinct from Indian *dohā*; and ornate poetry, for which Mindröling became famous. (Mindröling's curriculum demonstrates a strong focus on literary arts and ornate poetry in particular, as I discuss in more detail in chapters 4 and 5.) Terdak Lingpa's range and the apparent enjoyment he took in playing with diverse forms express a kind of literary aesthetic of impartiality.

In addition to his stylistic range, the range of Terdak Lingpa's correspondents from different regions and schools helps demonstrate how connected he was across the Tibetan Buddhist world. To illustrate this point, he corresponded with the Sixth Dalai Lama in a lengthy and detailed letter on Great Perfection practice in Central Tibet during their day and the need to protect and support Mindröling as a reliable center for the Nyingma tradition.[55] Other noteworthy recipients include multiple Ganden Podrang regents, including Sangyé Gyatso.[56] He addressed letters to the young Polhané, who studied at Mindröling and would become Tibet's secular ruler for much of the eighteenth century.[57] Beyond Central Tibet, he corresponded with other political leaders from across Tibetan cultural regions including Degé, Chamdo, Kongpo, Amdo, and Dolpo. He also wrote to major teachers from all the Tibetan Buddhist schools including the head Sakya Lama,[58] as well as Bön masters.[59] His less famous correspondents included meditators and practitioners who sought his advice on their practice. There were numerous women. Much like the men he exchanged letters with, the women were practitioners, sponsors, or local rulers.

There are notable parallels between the form and the content of his letters. For instance, the less formal letters composed in direct response to a specific query tend to offer pragmatic advice. The more formal letters, for instance those composed in ornate poetry, tend to have more idealistic Buddhist advice. An example is "Life is impermanent, therefore you should spend all your time and energy practicing Dharma. Everything else is a complete waste."[60] This kind of advice from lamas to students is of course common. Although it is crucial from a Buddhist perspective, it remains theoretical without a clear means of practical application. By contrast, in Terdak Lingpa's less formal letters, the messages tend to be more pragmatic and nuanced. They display a tolerance for complexity and ambiguity that is necessary in applying ideals to reality. I provide examples below.

He also makes frequent and knowledgeable reference to the writings of historical masters such as Sakya Paṇḍita, the famed thirteenth-century hierarch of the Sakya school who helped establish the traditional Indian Buddhist fields of knowledge in Tibet, and Tsong Khapa, who was retroactively credited with founding the Géluk school. He proves himself a knowledgeable historian. For example, in a letter to the regent, Sangyé Gyatso, he explicates historical topics such as the history of the term for Tibetan Buddhist debate,[61] and in another he writes about the family of the young Sixth Dalai Lama.[62] He writes about the codification of the Tibetan calendar and in particular the correct and timely celebration of Buddhist holidays,[63] and a Tibetan imperial effort to equalize the rich and poor during the emperor Muné Tsenpo's reign in the eighth century.[64]

He also corresponded with colleagues about Sanskrit and Tibetan grammar and poetics;[65] medicine, a subject of study for which Mindröling was famous; ethical statecraft; and rituals for repelling enemy armies (dmag zor).[66]

Terdak Lingpa's letters also show a keen interest and expertise in artistic media, ritual practices, and material culture. This reflects Mindröling's fame as an authoritative center for ritual activities. In many examples from among these letters Terdak Lingpa offers instruction and advice on how to make mandalas and statues, recipes for medicinal pills with specific instructions for gathering plants, and decorations and ornaments for use during Buddhist holidays and ceremonies.[67] His letters specify the material offerings that should be made upon the enthronement of a new Dalai Lama[68] and give more general guidelines for making material offerings. In one particularly striking example of attention to material culture and the significance of aesthetics in Buddhism, Terdak Lingpa instructs his correspondent to view all material objects, whether intended for ritual purposes or quotidian use, as physical reminders of the nature of reality, and thereby as supports for Buddhist practice.[69]

In his letters to temporal rulers and officials, the driving question for Terdak Lingpa seems to be how to conduct oneself responsibly in an official capacity while maintaining one's Dharma practice and acting in accordance with Buddhist values of equanimity and compassion. From the frequency with which these themes arise, it is clear that this was a central area of interest for him and a topic that his contemporaries sought his advice on. This pragmatic approach in turn shaped the pedagogy at Mindröling.

For instance, in one letter, he responded to a disciple who had been engaged in an elaborate daily ritual practice but was then promoted to a high position in the government and no longer had time for the full practice. In response to this official's query about how to balance his new commitments, Terdak Lingpa writes, "Because of your positive karma and the effects of your practice on your character, a higher official took notice of you."[70] He goes on to say, in sum, "Now you've been promoted, you don't have enough time to do all the practices I instructed you to do, therefore amend your daily practice in the following way. . . ."[71] Terdak Lingpa provides details about how to abbreviate the prescribed practices. The thrust is that if the letter's recipient follows the new instructions, he can do his official worldly duty as well as fulfilling his religious commitments.

In another example of practical advice, in this case to the Fifth Dalai Lama's regent, Sangyé Gyatso, Terdak Lingpa avers, again in sum: "You're a busy political leader. If you try to build a three-dimensional Kālacakra maṇḍala, it will take a long time and require a huge physical space. The real value of the maṇḍala depends on the quality of the practitioner's mind. Don't worry about building a physical maṇḍala; visualize it instead, just visualize it well."[72] It seems the regent had written to Terdak Lingpa with the intention of building a massive mandala. Instead, Terdak Lingpa counsels the regent to be pragmatic and use his imagination instead. In another letter, he writes, "By being balanced in how you treat people in your role as a leader, you are practicing the Dharma."[73] And in a letter on Dharma practice for royalty (*rgyal po chos lugs*), he writes, "If in your official work you focus on the three jewels, and on benefiting others, you will avoid becoming small minded and petty in your concerns." In the same letter, he also writes, as a leader "be reasonable, be egalitarian," and in meting out punishments, "be like a compassionate mother correcting her beloved child."[74]

Both the diversity of Terdak Lingpa's correspondents and the pragmatism of much of his writing demonstrate an ecumenical worldview that sought to integrate Buddhist philosophy with daily life, allowing for the particular demands and commitments of his diverse students. Beyond nonsectarianism per se, Terdak Lingpa's expression of the *rimé* ideal demonstrates a holistic sense of being unbiased and nondiscriminatory *in general*. When this ideal is applied to real-life situations, one of its manifestations is indeed an open engagement with members of other Tibetan Buddhist schools. But that is only one of many expressions of this worldview.

Women Correspondents

I suggest that Terdak Lingpa's respectful engagement with female disciples is another practical example of his application of Buddhist philosophy to his worldly endeavors. While Mahāyāna Buddhist philosophy posits that gender is an empty construct and the categories of "male" and "female" ultimately are nondual, there are countless examples of inequalities between the sexes in the history of Buddhism, ranging from androcentrism to misogyny.[75] For example, currently Tibetan Buddhist women do not have access to full monastic ordination, so all nuns are novices, regardless of their level of training, knowledge, or accomplishment.[76] And whereas life stories of male practitioners typically recount the decision to devote one's life to the Dharma as a joyous and celebratory occasion, in stories about women this decision is typically rife with struggle and resistance from their families and communities.⁷⁷ This might suggest that Terdak Lingpa would treat his female interlocutors differently from his male interlocutors.

On the contrary: if the letters were not addressed by name with female titles provided, it would be difficult to infer the gender of the recipient because the content of letters to women does not differ much from the content of letters to men. In the letters to females, he uses titles for women that are the direct equivalent to those used for his male disciples: "female Dharma practitioner-donor" (*chos mdzad ma*),⁷⁸ "female meditator and knowledge holder" (*sgom ma rig 'dzin*),⁷⁹ and "female ruler" (*dpon mo*).⁸⁰ One subtle and important difference is that his letters to women seem to convey a slightly more idealistic approach than his letters to male disciples.

A Letter to a Woman Grieving Her Child

As an example of a letter to a female disciple, the following is an excerpt from a condolence letter to Sonam Pelzom, whom he addresses as a "female ruler," following the death of her son. Sonam Pelzom is the name of Terdak Lingpa's sister. He wrote a number of letters to a woman with that name, although I have not verified that this correspondent is indeed his sister. It is possible, although not certain, that in this letter Terdak Lingpa is giving his sister advice about how to survive the devastating loss of her child. Alternatively, the letter might be riffing on the Buddhist trope of the pain of losing one's only son as an impulse for renunciation.

This is a *gur* (*mgur*)-style poem, written in lines of eight syllables with a melodic meter that is not entirely consistent across the verses and was possibly sung.⁸¹ I render it here in lines that are approximately sixteen syllables, in an effort to maintain the regularity of the line length.

Conceptual thought gives rise to pleasure and to pain.
Nothing exists but luminous emptiness—one's mind.

Come what may—transformation comes without action.
Looking toward one's own true nature, it blissfully dawns.

Now that we have won these precious human bodies,
it's crucial to join experience and Dharma as one.

Working endlessly, there are so many things to do.
Cast off the distraction of indiscriminate work.

While subduing foes, there are so many to subdue.
Overcome the foes of the afflictive emotions.

Harmonize with kin, although they're easy to resent.
The companions of this life are the cause of duḥkha.

Despite hoarding wealth, it's difficult to be content.
Now, resolve to be revolted—this is profound.

As soon as you're deceived by an object of the mind,
rely wholeheartedly on the undeceiving jewels.

Bereft of your beloved child, your only son,
you must crush your discontented state of mind.

This is the meaning of luminous emptiness.
Rest easy in a state of nongrasping awareness.

In the six realms the bond with one's parents is so deep,
but it's useless to be biased by love and by hate.

Aware of equality and equanimity—
does self-liberation not exist in great bliss?

The true essence of mind is free from mental constraints.
With the everyday appearance of pleasure and pain—

Just as the colors of the rainbow don't stain the sky,
don't grasp at the expanse, rest in the state of the sky.

Since castles of earth and stone will all come to ruin,
commit to bind the body in its primordial state.

There is scant meaning to be gleaned from idle speaking.
Instead, recite the pure *yidam* deity's mantra.

Why carry the burden of mental misery?
Through continuous nongrasping, just abandon it.

The activities of indiscriminate distraction—
transform them into the wish for virtuous karma.

The pleasures of this life only last for an instant.
Instead cultivate the pleasure that lasts forever.

The expression of words can confound the intellect—
contemplate what the teacher points out with his finger.

Value the condensed essence, not the many meanings.
Strive for the method that integrates this with your mind.[82]

In the first verse translated above, the promise of bliss and the warning about the danger of conceptual thought introduces this teaching on joining experience and Dharma. This is an expression of the familiar theme of integrating religion and life in the world, but here the reference is stripped of any political valence to focus on the recipient's experience of mourning. Terdak Lingpa focuses on the busyness of life's projects and asserts that meaningless work should be abandoned. After all, what work *really* matters after the death of one's child? From Terdak Lingpa's perspective, there seems to be no need to specify—in the early phases of grief, all work might appear indiscriminate and meaningless. In the glaring pain of loss, what is really necessary suddenly becomes clear.

Here again is a classic piece of Buddhist advice made famous by Śāntideva—rather than fighting against external enemies, one should battle the real culprits of mental afflictions and negative emotions, striking at the actual root of conflict and strife. The verse about resenting annoying relatives takes on a special meaning if the recipient is in fact his sister! The candor of the statement reflects Terdak Lingpa's pragmatism—the loss of loved ones does bring suffering, and obligations to loved ones can cause everyday dissatisfaction since familial responsibilities can be burdensome, even in the best of times.

He turns then to consider the futility of wealth in times of profound sorrow. The crux of the advice: the recipient must somehow deal with the pain of her loss, and "crush her discontented state of mind," but how? In a beautiful and graceful application of Great Perfection teachings, Terdak Lingpa states that *this* is the real purpose of recognizing the natural mind, "resting easy" even under unthinkably adverse emotional circumstances.

Terdak Lingpa once again asserts the vital importance of impartiality, when he says, "it's useless to be biased by love and by hate," while acknowledging the power of bonds between parents and children in all six realms of saṃsāra (the realms of the gods, demigods, humans, animals, hungry ghosts, and hells).

The following three verses, rich in sensory imagery, evoke bliss, pleasure and pain, and the colors of the rainbow in quick succession. The rainbow is one of the few visual images in the poem. Here Terdak Lingpa makes plain the point that the rainbow does not alter the state of the sky any more than mental constructions, whether painful or pleasurable, stain the mind, and repeats the word "sky" with a new focus, not on the rainbow but on the expanse in which it appears.

Then Terdak Lingpa turns to the experiences and expressions of body, speech, and mind. Material wealth and comforts are also passing, he reminds her, as everything she builds will change and eventually come to ruin. Having outlined the correct attitudes toward physical embodiment, which should be disciplined in keeping with the primordial state; speech, which should be used for mantras rather that idle talk; and mental states, which should give up grasping, Terdak Lingpa turns to the effects of the actions of the body, speech, and mind. He then reminds Sonam Pelzom of impermanence and the fleeting nature of all experience, invoking an alternative pleasure of awakening as one that "lasts forever."

Finally in a self-reflexive turn he comments on the risks of using words to teach, since they can instead "confound," and he stresses the importance of extracting the essentials rather than any extraneous aspects of his own poetic use of language in the letter. He encourages the reader to focus on his main point rather than being distracted by the confounding potential of language. He ends by asking Sonam Pelzom to follow his finger to the condensed, profound meaning he intends to reveal to her, rather than getting lost in all the possible interpretations of his words.

These succinct and (in the Tibetan) musical verses are quite ordinary in their Buddhist messages. Yet, the brevity of the literary form packs a punch, especially when conveying this emotionally intense content. Why might Terdak Lingpa have addressed the topic of how to cope with the loss of a child (whether actual or metaphorical) in this particular poetic form? Although I cannot answer this question with certainty, I suggest that the literary features of this form, including the short lines and melodic meter, combine with conventional Buddhist teachings to convey his counsel to a parent whose child has died more effectively than prose or ornate verse could have. The lucidity he seeks to impart is glaring, painfully so, in the spareness of the form. More generally, the *gur* form, with its freedom from elaborate metaphors and its short clean lines, has a literary affinity with this kind of Great Perfection instructions that invoke naturalness and nongrasping awareness.

An Acrostic Letter to an Aristocrat

Terdak Lingpa used other forms to convey different types of messages. For instance, in the verses just below, he employed a showy acrostic (or a-b-c) form to give a student permission to begin Great Perfection practice. The form allows him an entertaining means to provide a warning about what sort of aesthetic interests are important (such as training the senses to be clear and discerning) and what sort are distractions (such as fashionable hats).

In this subtly humorous example of his expertise, Terdak Lingpa employs the acrostic form to address a student named Namka Wangjor. In English-language literature, the acrostic is associated with children's rhymes, but in Tibetan literature it is an extremely difficult and highly cultivated poetic form. Terdak Lingpa simultaneously encourages the student to practice, rebukes him for engaging in petty behavior, and shows off his own literary virtuosity. To demonstrate the formal qualities, I present the full translation first with a brief commentary afterward. Notice the many references to the senses, and the discernment between sensory alertness on the one hand and misguided concerns with materiality on the other:

Attention that's expansive like a water lily's petals,
best-intentioned for the people of the Snowland,
compassionately soothing, a rainfall cool as camphor,
desperate as I am, Guru Rinpoche keeps me in his mind.

Ever mindful from afar, be unremitting.
Forget not a man's clothing style and signs of ranks come and go.
Give up the delusion that making a living is everything.
Have pristine motivation, like the lone full moon each month.

In solitary places such as groves of palm trees,
just forget all that's ordinary and distracting.
Keep at it and you'll achieve freedom on your own here and now.
Let it be today that you accomplish the ultimate aim.

Mastering the practices of the *pāramitā*,
now you know the path of transcendence. Obstinate beings, like cattle,
     are difficult to tame.
Persevere in liberating them without exception.
Quite a subtle spark, the size of a mere sesame seed,
really can ignite everything with its scorching heat.

Stave off wild and careless behavior,
take up the cultivation of vividness and true memory.

Undue concern with superficial fashions such as hat styles,
and vainly collecting silk brocades takes time away from the teachings.
What we call "partiality" comes about; be nondivisive,
excellently demonstrating that noblemen can be liberated.

Your courtyard's enclosure cannot fend off the army of death.
Zipping about, crossing passes and rivers, you flee, but nowhere is safe.
Abandon the illusory body of meat, blood, and bones as a corpse.
Bits of dirt and stone, don't you see?

Cast off excessive laziness, comfort, and idleness.
Dzogchen is the right path for you to practice now.

Extreme in your application, having marshaled that effort,
fantastic! Accomplish the meaning of this life.

Thus advised Gyurmé Dorjé to Namka Wangjor.[83]

The references to nobility and current fashions suggest that the recipient was a lay member of the aristocracy; thus this letter provides some insight into how Terdak Lingpa engaged with the many lay disciples affiliated with Mindröling. Through his attention to the right and wrong type of aesthetics, Terdak Lingpa guides the student toward "vividness and true memory" and away from "hat styles" and "signs of ranks." The Buddhist content is not so different from that of the letter to Sonam Pelzom. What is distinctive is the density of aesthetic, affective, and emotional imagery and references in this more ornate letter. Terdak Lingpa uses a sensory image in every verse. He invokes images from Tibetan as well as Indian natural environments—notice his mention of palm trees, an unlikely sight on the high Tibetan plateau. He includes a range of pleasant and frightening figures: water lily petals; a rainfall cool as camphor; the lone full moon; groves of palm trees; a subtle spark; a sesame seed; scorching heat; passes and rivers; the army of death; the illusory body of meat, blood, and bones as a corpse; bits of dirt and stone.

Notice too the emotionally charged terms, again both pleasant and unpleasant: attention that's expansive; soothing; desperate; partiality; nondivisive; excessive laziness, comfort, and idleness. There is a clear call to resist one's enthusiasm for superficial and distracting aesthetic concerns: clothing style and signs of ranks; superficial fashions; vainly collecting silk brocades; a courtyard's safe enclosure. By contrast, in order to show that "noblemen can be liberated" (perhaps there is some doubt about whether this is possible!), he calls for the embrace of the sensory state of "vividness," through which one discerns what really matters and what's a passing fashion.

Conclusion

In his two letters to Terdak Lingpa, the Dalai Lama frames the younger man's extraordinary characteristics as a famed visionary within the undulating context of his mutually dependent and defining connections. His greatness exists in and through his relationships. According to the Dalai Lama's letters, Terdak Lingpa is primarily constituted by his relationships with the Dalai Lama himself, past incarnations, a consort, and the Tibetan people. Through these relationships, Terdak Lingpa is portrayed as a fully enlightened buddha, beyond the limitations of convention austerities, utterly perfect in his ability to teach in accordance with the capacities and sense perceptions of the people who need his instruction.

The connections the Dalai Lama points out between Terdak Lingpa and Padmasambhava, Vairocana, Dorjé Lingpa, and Ratna Lingpa represent the fulfillment of great masters' previous endeavors and aspirations. The Dalai Lama implies these connections are so strong that Terdak Lingpa could not avoid them, even if he wished to. Through the strength of the interdependent connections, his own career was latent in their previous deeds just as their aspirations continue to bear fruit through his current activity. The Dalai Lama paints a scene of a powerful momentum through Tibetan history, causing each of the incarnations to be moved to greatness in his own time, fulfilling the continuously accumulating efforts of his predecessors for the benefit of the Tibetan people.

The connection to Ngödrub Pelzom is the most extraordinary relationship conveyed in these two letters. Relationships between reincarnate lamas and buddhahood, teacher and student, or consecutive incarnations are common in Tibetan literature, but open treatment of tantric consort relations is more rare. Whereas the Dalai Lama might have referred to her throughout the letter with the honorific, euphemistic, and somewhat obscuring "secret consort," instead he employs an array of terms that together paint the picture of a nuanced relationship with social and political ramifications as well as tantric ones.

The emphasis on relationships and auspicious connections or *tendrel* is closely related to the dialogical nature of letters. This aspect of the correspondence illustrates the expression of a central Buddhist concept in the lives and communication of two major Tibetan Buddhist masters. Indeed, the concept is the armature of the Dalai Lama's compositions. In Tibetan, *tendrel* is a rich and complex term that has active philosophical and colloquial meanings. It can refer to "'coincidence,' 'circumstances,' 'omen,' a 'connection' with a particular teaching." The term can apply to a ceremony or auspicious event, in this case Terdak Lingpa's enthronement ceremony.[84]

Rather than presenting a portrait of an important person with connections, the Dalai Lama's letters to Terdak Lingpa suggest that from his perspective, the important person *is* his connections. In other words, *tendrel* are not only a reflection of greatness; they constitute greatness. Each of Terdak Lingpa's relationships fulfills crucial aspects of Terdak Lingpa's person. The concept of *tendrel* is important since these relationships are the ligaments holding together the larger networks that undergirded Mindröling, including monastic and family group networks, and the Tibetan aristocracy.

In particular, the Dalai Lama's treatment of the relationship between Terdak Lingpa and Ngödrup Pelzom is striking in the explicitness and enthusiasm with which he celebrates it. The very fact that the Dalai Lama took notice of Ngödrup Pelzom's arrival at Mindröling might come as a surprise, given his position as an ordained celibate monastic leader of the Géluk school. But the Dalai Lama evidently was invested in Terdak Lingpa's tantric and visionary practice. He need not have been scandalized by Terdak Lingpa engaging with an actual consort (as opposed to visualizing a consort), since Terdak Lingpa's vows, unlike those of a monk, did not require celibacy. Because he was a visionary Treasure revealer, his relationship with Ngödrup Pelzom was vital to the success of his practice.

Terdak Lingpa's connection with the people of Tibet is also noteworthy and sheds light on the role Mindröling would come to play. The Dalai Lama situates Terdak Lingpa's greatness within the context of Tibetans' collective merit; he suggests it is due partly to their good karma that Terdak Lingpa exists. In the grandest terms, the Dalai Lama states in both letters that Terdak Lingpa, and by extension Mindröling, had a special function of nourishment and fulfillment for the Tibetan people.[85] The Fifth Dalai Lama's efforts to consolidate a greater Tibetan polity relate directly to his vision of Mindröling as "a grove of wish-fulfilling trees in the dark forest of Tibet."

Throughout the Dalai Lama's letters, rich in allusion and Indic-inspired metaphor, he shows great esteem for the much younger lama, visionary, and founder of Mindröling. At the same time, he stakes a claim for Mindröling within his plan for Tibet. Virtually every element of the letters fits within the celebration or acknowledgment of *tendrel*, as formative interdependent connections and their networks.

The letters make clear that the Dalai Lama held the events of the enthronement and the arrival of Terdak Lingpa's consort at Mindröling as very significant. They also mention sizable donations of material objects such as robes, bells, and vajras, sent along with his letters. Writing as the principal patron of the newly established Mindröling, the Dalai Lama is exultant while also displaying a marked gravitas, formality, and respect. His letters have a rhetorical intensity and literary flair that verge on the grandiose in some passages, revealing a very specific sensibility. While this is partly a reflection of the high literary aesthetic of the time and the Dalai Lama's own florid style, the formality also suggests these occasions were important events.

Further, although these two letters fill only six Tibetan folios combined, they offer insight into fine points of tantric practice for which the Mindröling lineage was renowned, Buddhist statecraft and the Tibetan concept of unifying religious and worldly spheres, Tibetan literary aesthetics, and "patron-priest" (mchod yon) dynamics (here the Dalai Lama is Terdak Lingpa's patron), to name some of the most salient elements. They also demonstrate the Dalai Lama's characteristic and influential prose and poetry styles.

The themes of the letters were primary concerns of the Dalai Lama in his efforts to consolidate a unified Tibetan identity and polity. Terdak Lingpa, and by extension the institution of Mindröling, was critical to that project, particularly in regard to joining correctly and successfully the two traditions of worldly and Buddhist authority. Since the Dalai Lama was an arbiter of taste and style as well as a political and religious authority, how he expressed himself can reveal fine points about early modern Tibetan aesthetics.

When considered together, Terdak Lingpa's collected letters provide perspective on Mindröling's founder as a teacher who encouraged rigorous Buddhist practice, candid self-reflection, and attention to detail in conducting ritual, even if the rituals needed to be abbreviated. Mindröling was famous for the excellence and clarity of its ritual traditions, which were connected to aesthetics through their focus on the senses and objects of the senses, yet Terdak Lingpa made allowances so that disciples could integrate Buddhist practice into their daily lives—implying that it is better for a busy official to do a shortened practice than not to practice at all.

Terdak Lingpa's interpersonal connections spanned the vast terrain of the Tibetan Buddhist cultural area, from Ngari in the west to Kham and Amdo in the east. Men and women in the highest positions of government, society, and religious authority sought his counsel on philosophical, historical, ritual, and political subjects. His advice consistently reflects a concern with integrating Buddhism into being in the world, bridging potential gaps between soteriology and normative claims about good Buddhist behavior with practical issues of daily life. He also demonstrates a consistent interest in cultivating and engendering impartiality. The style and content of his letters as well as his engagement with men and women alike reveal an aesthetic of impartiality and a perspective that seeks to balance being discerning with being nondivisive.

In these two letters Terdak Lingpa advises a laywoman and a layman, both apparently members of Tibet's ruling class. He seems to have delighted in diverse literary forms, revealing the sensibilities of Tibetan literati. Thus, the letters provide a window onto some of the social dynamics at play in Lhasa's cosmopolitan milieu during the time of Terdak Lingpa and the Fifth Dalai Lama's rule.

But Mindröling was first and foremost a center for celibate monastics. To understand how Terdak Lingpa interacted with the monastic population and what the intended role of Mindröling was in its first few decades of existence, in the next chapter I analyze the constitutional guidelines he created to inculcate the values expressed in his letters and to govern the Mindröling community.

FOUR

Training the Senses

Aesthetic Education for Monastics

Students of the highest capacity ... should also study the other fields of
knowledge, as much as they are capable. This is the armor that will protect
one's future goals and must not be allowed to fall away.

—TERDAK LINGPA, MINDRÖLING
MONASTIC GUIDELINES

DURING THE EARLY years of Mindröling monastery's history, what did
the monks study, how did they spend their time, and what were the founders' educational and institutional priorities for the monastic population?
How were students trained in the ritual, scholarly, and artistic practices for
which Mindröling became famous? In this chapter I address these questions by analyzing selections from Mindröling's constitutional guidelines
(*bca' yig*),[1] with a focus on the section that outlines the curriculum of study.[2]
Composed by Terdak Lingpa, the detailed and colorful monastic guidelines
explain the monastery's rules and regulations, curriculum, and yearly calendar, including rituals to support the Dalai Lama's government. As the
epigraph demonstrates, Terdak Lingpa was committed to training students
in the worldly fields of learning—the arts and sciences—as well as the study
of Dharma. Both were elemental to a Mindröling education.

A New Model for Nyingma Monasticism

When Terdak Lingpa founded Mindröling, he was in the complicated position of establishing a new monastery that would help clarify and safeguard
the Nyingma school *qua* school, in contrast to a previously diffuse array of

Figure 4.1 Interior of Mindröling monastery with statue of Terdak Lingpa, 2009. Photograph by Aaron Fox

ancient Tibetan traditions and lineages.[3] At the same time, he had to meet the demands of various Tibetan, Mongol, and Qing supporters of the Dalai Lama's Ganden Podrang government and the dominant Géluk establishment. This meant that Terdak Lingpa had to negotiate and mediate prejudice against Nyingma practitioners in order to build a stable new monastery.

As an illustration of anti-Nyingma prejudice, in the Dalai Lama's autobiography he recounts an instance in which an advisor tells him, under desperate circumstances, "Practice the Nyingma tradition! The proverb says: 'If it is good for the wound, even dog fat (is fine)!'"[4] This proverb encapsulates the disparaging attitude some members of the Géluk school held toward Nyingma traditions during the time Mindröling was established. The speaker acknowledges that Nyingma practice, which in this case involves ritual violence, may be effective under some circumstances. However, he does not have much respect for the tradition in general, which he equates with dog fat. The Dalai Lama's Nyingma affiliations are well documented. The ritual dagger depicted in his belt is visual evidence of his commitment to the Treasure tradition in particular (see figure 3.2). However, his official sponsorship of Terdak Lingpa's new monastery did not guarantee that other members of his school would approve of it.

Against this backdrop, the monastic members of Mindröling had to uphold the values most important to the Géluk school, including celibacy, while crystallizing the qualifications for which Nyingma practitioners were valued most. They would do so under the codirection of the hereditary posts of the noncelibate senior chair and the celibate abbot of the monastery. Mindröling would also provide a home for Terdak Lingpa's family lineage, both men and women. The monastery would integrate his collection of rediscovered Treasure teachings, associated with Padmasambhava and Yeshé Tsogyel, as well as his collection of Nyingma *kama* (*bka' ma*), the spoken teachings considered to be the words of the Buddha, passed from teacher to student over generations.

The curriculum would not be limited to Buddhist subjects. Terdak Lingpa's ancestors were renowned for expertise in the arts and sciences known as *rikné* (*rig gnas*)—literary arts, astrology, and medicine in particular—as much as for esoteric Great Perfection philosophy and meditation and tantric ritual expertise. A Mindröling education would integrate more secular topics with monastic decorum, adherence to appropriate vows, the study of Mahāyāna philosophy, and expertise in tantric ritual performance, most notably large-scale public rituals.

Part of the phenomenon of Mindröling is that its curriculum and ritual liturgies came to serve as models for other Nyingma monasteries across diverse Tibetan cultural regions. Beginning in the eighteenth century, its curricular and ritual traditions spread from Mindröling to Kathok monastery, one of the six "mother" monasteries of the Nyingma school.[5] All six of these monasteries were founded (or in the case of Kathok, expanded and reenvisioned) during the seventeenth or eighteenth century, around the time Mindröling began to flourish.[6] Jann Ronis notes the "ascendency of Mindrölling Monastery's teachings" in his study of the transformations Kathok underwent in the eighteenth century.[7] He demonstrates the adoption of Mindröling's spoken teachings and commentaries, most significantly those related to the *Guhyagharba* tantra. Terdak Lingpa compiled and edited these teachings and Dharmaśrī composed the most influential commentaries. Leaders of the Eastern Tibetan monastic communities imported aesthetic practices related to dance, mandala drawings, chants, music, and more at the other major Nyingma institutions.[8] In turn, the other mother monasteries disseminated Mindröling's traditions to their own branches and affiliates. Kathok, Dzogchen, Palyul, and Shechen monasteries in Eastern Tibet all adopted Mindröling versions of these practices and trained their monks in Mindröling's aesthetic traditions. Over time, some would also shift toward a focus on literary arts, in keeping with the Mindröling model.[9]

A Buddhist Field of Merit in a Time of Strife

Terdak Lingpa, in consultation with his brother, the second Mindröling abbot Dharmaśrī, incorporated all these priorities in the monastic guidelines and curriculum with the aim of clarifying, safeguarding, and spreading Nyingma traditions. To do so, they had to account for a diverse range of patrons and critics vying for power on the Tibetan political and religious stage. The guidelines reflect concerns about environmental and supernatural entities as well as human ones. Terdak Lingpa warns students to follow the guidelines not only to please laypeople and sponsors but also to avoid disturbing the local protectors, who might seek revenge if the rules are broken.[10] These demands proved daunting during a period of sectarian strife and early modern Central Tibetan state-building efforts on the part of the Dalai Lama and his cohort.

The main goal stated in the curriculum is to cultivate Mindröling as a "field of merit." This reflects a classical Indian Buddhist premise that monasteries benefit the laity because monks and nuns conduct productive rituals, negotiate with supernatural forces, and generally maintain behaviors deemed to be virtuous and conducive to the continuation of the Buddha's teachings and the well-being of the broader community. A good monastery creates a font of positive karma while perpetuating Buddhist teaching and practice. This is a conventional claim about monasteries that appears across Buddhist societies.[11] Even so, it deserves attention as the stated purpose of the curriculum.

For Terdak Lingpa, cultivating a field of merit required a particular approach to education. The curriculum displays a structure that enables continuity while allowing for adaptation to changing social norms and accommodates a diverse body of students. Given the focus on ritual expertise and the worldly fields of knowledge, this was in part an education in aesthetics, meaning not merely a concern with beauty or a philosophy of art, but rather all that concerns the senses and the objects of the senses. In this way the curriculum provides an overview of the aesthetic education for monastic members of Mindröling, with the rationale that this training will contribute to the generation of merit. The rules and regulations as well as the curriculum were, at least rhetorically, all in the service of this aim. Before analyzing how these concerns play out in the curriculum, it will be helpful first to consider the genre of monastic constitutional guidelines in general.

Tibetan Monastic Constitutional Guidelines

Most large Tibetan Buddhist monasteries, many small monasteries, and in some cases groups of students devoted to a particular teacher have written constitutional guidelines similar to Mindröling's, although Terdak Lingpa wrote a particularly detailed and vivid example.[12] In *The Monastery Rules: Buddhist Monastic Organization in Pre-Modern Tibet*, Berthe Jansen provides an invaluable survey of such documents, reflecting the breadth and practical utility of these texts. Her work reveals that monastic guidelines make up a significant, if difficult to define, area of Tibetan literature. Like the Tibetan letters I analyze in chapter 3, this porous genre provides a rich source of information pertinent to the study of Tibetan cultural production as well as social history. Such guidelines can act as manifestos; proclaim rules and regulations; state the monastery's purpose; describe its ritual and educational practices; outline the daily life of its inhabitants (including dress, food, discipline, how to deal with illness, rule breaking, etc.); describe the ideal relationship with the monastery's surrounding community; and list branch and affiliate monasteries. These documents are extremely useful in providing material about Tibetan Buddhist life and history beyond the stated ideals that appear in more doctrinal genres of Tibetan literature.

There was an increase in the production of constitutional documents in the seventeenth and eighteenth centuries, during the time when Mindröling was founded. In many cases patrons or members of a monastery commissioned the author to write guidelines. At Mindröling the founder himself composed the text in 1689; it was revised and augmented subsequently by his brother the scholar-monk Dharmaśrī in 1708. Terdak Lingpa did not articulate an explicit motivation for writing the guidelines when he did, about thirteen years after he founded the monastery, but he generally acknowledged the need for clear rules and regulations. It appears he sought to provide a normative structure so his successors could continue the institutional project as he intended.

In this sense, the guidelines served the dual purpose of governing the monastery from within and protecting its good reputation from without. In particular, Terdak Lingpa sought to prevent patrons, sponsors, and visitors from witnessing undisciplined behavior, which would jeopardize the monastery's sources of material support and protection. He also sought to overcome suspicions based on old Tibetan stereotypes of Nyingma practitioners due to their association with literal (rather than visualized) sexual tantric practice and ritual violence,[13] and to show that Mindröling's monks were rigorous in upholding their monastic vows despite the fact that the senior chair of the monastery was not a monk. As other monasteries were being destroyed or forcibly converted to the Géluk school, the stakes were very high.

While these documents are not strict contracts that must be followed to the letter, monastic guidelines do set up expectations for how members of the community should behave, clarify the purpose of behaving in the prescribed way, and explain what to do if someone breaks the rules. In this way, they define what it means to be a part of that particular community. They set norms for how to behave. The institutional authorities, the members of the monastic community, the wider society, and potential patrons can all refer to these when questions or conflicts arise. In the Tibetan monastic context, these guidelines arguably were more significant for members than translations of the Indian Buddhist canonical monastic code, the Vinaya, which in most cases, including at Mindröling, only the most advanced and fully ordained students are invited to study.[14]

Tibetan Buddhist monasteries treat these documents in a variety of ways. In some cases they are readily accessible, and in other cases only authorized members of the community, such as the disciplinarian, can read them. At Mindröling, today at least, the 1689 guidelines are publicly available. Contemporary monastic leaders have allowed for adaptations due to changes in time and place, and yet members of the monastery maintain the 1689 document's basic authority because Terdak Lingpa himself composed it.[15]

At Mindröling and in many other cases where the guidelines are not restricted, the outward-facing communications embedded within them can give sponsors who support the monastery a clear understanding of how they should expect monks and nuns to behave.[16] In this regard, some such documents were (and are) publicly performed, for instance read aloud by the monastery's disciplinarian, sometimes with proverbs added for illustration.[17] Others were displayed prominently on the monastery walls.[18] In some cases, only the relevant monastic authorities have access to read and implement the documents; in particular, members of the Géluk school tend to guard the monastic guidelines as secret.[19] By contrast, today the original Mindröling guidelines are published alongside other major institutional documents composed by the founders. They are accessible to anyone who chooses to read them.

An Overview of Mindröling's Monastic Guidelines

Beyond the details of the curriculum, the constitutional guidelines give insight into the general culture and ethos of Mindröling and offers windows onto concerns and conflicts that arose in the community. For instance, the guidelines explain how to help poor monks who fall ill and cannot afford to pay for private medical care, and how to determine which students are suited to undergo solitary meditation retreats and which students need to remain within the structure of the monastic community.

The authors also wrote extensively about how to safeguard monks from breaking their vows of celibacy, in part by prohibiting women, including the monks' mothers and sisters, from visiting the living quarters. It is worth pausing on this point. Celibacy is a major concern for all monastic communities, but Mindröling also became known for the strength of its women practitioners and teachers, beginning with Terdak Lingpa's mother, Yangchen Dolma, and his daughter Mingyur Peldrön and continuing up to the present. There was also an affiliated community of about thirty nuns connected to the monastery. For this reason, it might come as a surprise that Terdak Lingpa designed extremely strict rules against the presence of women in many areas of the monastery, particularly the living quarters. The guidelines state that whether a woman is of high or low social status, and regardless of whether she has relatives living at the monastery, she is not allowed to visit any part of the monastery beyond the main temple, and she can under no circumstances stay the night.[20] By contrast, Terdak Lingpa, who was not a monk, had abundant contact with women, as recipients of his Great Perfection meditation instructions, as sponsors of the monastery, as family members, and as tantric partners. Likewise, he was very close with the female members of his family, especially his daughter Mingyur Peldrön, to whom he passed on the full range of his teachings. But protecting the monks' vows of celibacy was a clear and central concern.

Other significant concerns reflected in the guidelines include how to manage the monastery's wealth and how to keep track of the valuable artistic and ritual objects acquired through donations. Terdak Lingpa provides guidelines for mundane concerns such as which members of the population may pick fruit from the local orchards (novices and laymen are allowed, ordained monks may not) and how often pupils should get together for afternoon tea. There are also strict rules regarding smoking and alcohol consumption, which was forbidden,[21] and rules about fighting.[22] The guidelines warn against coercing the families of new pupils to make large donations to the monastery. They provide direction on whether and how members of the monastery can engage in lending money to laypeople and safeguards against the monks seeking to profit from predatory lending.[23] The guidelines also restrict the duration of time that a student may spend away from the monastery, according to how far away from Mindröling their family lives. The fact that Terdak Lingpa added a clause for those who lived more than one month's journey from Mindröling indicates the presence of pupils from very distant locales, underscoring the wide scope of Mindröling's network. The guidelines also stress the importance of treating laypeople well and particularly warn against mistreating people in service positions, for instance porters and helpers in guesthouses.[24] The guidelines also contain rules and regulations for dealing with graffiti.[25] And Terdak Lingpa warns against engaging in gossip, physical brawls, matchmaking, and sectarianism. These guidelines paint a vivid picture of the community, indicating the types of problems and conflicts that arose and providing a sense of the institutional culture of the monastery.[26]

The Curriculum Section of the Mindröling
Monastic Guidelines

Here I offer a translation of the curriculum section of the guidelines, followed by an analysis of the contents. Terdak Lingpa's outline for the course of study reads as follows:

Principally, since the primary cause of the accomplishment of awakening depends on study and contemplation, after having initially joined the monastery, students should not develop bad mental habits nor become spoiled. Having relied on the master of the monastic courtyard and each individual division's teacher, begin with training in modestly practicing all the four modes of conduct [eating, walking, sitting, lying down]. From there, through reading aloud, ritual, Dharma practice, and so forth, the mind should become deeply clear and pure though skillful instruction, rather than becoming rigid. In accordance with the conditions of each individual's understanding, grasp as many daily lessons as one can. That is to say, with the exception of periods of travel for monastic duties, illness, and so forth, regular lessons should be given and received every day without fail, as much as the teacher and student can manage, similar to the example of an anthill and honey.[27] Both master and student should generate a sense of responsibility in producing the highest aspiration.

In accordance with the conditions of understanding, the examinations can be given collectively or else the three-part examination series can be given incrementally. Whichever approach is taken, students should pass the examinations within five years. If both teacher and student remain indifferent, and one day the limit of five years is reached, that is not suitable.

For up to fifteen years,[28] for every five daily lessons taken, the student must do one day of young people's work.[29] For every ten daily lessons, the teacher must offer a porkang's worth of butter lamps.[30] If the student does not meet the requirements after sixteen years of preparation for the examinations, it is the individual student's responsibility to pay the penalty rather than the teacher's. The individual's teacher, the master of the courtyard, and the disciplinarian all must agree on the calculation of that penalty. When the rotating positions of master of the courtyard and disciplinarian change over, the individuals who take up those posts should uphold the previously agreed-upon penalties.

After that, in accordance with each individual's intellectual approach, one should study and contemplate to become deeply self-reliant in the visualization stage of the appropriate ritual practice.

As for melodies, chanting, instrumentation, offerings, mandalas, lama dances, and so forth, do not sit idly "donkey-handed" during rituals and do not remain silent in the liturgies. These practices are to be internalized genuinely as indispensable aspects of the activities to be maintained in our particular monastery.

Then, in accordance with each respective student's approach to understanding, study the detailed commentary and the general essence of the Secret Essence (*Shri Guhyagarbha*) tantric cycle, as the pedagogical exegesis that constitutes the stable center of our Mindröling system. Through memorizing the words and understanding the meaning, receiving the pointing out instructions and explanations, listening and so forth, attain the position of a scholar.

Regarding those students of the highest capacity, they should study a suitable amount of monastic discipline, the Perfection of Wisdom (*phar phyin*) teachings and so forth, as well as the textual system of the Sūtra Vehicle (*mtshan nyid theg pa'i gzhung*). They should also study the other fields of knowledge [besides Dharma], as much as they are capable. This is the armor that safeguards one's future goals and must not be allowed to fall away. As for the teacher, do not remain indifferent but arouse the highest aspiration to enter into the stream of being of another. This opportunity is not to be wasted.

In both summer and winter practice sessions, the explanation of the tantras should be studied and contemplated. In both autumn and spring practice sessions, request the *prātimokṣa* vows, together with empowerments, instructions, oral transmissions, direct instructions, and whatever will lead to one's own development and liberation. In particular, practice daily training in the *prātimokṣa* and bodhisattva vows, gaining a general sense of how to engage in the vows without error.

As for those students who are interested in the Development Stage practices, devotedly propitiate whichever of these meditational deities is appropriate for at least six months—Fierce and Peaceful Guru Padmasambhava (*bla ma zhi drag*), the Great Compassionate One (*thugs rje chen po*), The Illusory Manifestation (*sgyu 'phrul*), The Eight Pronouncements (*bka' brgyad*), Kilaya (*phur pa*), Yamantaka (*gshin rje gshed*), and so forth. Through continuous meditation and uninterrupted recitation, training these three—the body, sense perceptions, and mind—as the wheel of pure boundless wisdom, perform the practices of the twenty-eight samayas and so forth, unerring in accepting and rejecting the distinctions between perceived phenomena.

If principally doing the Completion Stage, focus on the two *Heart Essence* teachings (*snying thig rnam gnyis*), The Vajra Bridge (*rdo rje zam pa*), instructions on Terdak Lingpa's newly revealed Treasures, the oral explanations, and so forth. Follow whichever experiential instruction is appropriate according to one's personal experience. Having relished, repented, and requested, don't lose out on the four occasions because of obscurations.

For the highest caliber individual, community and solitude are the same. Solitude is best for increasing virtue; however, for middling and lower caliber individuals who stay in an isolated place, the mind is not disciplined. Left to their own devices, they lose control to laziness and idleness. Some even turn out to be unable to give up intoxicants and evening meals.

Become a genuine community of monks that gathers in harmony with the doctrine. Perform activities in keeping with the teachings. In order to accomplish the marvelous two purposes [of benefiting self and other], even if one becomes discouraged with the monastic community, one should not be overly carefree in one's attitude nor go on talking about going into solitary retreat. If a student has a certain spiritual practice that requires staying in retreat for a set period of months or years, they should keep the general rules of the monastic community intact while staying at the retreat location known as the Land of Bliss. After leaving there, just as before, it is essential not to generate conflict within the community.

In brief, through the activities of studying, contemplating, and meditating day and night, heavy with the weight of learning, discipline, and nobility, become a field of merit, worthy of praise by the wise.[31]

In designing this brief curriculum section of the monastic guidelines, Terdak Lingpa establishes a course of study and practice for his new monastery that other Nyingma monasteries could reproduce through training their own monks. He pays special attention to the artistry of the tantric ritual performances for which the monastery would become renowned, thanks in part to the founders' careful scholarship, and in part to their staging of large-scale public performances that attracted visitors from across Tibetan Buddhist regions. The first of these took place at Mindröling in 1691.[32] Such performances would help to clarify and solidify the bases of the Nyingma school. This project went in tandem with the Dalai Lama and the regent, Sangyé Gyatso's, efforts to unify a Tibetan polity through an array of ritual, intellectual, cultural, and scientific initiatives.[33] These mutually contributed to what Jacques Rancière calls, albeit in a different context, "a community of sense . . . a frame of visibility and intelligibility that puts things or practices together under the same meaning, which shapes thereby a certain sense of community."[34] For Terdak Lingpa to accomplish these aims was no simple task, and the curriculum displays a delicate balance of institutional priorities, all presented in his distinctive authorial voice, including a taste of his sense of humor and areas of potential frustration.

In the first section of the curriculum translated above, Terdak Lingpa describes basic training and deportment for monks who have recently entered the monastery. The guidelines become more specific as the curriculum progresses, attending to ritual arts, fields of worldly learning, and areas of meditative and practical expertise that students might develop. The curriculum culminates in a strongly stated proclamation about the factors students must weigh when considering solitary meditation retreat beyond the monastery's walls.

Terdak Lingpa starts by setting the basic parameters for training at the monastery, establishing standards of deportment and intellectual qualities and setting the rigorous tone of the curriculum. This reflects his concern with the students' *habitus*, their way of being in the world, their attitudes, dispositions, and demeanor. Thus he begins to establish the sensibility he seeks to generate in his students. "Principally, since the primary cause of the accomplishment of awakening depends on study and contemplation, after having initially joined the monastery, students should not develop bad mental habits nor become spoiled. Having relied on the master of the monastic courtyard and each individual division's teacher, begin with training in modestly practicing all the four modes of conduct [eating, walking, sitting, lying down]."[35]

The attention to deportment is common in Buddhist monastic guidelines, which generally are concerned with how to behave. Positive mental and physical habits are presented as being basic necessities. Behaving properly and carrying oneself with dignity and respect is presented as the baseline for membership in the monastery. His attention to study (here distinct from "meditation," which he addresses later in the curriculum) also indicates that intellectual learning is essential for achieving Buddhist awakening.

Next Terdak Lingpa outlines the requirements for general education and indicates the style of teaching and learning he seeks to inculcate: "From there, through reading aloud, ritual, Dharma practice, and so forth, the mind should become deeply clear and pure through skillful instruction, rather than becoming rigid."[36] According to this statement, training at Mindröling requires a mental state that is vigorous and disciplined, clear and pure, but not rigid. While avoiding laziness and idleness, students should be supple-minded, in a style that resonates with Great Perfection teachings on natural wakefulness. He then turns his attention to the importance of daily lessons, based on the student's capacity:

> In accordance with the conditions of each individual's understanding, grasp as many daily lessons as one can. That is to say, with the exception of periods of travel for monastic duties, periods of illness, and so forth, regular lessons should be given and received every day without fail, as much as the teacher and student can manage, similar to the example of an anthill and honey. Both master and student should generate a sense of responsibility in producing the highest aspiration.

Terdak Lingpa uses the metaphor of an anthill here to encourage students and teachers alike to work as hard as they can, with the enthusiasm of ants attracted to honey, tirelessly returning again and again for more. In this spirit, even general education should inspire an energetic pursuit of the "highest aspiration."

Next he introduces Mindröling's three-part system of examination. The examinations are required for all students to ensure that they are prepared for the more advanced and individualized study that follows. "In accordance with the conditions of understanding, the examinations can be given collectively or else the three-part examination series can be given incrementally. Whichever approach is taken, students should pass the examinations within five years. If both teacher and student remain indifferent, and one day the limit of five years is reached, that is not suitable."[37]

Terdak Lingpa also explains what should be done if the exams are not passed successfully. "For up to fifteen years, for every five daily lessons taken, the student must do one day of young people's work. For every ten daily lessons, the teacher must offer a *porkang*'s worth of butter lamps. If the student does not meet the requirements after sixteen years of preparation for the examinations, it is the individual student's responsibility to pay the penalty rather than the teacher's."[38]

It appears that the individual student's capabilities and plans determine how long it takes to prepare for the examinations, how they structure the actual examination process, and what the consequences of failure are. If after fifteen years the student has failed to pass the examinations, both teacher and student are punished; teachers are required to offer butter lamps and students must do menial labor. After sixteen years, the penalty for failing falls on the student alone.[39] This tells us that during Terdak Lingpa's time, some students took many years to pass the examinations, and some failed. This was a strenuous and extensive course of study. Both teacher and student are held accountable for the student's progress or failure, providing a hint of Terdak Lingpa's pedagogy.

Next the curriculum gives a rough schema of the hierarchy of authorities who were involved in the examinations and related punishments: "The individual's teacher, the master of the courtyard, and the disciplinarian all must agree on the calculation of that penalty. When the rotating positions of master of the courtyard and disciplinarian change over, the individuals who take up those posts should uphold the previously agreed-upon penalties."[40] This provides a sketch of the monastic bureaucracy and system of governance, which was organized according to rotating positions of authority.

After the examinations, education becomes more specific to the individual. The next part of the curriculum establishes courses of study and practice, indicating the ritual activities, stages of meditation, and texts appropriate for various types of student: "After that, in accordance with each individual's intellectual approach, one should study and contemplate to become deeply self-reliant in the visualization stage of the appropriate ritual practice."[41]

Next comes the training in the artistic media central to Mindröling's institutional identity as a major center for ritual activities, which demonstrates the role of aesthetic education at the monastery. "As for melodies, chanting, instrumentation, offerings, mandalas, lama dances, and so forth, do not sit idly 'donkey-handed' during rituals and do not remain silent in the liturgies. These practices are to be internalized genuinely as indispensable aspects of the activities to be maintained in our particular monastery."[42] This list of ritual activities, although not comprehensive, provides an overview of the types of aesthetic training Terdak Lingpa designated as crucial to Mindröling. These were the techniques other Nyingma monasteries adopted in training their own monastic populations.

The tone here suggests not all members of Mindröling took this aspect of their education as seriously as Terdak Lingpa wished. Some apparently performed rituals in a clumsy, "donkey-handed" manner, and some must have sat silently when they should have been chanting the memorized texts.

This jibe reflects Terdak Lingpa's frustration with monks who did not practice the rituals well and gives us a taste of his sense of his style as a writer. It was crucial that students learn proper performance of ritual arts since Mindröling's prestige was established in part by its public rituals, which attracted sponsors and practitioners and shaped Nyingma monastic ritual practices more broadly.

Notably, in regard to ritual expertise, Terdak Lingpa does not mention individual paths, insisting that all students at the monastery, of all capacities, should take these artistic media seriously. Education in ritual practices is basic aesthetic education. Ritual spectacle and experience are crucial in generating a shared sensibility as well as systematizing the calendar and relationships to time. Mindröling was and is renowned for excellence in all ritual media, even including the production of incense. All are associated with offerings designed to appeal to the senses of the deities, based on records of Terdak Lingpa's visionary insights.[43]

With the importance of students' ritual dexterity and competence established, Terdak Lingpa underscores the necessity to internalize Mindröling's main tantric system through memorization and analysis of the *Guhyagarbha tantra* (*dpal gsang ba snying po'i*): "Then, in accordance with each respective student's approach to understanding, study the detailed commentary and the general essence of the Secret Essence (*Shri Guhyagarbha*) tantric cycle, as the pedagogical exegesis that constitutes the stable center of our Mindröling system. Through memorizing the words and understanding the meaning, receiving the pointing out instructions and explanations, listening and so forth, attain the position of a scholar."[44] Terdak Lingpa celebrates the role of the scholar, calling on students to take seriously their engagement with the main source materials of the tradition.

He then outlines the study of monastic discipline and Mahāyāna philosophy the most capable students should pursue: "Regarding those students of the highest capacity, they should study a suitable amount of monastic discipline (*'dul ba*), Perfection of Wisdom (*phar phyin*) teachings and so forth, as well as the textual system of the Sūtra Vehicle (*mtshan nyid theg pa'i gzhung*)."[45] While the foundation was tantric ritual practice, exoteric subjects were part of the 1689 curriculum as well.

Crucially, Terdak Lingpa includes extra-Buddhist subjects in the curriculum: "They should also study the other fields of knowledge, as much as they are capable. This is the armor that safeguards one's future goals and must not be allowed to fall away."[46] These subjects are divided into the five major fields and five minor fields. The major fields are: arts and crafts, logic, grammar, medicine, and "inner science" or Dharma. The minor fields are: synonyms, mathematics and astrology, drama, poetry, and composition. Note the focus on the literary arts of grammar, synonyms, poetry, and composition, vital to Mindröling's identity. The monastery became the main Central Tibetan hub for learning in the worldly subjects. Including these areas should not be taken for granted; Tibetan Buddhists of Terdak Lingpa's day debated the proper approach to these fields, and some doubted whether the more secular disciplines could contribute to enlightenment.[47]

In addition to the monks who are the main focus of the curriculum, laypeople came to the monastery to study these subjects as well. Monks acted as tutors in the homes of aristocrats, besides working as teachers in Lhasa's schools. The curriculum shows that training in these subjects was important from the monastery's earliest days.

The metaphor of worldly knowledge as armor is a striking choice. More often, proponents of these subjects associate them with omniscience, but here Terdak Lingpa makes a different point. He equates worldly knowledge with power, or at the very least, protection from harm. At the same time, the curriculum makes it clear that, for capable students, studying these subjects was essential to making Mindröling a field of merit.

Terdak Lingpa then establishes a basic seasonal calendar, all the while drawing attention to the needs of the individual, calling for "whatever will lead to one's own" awakening, with a strong focus on monastic and bodhisattva vows:

In both summer and winter practice sessions, the explanation of the tantras should be studied and contemplated. In both autumn and spring practice sessions, request the *prātimokṣa* vows, together with empowerments, instructions, oral transmissions, direct instructions, and whatever will lead to one's own development and liberation. In particular, practice daily training in the *prātimokṣa* and bodhisattva vows, gaining a general sense of how to engage in the vows without error.[48]

Only later in the curriculum does Terdak Lingpa turn his focus to meditation practice, again offering an array of paths for individuals. He directs "those who are interested in the Development Stage"[49] to proceed in one of a variety of ways, engaging with the appropriate text focused on an appropriate deity for the appropriate amount of time:

As for those students who are interested in the Development Stage practices, devotedly propitiate whichever of these meditational deities is appropriate for at least six months—Fierce and Peaceful Guru Padmasambhava (*bla ma zhi drag*), the Great Compassionate One (*thugs rje chen po*), the Illusory Manifestation (*sgyu 'phrul*), the Eight Pronouncements (*bka' brgyad*), Kilaya (*phur pa*), Yamantaka (*gshin rje gshed*), and so forth. Through continuous meditation and uninterrupted recitation, training these three—the body, sense perceptions, and mind—as the wheel of pure boundless wisdom, perform the practices of the twenty-eight samayas and so forth, unerring in accepting and rejecting the distinctions between perceived phenomena.

Those students engaged in the more advanced Completion Stage should engage in "whichever experiential instruction is appropriate according to one's personal experience."[50] In particular:

Focus on the two *Heart Essence* teachings (*snying thig rnam gnyis*), *The Vajra Bridge* (*rdo rje zam pa*), instructions on Terdak Lingpa's newly revealed Treasures, the oral explanations, and so forth. Follow whichever experiential instruction is appropriate according to one's personal experience. Having relished, repented, and requested, don't lose out on the four occasions because of obscurations.

The final section of the curriculum concerns whether students should leave the main monastery area, temporarily giving up lessons with their teachers and pausing their participation in the large-scale ritual activities, to engage in solitary meditation retreat in a nearby area designated for this purpose. This appears to have been a vexed question at the time of the curriculum's composition, given the critical tone and the relative length of the section. Again, Terdak Lingpa demonstrates a pedagogical method of creating a structure that allows flexibility for the individual: "For the highest caliber individual, community and solitude are the same. Solitude is best for increasing virtue; however, for middling and lower caliber individuals who stay in an isolated place, the mind is not disciplined. Left to their own devices, they lose control to laziness and idleness. Some even turn out to be unable to give up intoxicants and evening meals."[51] He indicates that those who are in solitary retreat must continue to follow the monastic guidelines, possibly suggesting that some retreat participants did not. The consumption of alcohol was a particularly sharp concern, indicated by the fact that the guidelines elsewhere provide directives for punishing laypeople carrying alcohol into the monastery.[52]

Terdak Lingpa devotes more space to this theme of whether to engage in solitary retreat than to any of the other stages of education addressed in the curriculum. He even directs students to refrain from going on and on about how great retreat is once they return to the community setting. "Become a genuine community of monks that gathers in harmony with the doctrine. Perform activities in keeping with the teachings. In order to accomplish the marvelous two purposes [of benefiting self and other], even if one becomes discouraged with the monastic community, one should not be overly carefree in one's attitude nor go on talking about going into solitary retreat."[53]

Terdak Lingpa thus clarifies who should undertake solitary retreat—only the best students, and only if they follow the rules and do not disrupt the harmony of the community when they return. This suggests a distinction between members of the community in more conventional monks' roles within the monastery walls and those in retreat. Terdak Lingpa's discouraging tone suggests that some unqualified students wanted to engage in retreat, and that some qualified students did not uphold the monastic rules, or sparked conflict in the community when they returned. This suggests that solitary retreat carried a degree of prestige in the Mindröling community, as well as an opportunity to get out of the mundane duties of monastic life, including the all-important ritual activities that reinforced the monastery's ties to the broader community.

Taken as a whole, the curriculum suggests that the monastery needs different kinds of practitioners in order to function as a place of learning, ritual, contemplation, and enlightenment. It needs ritual experts, good writers and scholars, and meditators. The curriculum ends with the fundamental institutional and soteriological aim: "through the activities of studying, contemplating, and meditating day and night, heavy with the weight of learning, discipline, and nobility, become a field of merit, worthy of praise by the wise."[54]

Training Diverse Members of the Mindröling
Monastic Body

A sense of accommodating the individual appears to reflect Terdak Lingpa's pedagogical approach and the relative diversity of the monastic body at Mindröling. While awakening is presented as the ideal aim, not everyone has the same capacities, inclinations, or vocation. Throughout the curriculum, Terdak Lingpa articulates that the course of study should be "in keeping with the individual's capacity for understanding." He qualifies each element of the educational process with phrases like "as much as they are capable" (*ci nus su*) and "in keeping with one's own intellectual approach" (*rang rang gi blo gros kyi 'jug sgo dang sbyar ba'i*). These phrases are not extraordinary in and of themselves; however, Terdak Lingpa uses them frequently enough to suggest a predominant theme. Phrases of this general type occur more than a dozen times within the three-page curriculum section of the constitutional guidelines. Almost every stage of education outlined is followed by a phrase that indicates the training must be suited to the inclinations and capacity of the individual student. It is as if a professor were to compose a course syllabus (which is also an agreement between enrolled students, administrators, and those who might patronize or criticize the college) with an addendum of "as appropriate for the individual student" qualifying every section. Terdak Lingpa's approach is neither free-form nor rigid, but rather a systematic balance of step-by-step training, with each step punctuated by the acknowledgment that the particular path must be determined based on the student's capacity, interests, talents, inclinations, and context. This demonstrates that Terdak Lingpa was committed to a pedagogy that allowed for the individual needs of students, while creating a stable and reproducible educational framework that could serve as a model for other Nyingma monasteries and stand the tests of time.

The curriculum is concerned with teachers and administrators as well. It refers to a hierarchy of teachers who oversee the training and development of the students in the early phases of training before they have passed the examinations. Although the teacher's specific duties are not the main focus, Terdak Lingpa does mention that their roles rotated on a prescribed schedule, some taking up the position of tutor of a large group of students, others overseeing individual progress, and still others acting as disciplinarians.[55] In this section of the guidelines, no specific information is provided on how students were assigned to particular teachers, for how long they studied with any given tutor, or to what extent instruction took place in groups versus individually.

The curriculum suggests Terdak Lingpa sought to provide each disciple and each student at Mindröling with the appropriate training, in regard to both the method of instruction and examination and the content studied. It encapsulates the Mindröling sensibility; it uses language that reflects the Great Perfection ideals, encouraging a disciplined but relaxed attitude and open state of mind, while calling for expertise in the ritual and artistic practices for which Mindröling was renowned.[56]

The focus on the individual's educational path gives the impression of an environment that supported different types of practitioners, underscoring although not directly addressing the presence of monks at different levels of ordination as well as affiliated nuns and laypeople. Despite stereotypes of all Buddhists as meditators, in fact different types of Buddhist practitioners engage in radically different practices, some of which appear to be in contrast. For instance, a tantric practitioner who is not ordained as a monk or nun might engage physically in sexual yoga, whereas monks and nuns take vows of celibacy. Some monks might be suited to solitary retreat beyond the walls of the monastery, whereas others are better suited to ritual practice within the monastery with the support of the community. Some students excel in poetry and medicine, while others excel in the artistic media necessary for rituals. The brief curriculum accounts for this spectrum.

Moreover, Terdak Lingpa's activities as a noncelibate tantric practitioner might have raised eyebrows among the more ardent followers of the dominant Géluk school, whose members included powerful Mongols and Qing leaders as well as wealthy and influential Tibetans. This was all the more reason to ensure and to demonstrate that Mindröling monks were beyond reproach in their vows. And given the role the monastery played in conducting rituals connected to the new Central Tibetan government, it was imperative that its monks stand out as a flawless field of merit for sponsors.

Subtly, the curriculum places the onus of establishing Mindröling's collective worthiness on these diverse individual members. In that sense it transfers attention from the monastery's most visible and famous members, such as the author of the document, Terdak Lingpa, and his family to the nameless members of the past, present, and future. According to the curriculum, it is the students, not only the famous founders and teachers, who embody Mindröling's potential as a fertile field of Buddhist cultivation and awakening. Like the famous few, the many students can render Mindröling "worthy of praise." Some also needed to be practically equipped to take up roles as teachers themselves. In this regard, the arts and sciences were crucial.

The Power of Writing and Worldly Fields of Knowledge

Starting in the time of the Fifth Dalai Lama when Mindröling was founded, the most powerful Central Tibetan Géluk monasteries did not train most monks to write. In fact, the Dalai Lama disallowed training in the worldly fields of knowledge at the three main monastic seats of Drépung, Ganden, and Sera.[57] For a variety of pedagogical and political reasons, literary studies within the Lhasa-area Géluk monasteries focused on reading and recitation and excluded the written arts enumerated in the traditional fields of knowledge. By contrast, Géluk authors from other monasteries, especially in Eastern Tibet, wrote prolifically and expertly. Debate was the focus of education at the Central Tibetan Géluk centers, and writing is not essential for debate; reading and memorization are. The policy of repressing writing was intended partly to limit innovation and criticism through new compositions and partly to prevent monks from being drawn into politics. Monks from Central Tibet's main Géluk monasteries who required literary training went to Mindröling to study grammar, poetry, and other literary arts.[58] For that reason, Mindröling's focus on the worldly fields of knowledge in general and on the literary arts in particular was a precious commodity in the Lhasa region. This helps explain why an education at Mindröling was so valuable and why Terdak Lingpa included these disciplines in the curriculum.

Until the 1950s, Central Tibetan Géluk monks tended to downplay the relevance of new commentary and exegesis, stressing the completeness of their tradition's core teachings. By this logic there was nothing new in the sphere of Buddhist thought worth writing down, so there was no need for monks to learn to write unless they were bound for administrative or governmental careers. This assessment, in keeping with the research of José

Cabezón and Penpa Dorjee on the negative perception of writing at Sera monastery beginning in the eighteenth century,[59] suggests the energy that might have gone into training monks to write was directed instead into training them to read, memorize, analyze, and debate the core of the Géluk curriculum—five key Indian texts on five key subjects: Perfection of Wisdom (*phar phyin*), Middle Way philosophy (*dbu ma*), epistemology and logic (*tshad ma*), metaphysics (*mdzod*), and monastic discipline (*'dul ba*).[60] Two of these—Perfection of Wisdom and monastic discipline—are explicitly mentioned in the Mindröling curriculum. At the Géluk centers, some saw writing as a sign of hubris since it suggested the available texts were insufficient.[61] This stands in marked contrast to the Mindröling curriculum, which includes writing as an essential skill, at least for the best students who would go on to be teachers and tutors themselves.

It seems that monks at Lhasa's major Géluk monasteries, which were closely entwined with the Ganden Podrang government, would have been more likely to be drawn into politics and away from their religious practice if they were skilled writers. By not training them to write, the monasteries were shielding them from the danger of being qualified for political work. The result was that monks at Ganden, Drépung, and Sera learned how to read, recite, debate, and perform rituals, but only administrators learned how to write. For this training they turned to Mindröling. Although the large Géluk centers of learning in Eastern Tibet, such as Labrang (*bla brang*), were major fronts of literary production, many renowned monks and lamas also traveled to study at Mindröling due to its reputation for excellence.

Terdak Lingpa was not revolutionary in this regard. His inclusion of the worldly fields of knowledge in the monastic curriculum is in keeping with Sakya Paṇḍita's assertions about the importance of these disciplines in the *Gateway to Learning*. Sakya Paṇḍita stressed the necessity of these fields, sometimes called the "five sciences," for the attainment of omniscience, drawing on the canonical Indian source of the *Mahāyānasūtrālaṃkāra* for corroboration:

Without becoming a scholar in the five sciences
Not even the supreme sage can become omniscient.[62]

Various schools or colleges were instituted at Mindröling to accommodate students engaged in distinct educational regimes. There was a college for students who specialized in the arts and sciences, particularly literary arts, astrology, and medicine.[63] Students only graduated to this college after gaining mastery of the ritual techniques deemed essential to the functioning of the monastery. The *Lamp of Teachings* catalogue states: "When students know how to chant the monastery's liturgies, have memorized the texts, and know clearly how to do the rituals for the goddess (*lha mo*), the local protectors (*gzhi bdag*), and the smoke offerings (*lha bsang*), they are ready to enter into the College of the Arts and Sciences (*rig gnas slob grwa*)."[64]

The specialized curriculum included textbooks on astrology and mathematical calculation, verse and prose composition, and calligraphy in multiple Tibetan, Indic, and Mongolian scripts.[65] In particular, students studied a treatise on astrological calculation composed in verse by Dharmaśrī along with an introductory companion text.[66] These were also core texts at the Medical and Astrological College in Lhasa.[67] This commonality reflects an important institutional connection, and students in medicine sometimes alternated years in Lhasa and at Mindröling.[68] Students in the College of Arts and Sciences also studied a sixteenth-century grammar textbook by Nawang Chökyi Gyatso,[69] and later incorporated nineteenth-century texts by Yangchen Drupai Dorjé.[70]

The College of the Arts and Sciences is not referred to in the 1689 monastic guidelines, and the editor of the *Lamp of Teachings Catalogue*, who published his work in 1992, does not specify when it was founded. He also mentions a commentarial college (*bshad grwa*).[71] Some of the core texts were composed before or during Mindröling's founding period and might have been in use during its early days, suggesting that these specialized colleges were established early on. In any case, Terdak Lingpa's curriculum laid the groundwork for these institutional developments to shape Mindröling's approach to education.

Conclusion

This range of educational priorities, including the Buddhist and the worldly, reflects Terdak Lingpa and Dharmaśrī's commitment to an impartial pedagogy. By embedding the arts and sciences in the curriculum, Terdak Lingpa implies that worldly fields are important to the goal of awakening.

Explicitly he makes a more pragmatic claim—that worldly knowledge will protect Mindröling students, like wearing armor, and facilitate their efforts to make their way in the world. But Sakya Paṇḍita and Terdak Lingpa do not merely claim that study could be the root of good governance, high social status, or cultural production; rather, they associate it with awakening itself. And when extended to lay pupils bound for careers in politics (the subject of the next chapter), this model of enlightenment through education would be directly integrated back into worldly life through cultural production and governance. In this way the ultimate Buddhist goal of enlightenment ideally could be joined with the relative goal of turning out highly educated and discerning people, ready to lead and govern.

The main areas of concern throughout Terdak Lingpa's constitutional guidelines were safeguarding the monks' vows of celibacy, dealing ethically and systematically with material donations, and mediating between the monastery's inhabitants and the local population, with a focus on cultivating behavior that would not upset the laity or give the monks a bad reputation. These factors reflected the priorities of patrons of the Géluk school that controlled the Central Tibetan government and of the founders of Mindröling, who sought to systematize their own Nyingma school's practices while supporting the Fifth Dalai Lama's and Desi Sangyé Gyatso's efforts to create the religious, political, social, and cultural structures for a nominally unified greater Tibetan polity.

Beyond these general goals, the particular specialties of Mindröling were embedded in the curriculum through training in decorum, ritual arts, Great Perfection practices, and the fields of knowledge. Mindröling's renown in these areas, as well as the charisma of its visionary founder and his illustrious family, helped draw laypeople as well as the monastic population addressed in the guidelines. In the next chapter I introduce a few of the most famous lay alumni of the monastery and analyze their role in establishing Mindröling as a center for cosmopolitanism and cultural production.

FIVE

Taming the Aristocrats

Cultivating Early Modern Tibetan Literati and Bureaucrats

Again and again your mouth touches
my smiling red lips
as if they were your cup—
view pleasure and longing like this.

—DOKHARWA, IN *BIOGRAPHY OF MIWANG*

WHILE THE MAJORITY of students in the Mindröling community were monks, some were nuns, and some were lay aristocrats from the highest echelon of Tibetan society who resided at the monastery to study for a period of approximately two to four years. In this chapter, I focus on a few of the most prominent lay figures who studied at Mindröling during its first four decades. The erotic verse in the epigraph was composed by one such layman, Dokharwa, in a biography he wrote about a fellow alumnus called Polhané. Both learned to write ornate poetry (*snyan ngag*) like this at Mindröling and with tutors trained at the monastery.[1] Their subsequent works and careers invite us to consider another side of aesthetic education at the monastery and to reflect on how such an education connects Buddhist and worldly spheres.

What did a lay aristocrat in seventeenth- and eighteenth-century Central Tibet need to learn in order to be considered well educated and cultured? What were the characteristics of Lhasa's dominant cultural sensibilities, and how were they inculcated? How did education relate to other structures of power and authority, such as government hierarchies? To begin answering these questions, I will reflect on why Mindröling, as opposed to other monastic centers of learning, became a hub for training lay aristocrats.

Figure 5.1 Early eighteenth-century Lukhang mural with detail of Terdak Lingpa teaching students at Mindröling adjacent to detail of Terdak Lingpa discovering Treasure teachings.
Photograph by Thomas Laird

Why Mindröling?

During fieldwork and textual research for this book, I frequently encountered the view that Mindröling was *the* place for aristocrats to pursue higher education in Central Tibet until the 1950s. I wondered why, among the many monastic institutions already existing in Tibet in the late seventeenth century, and among the various Buddhist schools and powerful family groups, Mindröling attained the aura of being "the best monastery school for aspiring lay officials."[2]

As the previous chapters have shown, the reasons combine religious, economic, cultural, and political factors. Mindröling's prestige was rooted in part in the founders' status as members of the Nyö family group. This clan had a history of prominence in South and Central Tibetan areas, tracing back at least to the eleventh century. Members included Pema Lingpa, who helped establish the Bhutanese royal family's dominance and was an important transmitter of the Great Perfection practices for which Mindröling was famous, as well as the Sixth Dalai Lama. The institution of Dargyé Chöling, headed by Terdak Lingpa's father, was a respected center of Great Perfection practice long before Mindröling. The massive support from the Fifth Dalai Lama and his regent, Sangyé Gyatso, connected Mindröling to the central government. Affiliations to historic figures through reincarnation also played a role in Mindröling's appeal.

More immediately, the combined charisma of the visionary founder, Terdak Lingpa, and his brother the scholar-artist-monk Lochen Dharmaśrī attracted students and sponsors. Through their efforts, Mindröling became a new model of Nyingma institution that was suited to its particular time and place. At the same time it was symbolically and aesthetically linked to Tibet's imperial era and to the first Tibetan monastery, Samyé. While the founders drew on Tibet's Buddhist and imperial history, they also took part in Tibet's avant-garde, spurring innovation even as they drew on the past for inspiration and legitimation. In shaping the monastery, the founders referred to the ideal of an impartial worldview rooted in Great Perfection philosophy and practice, as well as the Two Systems of Dharmic and worldly expertise. Their mastery and codification of old traditions through methodical historiographical research and vigorous efforts to found an institution suited to the needs of their day all contributed to Mindröling's magnetism as a center for elite lay education.

Monastic Bodies

In the monastic curriculum, introduced in chapter 4, Terdak Lingpa uses a general term for "student" (slob ma) and does not refer to monks, nuns, or lay students specifically. Based on the overall tone and content of the document, it seems Terdak Lingpa designed the curriculum primarily for monks. However, the pedagogical methods and the subjects represented in the constitutional guidelines and the curriculum provide insight into why lay students would study at Mindröling and clues as to what they studied. This information is supported by biographical accounts that are the main sources for this chapter. The presence of lay students at the monastery underscores the need for an atmosphere of flexibility and a pedagogy focused on cultivating the strengths and capacities of diverse individual students.

Catering to a diverse monastic body is not unique to Mindröling. To some extent, all Buddhist monasteries and nunneries generate a variety of roles for different types of people—some are administrators, some scholars, some artists, some cooks, some ritual experts, some disciplinarians, and some (usually very few) are meditators. However, the question of diversity appears to have been especially salient at Mindröling, where the hereditary senior chair is held not by a fully ordained monk but rather by a tantric ritual expert, charismatic visionary, and scholar who marries and must have children in order to continue the lineage. The role, beginning with Terdak Lingpa, is defined in part by a transcendence of celibacy, which by contrast is fundamental to the social and religious roles of monks and nuns.

In part due to being organized around a hereditary lineage similar to a monarchy, Mindröling was home to women practitioners as well as monks and laymen. That said, women were represented in much smaller numbers than men, and aside from accounts of the life of Terdak Lingpa's daughter Mingyur Peldrön, the details of women's education are difficult to assess based on available sources. Except for female members of the family lineage, women generally spent their time outside the monastery walls at an adjacent retreat center for nuns.

Every member of the community, whether lay or ordained, female or male, took vows relevant to her or his station. Throughout Mindröling's formal literature, vows are one of the highest priorities, a theme reiterated throughout numerous institutional documents and reflected in the collected works of Lochen Dharmaśrī. This focus was an important factor in cultivating monastic discipline as well as a means of assuring lay sponsors that Mindröling was worthy of their material support.

The Fifth Dalai Lama reportedly encouraged Dharmaśrī, Mindröling's second abbot and a preeminent scholar and artist, to pay particular attention in his study of monastic discipline. Taking this advice to heart, Dharmaśrī composed a lengthy and influential commentary on the three types of Buddhist vows, which remains one of the two most significant works on the topic in Tibetan literature.[3] Especially given that many of the most famous Nyingma practitioners were fully ordained monks or nuns, Dharmaśrī's expertise on the subject played a significant role in setting Mindröling's reputation as a serious monastic institution, drawing sponsors and students, both lay and monastic.

What the Literati Need to Know: Mindröling's Likeness to a Liberal Arts College

Aesthetics, as that which concerns the senses and objects of the senses as well as an interest in the efficacy of beauty and elegance, were central to education at the monastery, which could include writing, ethics, philosophy, ritual performance, Great Perfection meditative practices, medicine, and astrology. Literary arts were paramount, and this was an important factor in attracting lay pupils.

Lay aristocrats valued language arts since fine calligraphy and skillful composition of verse and prose were marks of cosmopolitanism and crucial abilities for employment in the Ganden Podrang government. Elite lay students tended to arrive at Mindröling in their teens, after completing their basic education with tutors or relatives. This was in contrast to the much more numerous monks, many of whom began their studies at Mindröling as young children. The laypeople who studied there were prepared for positions of cultural prestige and political authority.

A primary function of Tibetan Buddhist monasteries is the performance of rituals that help meditate human relations, for instance with deities and the natural environment. That said, monasteries are also centers of civilization through literacy, learning, and cultural production, and at Mindröling education in the arts and sciences was central to the institutional identity. In this way, the monastery displays a likeness to a liberal arts college.

Among the most edifying parallels between a college and Mindröling is the institutionalized charisma of its great teachers. Those who held the positions of senior chair and abbot of the monastery also played complex roles vis-à-vis the Central Tibetan polity and society. From the beginning, the senior chair's and abbot's charisma and expertise held the monastery together in times of strife, drew sponsorship from aristocrats and the new government, and, most important for the purposes of this chapter, attracted students to Mindröling.

William Clark points this feature out in his study of the modern research university, arguing that what he calls "academic charisma" merges spiritual and political topoi.

> The original charismatic religious figure was the sorcerer, then later the priest and especially the prophet, the herald of a new cult. Regarding academia, part of academic charisma sprang from this topos—the teacher as spiritual or cultic leader. In the sphere of politics and economics, the original charismatic figure was the warrior, then later the general or king. Part of academic charisma sprang from this topos—the martial, agonistic, polemical cast of academic knowledge.[4]

Terdak Lingpa's and Dharmaśrī's roles in the early history of Mindröling reflect similar dynamics. Other salient parallels include the relationship of higher education and civil society, the place of "good taste" and aesthetics in perpetuating class hierarchies and shaping dominant worldviews, the connection between elite education and political authority, and the seemingly incongruous but interwoven purposes of education in shaping members of a given society. Examining Mindröling's curriculum, political engagements, and cultural production can shed light on diverse religious and secular educational models and demonstrate how aesthetic communities are formed and perpetuated beyond this particular study.

To elaborate, I propose a comparison with the charters of comparable American educational institutions. The Harvard and Yale charters of 1650 and 1701, respectively, provide useful analogs for Mindröling's constitutional guidelines, which Terdak Lingpa composed in 1689.[5] Composed around the same time in a radically different milieu, the Harvard and Yale charters are shorter and less detailed than Mindröling's constitutional document. They focus on the corporations that manage the resources of the institutions and describe general educational aims without providing the numerous examples and detailed explanations that characterize the Tibetan guidelines of Mindröling. That said, considering these documents allows us to reflect on Mindröling's foundations and the methodology and vision of its founders as they related to lay education.

The Yale charter declares that the institution was founded "wherein Youth may be instructed in the Arts and Sciences [and] through the blessing of Almighty God may be fitted for Publick employment both in Church and Civil State."[6]

And the Harvard charter states:

Whereas, through the good hand of God, many well devoted persons have been, and daily are moved, and stirred up, to give and bestow, sundry gifts, legacies, lands, and revenues for the advancement of all good literature, arts, and sciences in Harvard College, in Cambridge in the County of Middlesex, and to the maintenance of the President and Fellows, and for all accommodations of buildings, and all other necessary provisions, that may conduce to the education of the English and Indian youth of this country, in knowledge and godliness.[7]

These excerpts from Ivy League charters reveal similarities between the intentions of their drafters and the intentions of Mindröling's founders. There are parallel concerns with managing wealth donated by sponsors, since Terdak Lingpa addresses how offerings should be accepted and distributed and who should be allowed to accept resources intended for the monastery. Likewise, the effort to carry on a traditional style of education (the British system in the case of the charters, and the Indo-Tibetan Buddhist system in the case of Mindröling) in a new cultural context (colonial America or the newly unified early modern Central Tibetan polity). There is also a similar focus on studying arts and sciences under the umbrella of religion, with the aim to turn out well-trained leaders of church and state.

By contrast, the Ivy League documents limit their focus to the make-up of the corporations that manage the resources donated to the institutions, rather than going into the quotidian details of student and teacher behavior. In general, Mindröling's constitutional guidelines include a wider range of concerns and paint a more vivid picture of the ethos of the community, whereas the charters are mostly concerned with resources and the hierarchical structure.

Most important, in both the colonial American and Tibetan settings, the ideal is to integrate worldly knowledge with religious ethics and discipline. In the Tibetan case this directly relates to the concept of integrating Dharma and worldly life. Educating members of the ruling class in the arts and sciences within a Buddhist framework, inculcating a fundamentally Buddhist worldview, exemplifies the extended definition of the Two Systems conceptual structure.

Tibetan Lay Education and Literary Production at Mindröling

To illustrate the education of lay students at Mindröling, I draw mainly from two works by the accomplished author and civil servant Dokharwa Tsering Wangyal (1697–1763).[8] To begin, I consider *The Autobiography of a Cabinet Minister* (1762), the first documented example of a Tibetan lay autobiography.[9] In the following section, I analyze excerpts from *The Biography of Miwang* (1733), which he wrote about the life of Polhané.[10] Dokharwa also wrote what is arguably the first Tibetan novel in 1721[11] and compiled a Sanskrit-Tibetan dictionary. In addition to their valuable content, *The Biography of Miwang* and *The Autobiography of a Cabinet Minister* demonstrate the writing style of a Mindröling-educated layperson. Both reveal Dokharwa's extensive training and conditioning in literary aesthetics.

Dokharwa was a significant figure in the Central Tibetan government, rising to the high position of *kalon* (*bka' blon*) or cabinet minister, and was an icon of early modern Tibet's literary scene. Recognized as the reincarnated lama of an important Kagyu (*bka' brgyud*) monastery called Taklung (*stag lung*) that was converted forcibly to Géluk tradition, Dokharwa studied at Mindröling under Dharmaśrī.[12]

Dokharwa and Polhané and later Doring Tenzin Paljor (b. 1760)—himself the son of a Mindröling alumnus called Ngödrub Rabten (1721–1792) were among the few Tibetan laypeople to be the subject of life writing before the twentieth century.[13] The first two men studied with Dharmaśrī.[14] Biographies are common for Tibetan religious figures but much more rare for laypeople. The existence of such literary works about the lives of lay students underscores Mindröling's significance as a center for cultural production beyond a strictly Buddhist sphere.

Poetics, Prosody, Astrology, Devotion: Dokharwa's Studies at Mindröling

Dokharwa provides this account of his education before attending Mindröling, where he went to study when he was a teen. While studying at home under the guidance of a Mindröling-trained tutor: "the government accountant named Trögyal Palgön and the intelligent bhikṣu Losel of Mindröling monastery taught me the two chapters of the *Kāvyādarśa* one after the other, and at the end of these studies I took the written examination and passed."[15] Notably, the focus of this period of his early education was the Tibetan translation of the *Kāvyādarśa*, a seminal Sanskrit text on ornate poetry. This text has been immensely influential in Tibetan literature but is not generally associated with monastic education.[16] Accordingly, it is not mentioned by title in the official curriculum found within the Mindröling monastic guidelines. However, both monks and laypeople educated at Mindröling evidently studied it, as made clear by the account of the ordained tutor.

Dokharwa continued his study of *Kāvyādarśa* in his education at Mindröling proper, according to his account. Most important, he recounts studying poetics under the famed Dharmaśrī: "in the year of the Iron Hare (1711), when I was fifteen, I left to study at Mindröling monastery where I followed the great scholar and translator Dharmaśrī. I requested instructions on the third chapter of the Indian scholar king Daṇḍin's *Kāvyādarśa* and presented my examination [on this subject]."[17]

Beyond the instruction he received in poetry, he also learned astrology and Indic scripts from Dharmaśrī: "he bestowed upon me the complete teaching on astrology and its related diagram. I am grateful that he taught me the different scripts such as *Lanza* and *Wartu*."[18] Dharmaśrī was a preeminent scholar of astrological calculation during this period, composing the foundational textbooks that would be used at Mindröling's specialized College of the Arts and Sciences (*rig gnas slob grwa*) and at Lhasa's Medical College (*sman rtsis khang*).[19] Training in the Lanza and Wartu scripts is mentioned in the overview of the curriculum for monks as well, underscoring the significance of diverse writing skills in this cultural context.

At this point the young Dokharwa's education was interrupted due to Dharmaśrī being called away from Mindröling to attend to an Eastern Tibetan lama who was ill: "I planned to request the remainder of these teachings gradually. However, Chamdo Gyalwa Pakpala, the lampholder of the doctrine in Dokham was afflicted by illness and the great translator was invited to examine him. And so, my wishes remained unfulfilled."[20] This passage reveals that Dharmaśrī was respected as a scholar of medicine, one of the major fields of knowledge beyond Buddhism for which Mindröling became renowned. Dokharwa reports longing for his teacher (referred to here as the "great/incomparable translator") during the time he was away.

> In the Female Water Snake year (1713), I once again acted as the attendant of the protector and great translator and studied the complete text of the *Sarasavativyakarana*, the text on prosody called "The Source of Precious Things," and the remainder of the teachings on astrology. As I mentioned, I studied all these subjects—I studied them not under various tutors appointed by the great translator, but I enjoyed the experience of receiving these teachings directly from the great, incomparable translator himself.

The focus on literary arts and astrology and the importance Dokharwa places on learning from Dharmaśrī himself and no one else reflects Dharmaśrī's reputation and charisma as a teacher. Dokharwa continues: "At the completion of my studies in grammar, I was awarded the name of 'Tsangsé Gyépai Lodan' handwritten [by Dharmaśrī]. He always accepted me as his student with great pleasure, and repeatedly remarked to his attendants and others, 'It would good if this government official became a student of religion.' Alas, I was not fortunate enough to obtain such a rebirth."[21]

This passage raises an important point: it indicates that Dokharwa was not at Mindröling to study religion first and foremost, but for the more worldly subjects already mentioned. He marks this quote from his teacher with the regretful wish that he could be more focused on religion, while accepting that that is not his lot. At the same time he stresses how hard he worked to take advantage of the opportunity, reflecting nostalgically on the intensity of his younger self: "during the early and later years of my studies, when Dharmaśrī was giving me instruction, I exerted myself, studying diligently, never wasting my time in relaxation, nor leaving my doorstep unless for an emergency. I'd never spend time in holiday or festivity like today."[22]

In a fascinating marker of his break from conventional worldly engagements, he notes that he did not wash his hair during the last period of his time at Mindröling: "During the last six months of my study just before my graduation, I washed my hair only once. In order to wash my hair, I had to cut open my plaits with a small knife. I was known as one who was disciplined in his study and whose mind did not wander on the path of distraction." Although he mainly studied with Dharmaśrī, he also recounts meetings with Terdak Lingpa (here referred to as the Dharma King), who again focuses on the importance of his worldly studies, although he also provides initiations and empowerments:

At that time the Treasure revealer, Dharma King Rigzin Gyurmé Dorjé, was still alive. I was fortunate to have many chances to prostrate before and have audiences with him. When I prostrated before him, he would arise and respectfully touch heads with me instead. He would advise me, "Noble son, heavenly clan leader, you praiseworthy Tibetan nobleman, if you do not make efforts to study you will achieve nothing." In this way, he bestowed upon me much meaningful advice. At that time, I received many instructions, empowerments, and permissions belonging to the new Treasure tradition.

Dokharwa also studied with Terdak Lingpa's son, Pema Gyurmé Gyatso, who would become the second senior chair of Mindröling after Terdak Lingpa's death. (Tragically, Zungar Mongol troops murdered Pema Gyurmé Gyatso soon after he took the throne, as I discuss in the epilogue.) Although Pema Gyurmé Gyatso's collected works demonstrate that he was an avid poet himself, he did not instruct Dokharwa in literary arts, but rather provided him with a tantric empowerment that he took very much to heart: "From the Prince of Thung, Pema Gyurmé Gyatso, I received the great empowerment of the glorious Vajrabhairava with the assembly of thirteen deities. Perhaps it was from this time that an auspicious door opened by taking this deity as my supreme tutelary deity."[23]

He provides a brief but rich account of Terdak Lingpa's death, paying close attention to the sensory experiences, including sounds, scents, and sights, at the time of his passing:

During the latter part of my studies, the great Treasure Revealer, the Dharma King, having completed his teachings for the benefit of students in this realm, and in order to compel those who cling to permanence, passed away into the peaceful realm. There were many kinds of external omens marking his passing—divine music was heard from the heavens; scented fragrance was smelled; along with the appearance of wondrous rainbow-hued clouds among many other signs. When he departed to the realm of Vidyadhara ḍākinīs, I was in attendance at his funeral and made thorough and wholehearted prayers.[24]

This display of devotion for Terdak Lingpa, replete with aesthetic imagery of music, fragrance, and rainbow lights, seals Dokharwa's connection to Mindröling. The Biography of Miwang, which he wrote about his colleague, Polhané, who also studied at Mindröling as a young man, complements the picture he presents in his autobiography of the value and content of an education at the monastery.

Training a Future King: Polhané's Studies at Mindröling

Polhané studied at Mindröling from age fifteen to eighteen. He went on to become a commander in the Tibetan army and rose to the highest station of Tibetan political authority and the peak of Tibetan society, coming to be known as Miwang (mi dbang) a title meaning "Lord of Men," sometimes translated as "King." It applied to the person holding the highest position of temporal authority in the Tibetan government. He held that position from 1728 to 1747, during the reign of the Seventh Dalai Lama and on good terms with the Qing emperor. When various factions of Tibetans, Mongols, and Manchus were vying for power across greater Tibet, Polhané managed to rule a relatively stable polity. His success was based on strong diplomatic relations with influential Mongols and Qing leaders as well as his authority among Tibetans.

Later in life Polhané became a major ally and sponsor for Mindröling by collaborating with Terdak Linpga's son, the third Senior Chair Rinchen Namgyal, and Terdak Lingpa's daughter the Great Perfection master Mingyur Peldrön. Together they would rebuild the monastery after Zungar Mongols, who were fanatically anti-Nyingma, destroyed it along with the other major Nyingma monastery in Central Tibet in 1718, during a violent campaign to take the Central Tibetan area from the Khoshot Mongols under Lhazang Khan.

A lengthy section of the *Biography of Miwang* is dedicated to Polhané's training at Mindröling. The description of what he studied there and the account of Dharmaśrī's qualities and credentials as a teacher provide further evidence of the literary and aesthetic focus of education at Mindröling. The training went beyond the mechanical skill of writing, although those were certainly important for politicians and poets alike. Mindröling cultivated writers highly skilled in grammar, the science of metaphor, prosody, and poetics as well as multiple scripts and calligraphy styles.

The section of the biography devoted to Polhané's time at Mindröling begins with his journey there. The author then gives a brief overview of his studies and some fond reminiscences of daily life at the monastery. The conclusion of the chapter touches on the history of Polhané's connection to the Mindröling lineage and foretells the help he will offer Mindröling in its near future.[25]

Dokharwa recounts that when Polhané arrived on horseback at Mindröling with his uncle and a large retinue of attendants, Polhané was moved by his devotion to Terdak Lingpa. He keenly anticipated the meeting and showed standard Buddhist affective signs of connecting with a teacher, including spontaneous tears and the hairs of his body standing on end.[26] Once he is in the presence of the visionary tantric master, the young Polhané's attention to Terdak Lingpa's luminous countenance and flowing white moustache and beard, quivering in the wind "like a fly whisk," is full of sensory and emotional force.[27] His sensual focus on the lama's physical presence and appearance reflects the correlation between beauty and power in this context. This encounter makes clear that Polhané did not go to Mindröling for a dry or rigid course of study but expected to be transformed in complex and profound ways, rooted in and expressed through aesthetic experience. According to Dokharwa, Polhané too studied under only the best teachers. As a member of the aristocracy whose family made a sizeable donation of three hundred pieces of silver and other valuables to the monastery upon his arrival, Polhané had as his main tutor Dharmaśrī.[28]

To paint the backdrop for Polhané's studies, Dokharwa first provides the teacher's credentials and specifies what Polhané aspired to learn from him. The biography depicts Dharmaśrī's learning as extraordinary. His expertise covered all the fields of knowledge as well as the fine points of taste and aesthetics. He mastered ritual technologies, fine arts, and medicine. He was trained to speak with eloquence and to compose compelling and pleasing poetry, and was an expert in grammar and nomenclature. Dokharwa describes him as a master of astrology, tantra, ritual, logic, etymology, and the physical sciences. His formal aesthetic training, based in the Indic Buddhist tradition, gave him expertise in distinguishing between good and bad men, women, gemstones, textiles, horses, and other materials associated with wealth and quality. The biography also asserts that Dharmaśrī excelled in calendrical studies, important in Mindröling's official role vis-á-vis the Ganden Podrang government, since organizing and standardizing time was a central occupation of the early modern rulers. The final assessment was that Dharmaśrī, here framed primarily as Polhané's teacher, had gradually achieved mastery of all subjects related to Buddhism, aesthetics, exposition, philosophy, ritual, medicine and astrology, and literary arts.[29] Although Polhané could not have hoped to attain such mastery in his mere three years of study at Mindröling, this portrait of Dharmaśrī as an ideal scholar demonstrates the level of learning Mindröling was renowned for and hints at the aspirations of the lay aristocrats who studied there.

Polhané's education under Dharmaśrī is described as challenging, making him "like a cripple who endeavors to climb the rocky precipice of a terrifying cliff."[30] The progress of his studies from that point shows that similar to monks at Mindröling, who had to meet prescribed standards through study and examinations before engaging in visualization and solitary retreat practice, the lay students studied the worldly arts and sciences before focusing on Dharma.

The primary focus of Polhané's studies was literary arts.[31] In particular, Dokharwa tells us that Polhané achieved the highest honors for his skills in writing and composition. Further, after he had mastered various scripts used to write the Tibetan language, he went on to study six different Indic scripts. This raises the question of what use a wide range of Indic scripts would have served for a man like Polhané. Whereas good composition skills and elegant handwriting in multiple Tibetan scripts were of clear practical value for someone who would go on to be a political ruler and diplomat, learning Indic scripts must have served a largely symbolic purpose, aside from the possibility that he intended to communicate in writing with leaders from Nepal and India. Knowledge of this kind also signaled an impressive level of elite learning and cosmopolitanism, since it was associated with the perceived grace and authority of India as the birthplace of Buddhism. After Polhané had gained a firm basis in the subjects of handwriting, poetics, and astrology, his training in Buddhist doctrine began. The biography insists that he emerged from Mindröling well versed in literary arts and ripe with an awareness of Buddhist ethics rooted in the practical skills necessary for a successful ruler.

This focus in Polhané's education reflects the centrality of writing as a qualification for Tibetan leaders of his day. These accounts show that the training at Mindröling encompassed skills beyond Buddhist ritual and doctrine. While there are many examples of temporal rulers being empowered through *abhiṣeka* (*dbang*) rituals conducted by Buddhist lamas, the power of this aesthetic training exemplifies how an education like that gained at Mindröling impacted society more generally. Students of Mindröling such as Dokharwa and Polhané were endowed with the authority of being cultured and learned.

The Power of the Erotic in a Layman's Biography

Remarkably, a third of the section on Mindröling is devoted to Polhané's departure from his favorite lover. Their amorous exchange comes just after Polhané leaves his home behind "like a mouthful of spit," perhaps taking Siddhartha's departure from his royal home and family as a literary model.[32] In contrast to the apparent ease with which he departs from his spouse, he and his sweetheart speak to each other at length about the pain of separation and sing in romantic verse about how to cope with their mutual longing. The woman chides Polhané for abandoning her and, in the erotically charged passage excerpted below, he encourages her to let her natural surroundings soothe her until his return.

> She said such things, lamenting and singing, and as she wiped away the tears that moistened her face with her preciously jeweled fingers and part of her undergarment, she implored him. At that time, feeling the physical torment of separation and focusing his eyes intensely on her face without wavering, the excellent youth said:

> Although in the sky the full moon—the Treasure of Nectar,
> the Crystal Lord—departs to the western mountain,

before long, from the shoulder of the eastern peak,
a handsome, smiling face will shine forth, night-blooming lotus.

The Lamp of Existence, Inexhaustible Treasury of light,
great radiance that rests on the throne of the wooden horse—
having cleared the darkness from other places,
the sun's noble light will illuminate the world without delay.

Endowed with the superior marks and the virility of a royal lineage,
I, the precious youth, the beautiful White Umbrella,
having promptly returned as the ruler of Nyang Valley,
will bestow the balm of well-being and happiness, cherished woman.

Until then, when the river's flow is completely blocked by ice
and the touch of winter's unbearable cold is oppressive,
hold it in your mind that the massive snow mountain
is my youthful body, full-breasted woman.

When the long course of the sun spreading spring's glory
exhausts your body and mind,
perceive the melodious voice of the female cuckoo
as my affectionate words, adorable woman.

When your body hair is aroused by the cool southern breeze
during the rise of autumn, in the time of plenty,
consider the perfectly clear, limitless sky
to be my mind, lithe woman.

When the virtuous signs of summer's queen are spreading out
and you are wretched with the torment of missing me, your friend,
wish for all the wondrous colors of the night-blooming lotus
to be me, your loving friend, slender woman.

I am the one who stays on top,
lifted up from below by the beautiful woman
who is just like a noble horse—
direct your loving thoughts to this.

The gorgeous woman's hands
clutch my handsome behind,
just like a belt binds—
our friendship must not loosen.

Your ravishing fingers
clasp my pure white fingers
like a whip and reins—
this is how we engage with each other.

Again and again your mouth touches
my smiling red lips
as if they were your cup—
view pleasure and longing like this.

The grasping and gentle touch of your body against
your friend's handsome youthfulness
is like being clothed in fine garments—
this is what our lovemaking is like.

If the region's charming garden is secure,
the cuckoo, Messenger of Spring, will return at the appropriate time.
If the cool mountain does not shift,
the Five-Faced Lord, the lion, will always be your friend.

If the Water Treasure, the ocean, is not dried up by fire at the end of the age,
the Swan King will again and again engage in pleasure and play.
If the young girl is steadfast in her promises of friendship
I, her affectionate friend, will rush to take care of her.
Utterly reject the darkness of longing
and enjoy the experiences of this good age, beloved.

This is the sort of thing he said to his lover. They exchanged words of unbearable torment and expressions of longing. When the whole day had passed in such a discussion, they played together, were joyous, and made love in the nighttime. In that way the whole night passed in the festivities of pleasure. Finally the stars' radiance diminished and dawn's light pervaded the eastern sky. When the loving couple heard the third cry of the innkeeper's rooster, the young woman's mood became extremely somber and she spoke at length.[33]

There is a notable resonance between the sensuality of this episode and Polhané's first meeting with Terdak Lingpa, in which Polhané is portrayed as being deeply moved by the lama's physical beauty and luminosity. The erotic and the devotional are thus shown to be affectively related. In a similar blending, throughout the section of the biography related to Mindröling, allusions to politics are intertwined with descriptions of monastic training, as well as humorous anecdotes. This literary quality of the text reflects the concept of the integration of religion and worldly life as a prevalent aesthetic theme. Leaving his family, enjoying the affection of his passionate lover, meeting his teacher, and engaging in a course of study at the monastery are all treated with an equal hand and not compartmentalized. In a sense, the romantic unions act as metaphors for political unions and the political unions are supported by religious ties, in an interwoven network of relationships and connections.

Reflections on Literary Style and Secular Content

Dohkarwa's compositions adhere to Tibetan poetics adapted from classical Sanskrit Kāvya, its formal style as well as its imagery and use of metaphor. The influence of Sanskrit literature on Tibetan literature can be traced directly to the twelfth-thirteenth century Sakya Paṇḍita's commentary on and partial translation of Daṇḍin's *Kāvyādarśa*, which was one of the main sources for studying poetics at Mindröling, according to these accounts. The Indic influence is clear in Dokharwa's writing about Polhané, to such an extent that it could well be mistaken for a translation of the mixed prose-poetry work of Daṇḍin.[34]

In its content, Polhané's biography is a font of historical material on Tibetan high society, culture, and government during the cosmopolitan eighteenth century. Since much of the available Tibetan literature composed before the mid-twentieth century is cast in distinctly Buddhist terms, *The Biography of Miwang* offers a rare window into the life experience and values of a layman of the early modern period. The text is contained within a Buddhist cultural framework, but since Polhané was not primarily a religious figure, the author was free to address subject matter and employ style that would have been taboo, or at the very least controversial, in a biography of a lama or other religious professional who would be a more common subject of Tibetan life writing. In this way, Dokharwa offers a window into the aesthetic sensibilities of Central Tibet's lay ruling class, rooted in a Buddhist worldview but not restricted to Buddhist doctrine and practice.

Polhané's biography is not the only example of such erotic imagery in literature produced in Central Tibet around this time. The songs and poetry attributed to the Sixth Dalai Lama engage erotic imagery, if subtly. Anecdotes in the biography of Yolmo Tenzin Norbu where he describes erotic encounters with women and female figures in dreams and visions are another case in point.[35] Given the prominence of the authors and subjects of these sources, it appears that such writing had an audience among the Tibetan literati of their day. Perhaps the eroticism in this Polhané biography reveals an alternative Tibetan model of rulership.

That said, the biography was not block printed for some thirty years after it was written, just after the time of the author's death.[36] The delay might suggest there was some doubt about the response this work would inspire in the broader literary sphere, which was dominated by more doctrinal and monastic Buddhist genres.

The Rarity of Tibetan Lay Biography

Biography is a major genre in Tibetan literature. Literally translated as "complete liberation" (rnam thar), the most common Tibetan term for life writing applies to the stories of accomplished lamas and other religious adepts. By contrast, Polhané's biography, the title of which uses another term for life writing (rtogs brjod), is the story of a man famed not for his Buddhist accomplishments—although he is portrayed as showing reverence for the Dharma and devotion toward his teachers—but for his military and political prowess, and his amorous encounters with women. Taken together with similar works from the period, the erotic content of the biography suggests the strong influence of Indic literary aesthetics in the training both men received at Mindröling. The ease with all manner of subject matter further connects the Mindröling aesthetic with a cosmopolitan worldview. Polhané himself is purported to have asked Dokharwa to compose his life story. Although he specified that the writing should be accessible, it is instead a highly erudite and ornate text. Dokharwa's authorized telling spans genres of biography, epic, Buddhist literature, romance, and high art. Dokharwa portrays his subject as an aristocrat, a skilled political and military leader, a Don Juan, an ardent student of Buddhism, and a patron of the arts and Buddhist institutions.

Examples of writing composed by laypeople that might offer more insight into the education of a spectrum of Tibetan laity from this period are rare and understudied.[37] This is largely because most printing took place within the purview of monasteries, where Buddhism was the priority and worldly subjects only rarely would have been considered worth the arduous work of carving wood blocks and inking reproductions. Existing examples of lay writing show that letters, poetry, and songs were important overlapping genres among educated Tibetans in the seventeenth and eighteenth centuries, as they are today.[38]

The examples we have of laypeople's biographies make clear the centrality of poetry and lyrics among the early modern Tibetan ruling class. Those cited in this work include the Tibetan version of *campu* (mixed prose and verse) from the tradition of Indian Kāvya as well as the more strongly indigenous Tibetan form known as *gur* (*mgur*). Indic literary aesthetics had a strong influence on Tibetan aesthetics, a fact confirmed in accounts of Mindröling's lay education and exemplified in the erudite compositions of writers associated with Mindröling.

Fields of Knowledge: A Rubric for the Arts, Sciences, and Cultural Production

A strong attraction for young aristocrats like Dokharwa and Polhané to study at Mindröling was its reputation as the most prestigious place in Central Tibet to study the arts and sciences and in particular, literary arts, which were crucial to civil servants and the educated elite. Their education at Mindröling was framed by the rubric of the Tibetan term *rikné*, usually translated as "fields of knowledge" and sometimes glossed as "arts and sciences," or "culture." *Rikné*, from the Sanskrit term *pañcavidyāsthāna* meaning "the five sciences," encapsulates the basics of education in Buddhist cultures beyond Tibet and long predating Tibetan Buddhism, but in Tibet they took on a distinctly Tibetan character. With some variation, these disciplines bear a strong resemblance to the trivium and quadrivium that made up the seven "liberal arts" of medieval European universities.[39] However, the Buddhist list includes medicine, which is excluded from the European liberal arts model.

From at least the thirteenth century, thanks primarily to the efforts of the famed scholar Sakya Paṇḍita (*sa skya pan di ta*,1182–1251), these fields of knowledge were widely recognized among Tibetans as the basis of a good education.[40] By the time of Mindröling's founding in the late seventeenth century, they formally defined what a learned and cultured Tibetan person knew. Like all things Indian, the fields of knowledge carried the impenetrable aura of coming from the land of Buddha himself. The five major disciplines or fields are arts and crafts (*bzo gnas rig pa*), medicine (*gso ba'i rig pa*), grammar (*sgra'i rig pa*), dialectics (*gtan tshigs kyi rig pa*), and Buddhist doctrine (*nang gyi rig pa*). These are the fields generally invoked by the term *rikné*, but it also applies to a larger classification of ten fields of arts and sciences. These include the five already listed as well as poetics (*snyan ngag*), composition (*sdeb sbyor*), the study of synonyms (*mngon brjod*), drama (*zlos gar*), and astrology (*skar rtsis*). A further list of eighteen fields expands on related themes, which are of interest in painting the picture of what an educated Buddhist should know. There are six standard versions of the list of eighteen. To illustrate, the version attributed to the Abhidharmakośa (*chos mngon pa'i mdzod*) includes music (*rol mo*), sexual intercourse ('*khrig thabs*), earning a livelihood ('*tsho tshis*), computation (*grangs can*), elocution (*sgra*), administering medicine (*gso dpyad*), traditions of Dharma (*chos lugs*), craftsmanship or architecture (*bzo bo*), archery or the judging of archery ('*phong spyod*), logical argumentation (*gtan tshigs*), yoga (*rnal 'byor*), hearing (*thos pa*), remembering (*dran pa*), astrological analysis (*skar ma'i dpyad*), calculation (*rtsis*), optical illusions (*mig 'phrul*), history (*sngon rabs*), and historiography (*sngon byung brjod*).[41] While not all these categories are addressed directly in Mindröling documents, Terdak Lingpa's family, on both his father's and his mother's side, had long been known for expertise in these areas, encompassing Dharmic and worldly subjects.

The lists above, especially the five major fields (*rig gnas che ba lnga*) and five minor fields (*rig gnas chung ba lnga*), make it clear that Buddhist education in general is largely concerned with language and literary arts. Notice that grammar, dialectics, poetics, composition, and the study of synonyms make up five of the ten primary fields. And Buddhist doctrine per se is a small fraction of the core subject matter. This focus on language is evident in accounts of studying at Mindröling, forming a bridge between two of Mindröling's seemingly incongruent functions—training in esoteric Buddhist practices (which require a specialized knowledge of language) and training in the skills necessary for a bureaucrat.

Mindröling's position was firm even while it remained at least rhetorically on the margins of the Géluk-controlled political center. It remained strong even after Mindröling became a target of anti-Nyingma fanaticism and sectarianism, acted out in drastic violence as well as more subtle forms of persecution. Mindröling was razed to the ground by Zungar Mongols who were Géluk zealots in 1717–18. And even after it was rebuilt by Terdak Linpga's children and the Qing-supported Polhané, the Qing court expressed mistrust of the Nyingma school and suggested that official support for Nyingma institutions like Mindröling and its neighbor Dorjédrak (*rdo rje brag*) be curtailed and adherents be forced to convert.[42] The fact that Mindröling became so powerful and retained its power despite major obstacles underscores how significant its role was.

Networks of Lay Education

The Mindröling curriculum analyzed in the previous chapter demonstrates the pedagogical approach and the content of education at the main monastery near Lhasa. Recalling that Mindröling's influence extended beyond this central seat to its branches and affiliated institutions, in this section I turn to a Sikkimese example to illustrate how Mindröling's pedagogical methods for training laypeople shaped its affiliates.

The orientalist L. Austine Waddell's survey of Tibetan Buddhism, *The Buddhism of Tibet or Lamaism*, gives an account of the education system of Pemayangtsé monastery in Sikkim, providing a nineteenth-century example of Mindröling's educational influence. Closely associated with the Sikkimese royal family, it is listed in official monastery catalogues as one of the significant monasteries in the Mindröling network. Waddell's analysis is shaped by his Protestant chauvinist perspective. Keeping that in mind, his record of the content of education at Pemayangtsé illustrates the dissemination of the Mindröling aesthetic sensibility and worldview.

The bond between the two monasteries was solidified when Terdak Lingpa's daughter Mingyur Peldrön fled into exile at Pemayangtsé to escape the Zungar Mongol troops that ransacked Mindröling and killed members of her family.[43] According to Waddell, the Pemayangtsé curriculum presents a basic training in Buddhism that reads like a manual on etiquette and good manners. The type of training Waddell describes would have been valuable in shaping the behavior of the children who would go on to positions of power and influence. In particular, when a boy began schooling at Pemayangtsé, after a preliminary physical examination and the shearing of his hair, he would take up with a tutor, usually assigned according to his family connections. The tutor would teach him the alphabet and then teach him to read and recite short Buddhist texts. Waddell then leaves aside the textual aspect of the curriculum to focus on the "golden maxims of a moral kind."[44] The list begins with a version of the golden rule, "Do unto others," and moves on to the essential Buddhist value of prioritizing others over one's self. It also includes more specific injunctions related to speech, stressing the importance of tone, pithiness, and persuasive rhetoric. These rules all have roots in the Buddhist Vinaya, the code of conduct for monks and nuns from the Pāli Canon, which is foundational to Tibetan Buddhist monasticism. They also reflect the Mindröling guidelines. Waddell reports that young boys sent to the monastery as "probationers" would have their hair cut but otherwise would not go through any initial ritual initiation since the intention was not for them to become monks. They would continue to wear a layperson's clothes.[45] Waddell writes that that monks from Pemayangtsé monastery in Sikkim regularly traveled to Mindröling to study. This suggests such travel was common until at least the end of the nineteenth century, when he was writing.[46]

The practice of sending monks to study abroad was not limited to the Mindröling tradition, and it created wide networks of monks and nuns from distant regions who shared a common educational and practical experience. In addition, Nyingma monasteries all over the Tibetan Buddhist area based their curricula, to varying extents, on the model of Mindröling.[47] Due to the various circumstances explored throughout this work, Mindröling had elite status that it could pass on to its affiliated institutions and to its graduates.

It is significant that the Fifth Dalai Lama and his advisors discouraged the fields of arts and sciences at Lhasa's major Géluk monasteries at the same time he patronized the establishment of Mindröling, where *rikné* flourished.[48] The coincidence of these factors helped establish Mindröling as a pedagogical authority, shaping the tastes and intellects as well as the religious practices of ruling-class Tibetans. It might seem that Tibetan aristocratic families did not need to seek out pedigrees for their sons, since their elite position was secure across generations.[49] However, the seventeenth and early eighteenth centuries were unstable times, and the culture and literacy associated with Buddhist education were highly valued assets sought out by the Tibetan nobility. As power shifted from Tibetan to Mongol to Qing actors, the position of even the most prestigious families was precarious, not vis-à-vis the less privileged classes but in relation to other noble families and religious lineages. Those in positions of power need to carry the aura of a sensibility of mastery, eloquence, and elegance. A record of having trained at Mindröling, or to a lesser extent at one of its branches, served as a kind of consecration certificate, bringing a glint of Mindröling's aura to the man or woman who studied there, or in some cases to those who merely claimed to have studied there.

Further, an educational institution fit for aristocrats would have needed to inculcate the behaviors befitting an aristocrat.[50] Being educated at Mindröling reconfirmed the Dokhar, Doring, and Polha families' already strong aristocratic legacy, through the practical skills of literary arts and the cultural skills connected to etiquette and "noble" bearing. These included not only refined manners but also a facility with Buddhist views and practices. In turn, the success of former students, such as these three powerful figures, boosted the prestige and symbolic capital of the institution. They later went on to protect and patronize the monastery during times of trouble, as did generations of their descendants. In addition to bestowing an aura of honor and prestige, having studied there also led to a sense of allegiance that created a cohesive and lasting bond among the lay alumni of Mindröling.

The aesthetic community-building aspect of monastic education is important in creating bases of support and patronage for major monasteries. Small as the central monastery was, the prestige of Mindröling was a consequential and far-reaching force in generating the multilayered network that developed over time. Assembling students from different regions had the potential to create foundations for continuity of teachings and traditions and to join monastic communities separated by geography. It also facilitated communication between distant Tibetan Buddhist locales and helped extend the influence of the major monasteries' charismatic leaders, for instance through following their ritual liturgies and spreading their Great Perfection-style teachings.

Writing and Power

To extend the scope of the context in which we understand Mindröling's role as a center of Tibetan literature and writing, and to consider the ramifications this had for Mindröling's position of authority in Tibetan societies, it is useful to reflect on the work of some Continental theorists who have investigated the relationship between writing and authority. Consider Jacques Derrida's elaboration of Claude Lévi-Strauss's assertion that writing is fundamentally tied to power and more explicitly, that writing has always and everywhere developed with the basic purpose of enabling the powerful to dominate others. Derrida writes, "Writing itself, in that first instance, seemed to be associated in any permanent way only with societies which were based on the exploitation of man by man."[51] Further considering the social and class implications, Roland Barthes has also commented on writing's basic relationship to the aggressive stratification of social classes.[52] Mindröling's place at the forefront of Central Tibetan aristocratic society and cultural production is in keeping with Barthes's observations that writing's origin is rooted in class distinctions, since Mindröling's family lineage, members of the Nyö clan, were among Tibet's highest social echelon. The monastery's role as a site of education in the arts and sciences in general and writing skills in particular firmly situated it as a center of authority.

The ability to write well and to teach others how to write is a highly valuable asset and a key to power and influence. Twentieth-century sources that deal with the question of education in premodern Tibet assert that the most important practical aspect of aristocratic education was handwriting.[53] The fact that Polhané learned various scripts and stood out for his handwriting, and that Dokharwa's legacy was sealed through his diverse compositions, underscores the fact that Mindröling appealed to the upper classes because of its strength in the literary arts. This is in balance with the appeal of its prestige as an esteemed place of Great Perfection philosophy and ritual practice. Writing was a crucial skill for administrators (ordained or lay) of the eighteenth century, and administrator monks from Géluk monasteries, much like lay aristocrats, traveled to Mindröling specifically to learn to write.

While the children of Tibetan aristocrats did not study statecraft per se at Mindröling, they acquired subtle tools with which to perpetuate the powerful roles of their families. Buddhist signs of virtue and good behavior were cosmopolitan by dint of crossing linguistic and cultural divides across East, Inner, and South Asia. More particularly, students trained at Mindröling were steeped in the worldview that called for the joining of religion and worldly life. Buddhist deportment would have been inculcated at any monastery, but Lhasa's Géluk monasteries would not have offered the same combination of practical skills and cultural capital, since they discouraged writing in favor of studying skills necessary for debate.[54] Just as a liberal arts education at today's elite colleges and universities aims to cultivate a well-rounded way of being that prepares students for positions of power and influence, Mindröling offered a broad education, focusing on the Tibetan Buddhist equivalent of "liberal arts" through *rikné*. Georges Dreyfus's assessment of Géluk pedagogy versus Nyingma pedagogy further supports an analogy of the Nyingma pedagogy represented at Mindröling with the liberal arts model. He stresses that the Géluk model tends to include a few orthodox texts and highlights debate over commentary, whereas the Nyingma model incorporates a wider variety of texts and stresses the literary arts, which lend themselves to both Dharmic and worldly purposes.[55]

The education that aristocrats such as Polhané and Dokharwa received at Mindröling shaped them as Tibet's future leaders. Mindröling alumni were conditioned for positions of power through a broad spectrum of training in the arts and sciences, aesthetics, ethics, and Buddhist doctrine. This both instilled practical skills and bestowed prestige. These men's success in the complex sociopolitical milieu of the day was based on the fullness of their education. In particular, Polhané's relatively stable rule marked a critical juncture in Tibet's early modern history. The resolution of a bloody Tibetan civil war led to a sustained period of stability and prosperity under the auspices of the Qing emperor, but marked by a distinctly Tibetan cosmopolitanism that crystallized in part at Mindröling.

Wealthy Sponsors and Prestigious Students

Many of the patrons who made donations to Mindröling were highly influential members of the Ganden Podrang government, including successive Dalai Lamas and their regents. Other prominent sponsors included high-ranking lamas of other schools, celebrated noblewomen, and rulers from across the greater Tibetan area. These sponsors made sizeable donations of fine art and ritual objects that became important elements in Mindröling's material identity. Donors were often former students of Mindröling and its affiliates, or the parents of youths who were sent there for education. In that way donors and students went hand in hand.

The donations made by these wealthy lay patrons in connection to Mindröling's educational functions relate to the monastery's role as a center for cultural production. Careful accounts were kept of the material donations made by significant donors, and these objects became enshrined in Mindröling's various temples and recorded in its catalogues as well as in letters and biographies. More specific to education, the fetishizing of objects such as the teacher's chair, crown, books, and ritual implements at Mindröling, and the attention paid to monastics' begging bowls and robes in Buddhism more generally, are similar to the treatment of objects in the modern university such as the chair, the seminar table, and graduation caps and gowns.[56] Terdak Lingpa also stresses the importance of accepting the generosity of poor patrons as appreciatively as donations from the rich and powerful, implying that there was a spectrum of socioeconomic classes represented among the monastery's early sponsors.[57]

Visual depictions also attest to Mindröling's role in education for the ruling class. One example is found in the wall paintings in the Lukhang (*klu khang*) temple located behind the Dalai Lama's Potala Palace in Lhasa.[58] The temple was built by the Sixth Dalai Lama for his ritual use and contains rare, detailed illustrations of Great Perfection practices and yogic exercises. These remarkable paintings show a diversely arrayed group of people studying and practicing at Mindröling. They are situated on the wall immediately next to a narrative depiction of Pema Lingpa, a Nyö clan member who conducted historic visionary and institution-building activities in Bhutan. These paintings mark Mindröling as having a special relationship to the Ganden Podrang and the ruling class more generally. They also reflect clan connections and lineage ties between Terdak Lingpa and his Nyö relatives, including Pema Lingpa and the Sixth Dalai Lama. The visual image of Mindröling reveals it to be a place where people of various vocations congregate, study, and practice. The people shown in the Lukhang murals are not labeled. Rather, they are generic or anonymous examples of the different kinds of people who would gather to study and practice at Mindröling.[59] Mindröling's visual presence in images in the Lukhang reflects its prestige, since the Lukhang was designed for the personal use of the Dalai Lamas in their tantric practices. Such visual materials worked both to increase and to instantiate Mindröling's high status.

Nevertheless Mindröling was like other monasteries in Tibet and throughout the Buddhist world in its role as a center for ritual and a site where laity could support the monastic "field of merit" whose adherence to vows and ritual activities helped dispel pollution and generate balance in the community between natural and supernatural forces. The distinct factors of celibacy and ritual on the one hand and education in worldly fields of knowledge on the other were mutually reinforced and were equally important to Mindröling's success.

At the time when Mindröling was founded, the Tibetan aristocracy was arranged into a hierarchy in which a number of noble families occupied society's highest tiers.[60] The children of such families were candidates for positions of power in the government. How high they rose depended at least in part on their personal charisma and achievement, and whether they were in favor with higher-ups, be they Tibetan, Mongolian, or Manchu. Scant research has been done on the education of the aristocracy during this time period, but biographical accounts indicate that Central Tibetan lay aristocrats were schooled with tutors at home, at the official schools in Lhasa, and in some cases for brief periods with monk tutors in monasteries.[61] Notably, many of the teachers at the official Tsé Lobdra (*rtse slob grwa*) and Tsikhang (*rtsi khang*) schools in Lhasa where young aristocrats were trained for government service were from Mindröling.[62]

It was also common for aristocratic youths to study at home with tutors before pursuing studies at Mindröling. For instance, Dokharwa studied at home with his father and tutors before beginning his training at the monastery. And again, while Mindröling had a special status, it was not the only monastery where laypeople went for Buddhist training. For example, the constitutional document (*bca' yig*) from Sera monastery mentions donors who would stay in the monastery for a period of time to receive training and religious education. These donor-practitioners were called *chözé* (*chos mdzad*).[63] The custom is not surprising considering that monasteries were the main sites of intellectual, artistic, ritual, and philosophical production. If lay pupils studied among monks for a period of time, they could later return to lay life. It is hard to say how widespread this practice was, but it is instructive for understanding the broader phenomenon of Buddhist monasteries acting as cultural and educational centers.

When laypeople studied alongside clerics at the large Géluk institutions that were the centers of the new Tibetan government in and around Lhasa, such lay pupils were usually financial donors who wished to spend a brief period engaged in intensive Buddhist practice, and their training generally was confined to ritual.[64] Since members of the Géluk school wielded the greatest political influence at the time of Mindröling's founding, one might expect that young aristocrats would have attended Géluk monasteries. The fact that young men whose high social position directed them toward powerful political careers studied at a Nyingma monastery reflects Mindröling's special reputation as a place of higher learning. Regionalism, linguistic and cultural capital, and the relationship between religious consecration and political legitimacy all figured into establishing it as a heterotopic space that was both on the margins and at the center of Tibetan culture and society.

The careers of the sons of the Dokhar, Polha, and later Doring, families show that they certainly were at the apex of their social, cultural, and political milieu. The fact that these young men were not sent to one of the major Géluk monasteries, ostensibly much closer to the seat of political power and influence, is again a reflection of the complexity of Mindröling's relationship to the political center as a site of religious and cultural production. It carried clout like that of an Ivy League school, a training ground for future heads of state and arbiters of taste.

Mindröling as Heterotopia

In the liberal arts paradigm and at Mindröling alike, education is intended to transform the intellect as well as the character and sensibilities of the student. The ideal is not merely to produce knowledgeable graduates but to cultivate well-rounded human beings. Michel Foucault's theory of heterotopias or "other spaces" aptly frames this complex function.[65] According to Foucault, heterotopias exist as functioning places in all times and cultures, in contradistinction to imagined utopias. Heterotopias are real, but like utopias, they are distinct from everyday environments and engagements. A confluence of seemingly incongruous functions is one of their core characteristics. One of the primary examples Foucault invoked in illustrating this theory was the boarding school, a place through which young people pass in order to be transformed from children into educated, cultured members of society. This process of transformation is not limited to the formal work of education, which takes place through sanctioned books, organized tuition, and class time, but also includes a range of trainings and experiences, some officially sanctioned and some implicitly condoned by the institutional culture but inconsistent with the ostensible work of the school. Examples include exposure to literary and artistic content outside the bounds of the curriculum, sexual encounters, subtle taste-forming experiences, intimate relationships with mentors, and hazing. The whole person is shaped and the position he or she occupies in the world is determined in the educational process.

As is the case at modern research universities where military technologies are developed in laboratories next to poetry seminars and biology classes, students at Mindröling were exposed to seemingly contradictory subjects. The wide range of careers and the distinctive literature produced by lay Tibetan literati who were trained at Mindröling demonstrate that a rich range of trainings and experiences took place at the monastery. Especially illustrative of this point is the presence of erotic and romantic themes in the literature composed by students. This style of writing, which adheres to the highest formal literary standards and draws extensively on Indic models and aesthetics, stands out vividly in better known Tibetan literature, which tends to focus on Buddhist subjects. For a brief time aristocratic lay students left their careers, families and other worldly engagements to be transformed and shaped by Mindröling. When they emerged, ideally they were more "open minded," ethical, informed, skilled, and ready to rule.[66]

Conclusion

During Mindröling's first flourishing in the seventeenth and eighteenth centuries, the prominent aristocrats whose children studied there included the Dokhar, Polha, and Doring families. In keeping with the needs of these lay students, training in astrology came along with conditioning in deportment and taste, and calligraphy lessons were followed by instructions in the Buddhist view of reality as impermanent and illusory. It was as likely that a lay student would use his training to become a bureaucrat or diplomat as it was that he would become a pious Buddhist; and most likely he would do both. To cultivate people who were skilled politicians, refined aesthetes, and accomplished Buddhists, a gamut of subjects and trainings similar to the liberal arts were offered at Mindröling. This variegated education took place within the highly disciplined atmosphere of the monastic community. Just as monks and nuns were encouraged to be beyond reproach in upholding their vows, for the benefit of the lay pupils, the subjects taught at Mindröling had to bear the marks of cosmopolitanism, prestige, and sanctity, while also serving the students' practical needs, especially in terms of writing skills. For all these reasons, which can be summarized by the ideal referred to as the Two Systems (*lugs gnyis*), Mindröling served as a school for aristocrats, directly shaping the cosmopolitan tastes of early modern Central Tibet.

Since Mindröling was not an ostensibly political institution, the prominent concentration of cultural capital there would have been less visibly connected to the Fifth Dalai Lama's dominance and would have lessened the potential for rivals to emerge from within the politically dominant school. However, this prominence also made it vulnerable to attack by the Zungars. Later the Qing emperors recognized its stature and granted it protection when they targeted other Nyingma institutions.

As schools for aristocrats became better established in Lhasa, it might have become less common for lay pupils to study at Mindröling, since they received the same model of education at the most prestigious schools. For laypeople and monastics alike, the elite Mindröling "degree," or the mere claim to one, functioned like a consecration, providing graduates with a credential that bolstered their authority and connected them to others who shared their educational background. In turn, the educated nobility supported Mindröling by offering material and financial support, but also by continuing to seek out the Mindröling degree, thereby augmenting the array of famous names associated with the tradition over the generations. The work of the early graduates, especially Dokharwa, arguably constituted some of the pinnacles of early modern Tibetan cultural production.

Likewise, the same wealthy and powerful sponsors who paid for large-scale rituals and endowed the monastery sent their children to study there. The training at Mindröling and its satellite monasteries across the Tibetan region and schools in Lhasa was not strictly limited to a discrete sphere of "Buddhism" nor "politics" nor "culture." Rather, what might appear to be contradictory trainings happened in tandem. Lay pupils gained a great deal of cultural capital through their Mindröling training. This is reflected by the worldly achievements of graduates. Their successful careers in an extremely complex and changing milieu required a high level of diplomacy and cosmopolitanism since the major players were not only diverse Tibetans but also Mongols and Qing. The first phase of Mindröling's flourishing was cut short by the Zungar invasion, when the brutal destruction of the monastery and the execution or forced exile of its inhabitants threatened its very existence. This destruction and the subsequent revival are the focus of the epilogue.

Destruction and Revival

The Next Generation

TERDAK LINGPA PASSED away in 1714, when he was almost seventy years old. He is reported to have anticipated his passing and announced the arrival of *ḍākinīs* to escort him. He also made a prophetic statement about a time when he would be reincarnated in Eastern Tibet. This paved the way for the moment several generations later, in the late nineteenth century, when there was no male heir to the Mindröling throne, threatening the end of the hereditary lineage. At that time, Tertön Rangrik Dorjé (1847–1903), who was recognized as Terdak Lingpa's reincarnation, brought his son to Mindröling from Lumora monastery in the Nyarong valley of Eastern Tibet.[1] The son, Pema Wangchen, married the previous senior chair's daughter, thereby joining the family and continuing the lineage.[2]

When the charismatic founder Terdak Lingpa passed away, Mindröling was well established as a new Nyingma monastic center for ritual, scholarship, and cultural production. The physical structures were complete, with the porch of the main temple bearing a celebratory history of the monastery composed in verse by the Fifth Dalai Lama, Terdak Lingpa, and Dharmaśrī on its walls. The guidelines for students, including the curriculum of study, rules for deportment, and a detailed yearly calendar, were clearly defined. Following the death of Terdak Lingpa's brother Tenpé Nyima, who was the first abbot, Lochen Dharmaśrī had taken up that position, and his reputation as a great scholar and artist spread and drew students to Mindröling. Terdak Lingpa's children were prepared for their roles,

Figure 6.1 Early eighteenth-century portrait of Pema Gyurmé Gyatso.
Courtesy of Rubin Museum of Art

having been trained according to their strengths and the Buddhist vows appropriate to their particular practice, in keeping with Terdak Lingpa's expectations of their future responsibilities at the monastery.

Just a few years later, Zungar Mongol troops occupied Lhasa and sought to destroy the Nyingma school in Central Tibet, killing practitioners and destroying the material cultural supports for Nyingma practice. After such devastating losses, with family members executed, students scattered, and the monastery razed, how did the Mindröling community recover and continue its role as a center for Nyingma practice and cultural production? In this epilogue I address some of the obstacles Mindröling encountered in the eighteenth century, focusing on the circumstances around the Zungar attack. Next, I consider at the connections and alliances that allowed for the rebuilding and stabilization of Mindröling after this traumatic rupture. The primary relationship I consider is between Mingyur Peldrön, Terdak Lingpa's daughter and cherished disciple, and Miwang Polhané, Tibet's temporal ruler from 1728 to 1747 and an alumnus of Mindröling. Finally, I sketch a partial portrait of Mindröling's ongoing institutional identity.

The Second Senior Chair, Pema Gyurmé Gyatso

Terdak Lingpa's eldest son, Pema Gyurmé Gyatso (1686–1718), whose mother was Terdak Lingpa's second wife, Yönten Dolma (d.u.), was known for his remarkable intelligence. He was educated in the Dharma as well as the arts and sciences with the expectation that he would succeed his father as the second senior chair.[3] He caused significant concern in the family when he became a fully ordained monk rather than following in his father's footsteps as a noncelibate tantric practitioner. Significantly, Pema Gyurmé Gyatso cut his hair in a gesture of monastic renunciation. The other senior chairs at Mindröling, beginning with Terdak Lingpa, do not cut their hair as a part of their tantric practice.[4] With this symbolic act, Pema Gyurmé Gyatso went against the expectations of the family and the lineage. His rejection of his prescribed role and decision to cut his hair carried extraordinary weight in the community and have even been interpreted as leading to the destruction of the monastery.[5]

In other ways, he fulfilled expectations. He was an outstanding scholar and an avid poet, composing a commentary on the Tibetan translation of the *Kāvyādarśa* (*snyan ngag me long*) and multiple texts comprising his examples of poetic devices.[6] Lochen Dharmaśrī composed a brief biography in the form of a prayer for the second senior chair, in which he praised him in particular for his impartial (*ris med*) approach to teaching the Dharma.[7] As illustrated in previous chapters, authors used this particular note of praise—which would later come to be associated with nonsectarianism but is rooted in a longer history of Mahāyāna, Mahāmudrā, and Great Perfection philosophy—to describe Terdak Lingpa as well. It highlights the ideal of an unprejudiced, unbiased worldview. Following in his uncle Dharmaśrī's footsteps, Pema Gyurmé Gyatso also wrote about the three types of vows.[8] Thus the second senior chair exemplified some of the key characteristics and expertise for which Mindröling was renowned.

The Zungar Attack

Zungar troops entered Central Tibet during this time and targeted Nyingma institutions and practitioners in a bloody pogrom. They murdered first Dharmaśrī and then Pema Gyurmé Gyatso in 1718. These were just two of many brutal acts the troops committed during their occupation of Lhasa from 1717 to 1720. Mindröling oral histories recount that due to Pema Gyurmé Gyatso's great merit as a practitioner, the soldiers were unable to decapitate him despite several attempts. To help them, he explained how they could defile him sufficiently to overcome his extraordinary merit and kill him. Accordingly they covered his head in soiled clothing, and the polluting effects of this symbolic gesture enabled them to behead him. The story goes that the head of a cherished statue at Samyé monastery fell off at the same instant.[9] This echoes the ties between Samyé, Tibet's seminal Buddhist monastery of the imperial period, and Mindröling, which played a parallel role as a new Nyingma center with ties to the Ganden Podrang government in the early modern period. These murders were an immense loss for the Mindröling community, the surviving members of which were scattered into exile. Many of the temples, shrines, and courtyard that had been designed and constructed so painstakingly under the direction of the Fifth Dalai Lama, which Terdak Lingpa had envisioned as materially manifesting the Two Truths for the sake of those who needed physical support for awakening, were demolished.

The circumstances that led to the destruction of Mindröling were a complex combination of stark sectarianism, a radically shifting political climate in which various Tibetan, Mongol, and Qing forces vied for dominance, and likely a current of personal enmity between Mindröling's supporters and detractors. Most acutely, the Zungars were spurred into their anti-Nyingma fervor by Gomang Lama Lobang Puntsok, the younger brother of an army general, Tsering Dondrub. After having taken control of the area, Tsering Dondrub summoned all religious and lay people of the ruling class together to acknowledge his takeover. He demanded that they instruct the working-class people in their areas to recognize his ultimate authority. Soon afterward, Gomang Lama Lobang Puntsok advised his brother the general to tear the Nyingma school up by its roots by targeting teachers and destroying all the images, objects, monasteries, and texts associated with the Nyingma tradition.[10] The lama called for an attack on the monks from the Potala's Namgyal college (*rnam rgyal grwa tshang*) as well, perhaps because they were trained in tantric rituals associated with the Nyingma school. The Namgyal monks were gathered together on the banks of the Kyichu river, stripped naked, and forced to throw their robes in the water and stand before crowds of people in humiliation. The soldiers proceeded to utterly destroy the monasteries of Dorjé Drak, Mindröling, Chushar Tharpaling, and Sangngak Chöling, and many smaller Nyingma hermitages. They rounded up luminary lamas, including Dharmaśrī and Pema Gyurmé Gyatso, and cut their throats on the banks of the Kyichu.[11] As a result of prejudice against the Nyingma school's approach to tantric ritual practice, members of the Central Tibetan Nyingma monasteries were tormented, humiliated, and killed.[12]

The Second Generation

Following the murders of Mindröling's second senior chair and abbot, the destruction of the monastery, and a period of exile, Mingyur Peldrön and her brother Rinchen Namgyal (1694–1758), who would become the third senior chair of the monastery, returned to Central Tibet when the political situation had settled down. They rebuilt Mindröling and made efforts to create a more stable future for the lineage, with the sponsorship and

Figure 6.2 Thangka painting of Mingyur Peldrön.
Courtesy of Khandro Rinpoché

patronage of Miwang Polhané, who had studied under Dharmaśrī and was devoted to Terdak Lingpa.

Mingyur Peldrön's perspective on the bloodshed is recounted in broad strokes in Mindröling's monastic catalogues and her biography.[13] These accounts tell us that she and some of her younger siblings escaped thanks to the intervention of an army officer who had met with Terdak Lingpa shortly before the lama's death in 1714. During that meeting, Terdak Lingpa prophesied that the officer would have a chance to aid Mindröling in the future. He offered the man gifts of sacred objects and asked him not to forget their amicable connection. When chaos erupted in Lhasa about three years later and the Zungars set out to destroy Central Tibet's Nyingma monasteries, the officer who had met with Terdak Lingpa secretly traded posts with the commander assigned to sack Mindröling. In this way Terdak Lingpa's admirer was able to go to Mindröling instead.

When the troops approached Mindröling, rather than proceeding directly to the monastery, he set up camp for the night in the valley below the monastery and fired shots into the air as a warning to the inhabitants.[14] Mingyur Peldrön had been in a three-year meditation retreat until that very day. Emerging, she and a small retinue including her sisters and mother escaped and headed toward Sikkim. Her two younger brothers made their way to Nyarong in the Kham region of Eastern Tibet. When order was restored to the Lhasa region in a few years, they would return to Mindröling and begin the process of rebuilding.

But meanwhile Terdak Lingpa's scattered offspring helped secure the spread of Mindröling's traditions to the locales where they took refuge. Accounts of Mingyur Peldrön's sojourn in Sikkim reveal the high degree of respect the Mindröling lineage received beyond their local region. Further, the events surrounding her exile illustrate the strength of ties between ruling-class families and religious lineages. According to her biography, while in Sikkim she presided over large public teachings attended by thousands of people. The royal family extended an open invitation for the public to attend her teachings and receive blessings.[15]

During this period in Sikkim she established her reputation as a Great Perfection teacher of great renown. Textual as well as visual materials attest to her fame. Visual culture examples include the group portraits called "lineage trees" depicting the most important masters of the Mindröling lineage, which include Mingyur Peldrön's image. The inclusion of women in this visual representation is a rarity in Tibetan Buddhist art history. Also significant, the institutional ties between Mindröling and Sikkim's Pema-yangtsé monastery were solidified during her stay in Sikkim.[16]

In addition to Mingyur Peldrön's activities to spread Mindröling's ritual traditions, her stay in Sikkim bolstered sociopolitical bonds. Significantly, her younger sister married into Sikkim's royal family. This was arranged by Mingyur Peldrön's main contact in Sikkim, who formerly had studied at Mindröling and been close with her father and uncle.[17] The arrangement strengthened the connection between Sikkim's leading family and Mind-röling. Similar to the marriage alliance the Fifth Dalai Lama arranged between Terdak Lingpa and his first wife or secret consort Ngödrup Pel-zom, such strategic marital unions highlight the interweaving of powerful Tibetan Buddhist family groups, political power, and Buddhist schools and lineages of practice.

Rebuilding Mindröling

Mingyur Peldrön and Rinchen Namgyal's return to Mindröling marked the beginning of the monastery's second wave. To ensure the continuation of the family lineage, she passed their father's extensive teachings on to her younger brother so that he could take up the position of senior chair, since that role is closed to women. When she was a child Terdak Lingpa had predicted that she would have an indispensable role in maintaining the lineage, and Lochen Dharmaśrī is quoted in her biography as stating that the women of the lineage would carry it into the next generation.[18]

Mingyur Peldrön began repairing the damage to the buildings, temples, and many art and ritual objects. More subtly, she worked to make the Mindröling tradition less vulnerable to censure from more members of other Tibetan Buddhist schools, most especially members of the dominant Géluk school, who might disapprove of practices such as the taking of an actual (as opposed to visualized) tantric consort. Her biography reflects her anxiety around the themes of sexual yoga, the use of alcohol in rituals, studying the worldly fields of knowledge, and ritual warcraft.

After Mindröling had begun to be rebuilt, she began to develop relationships with powerful ruling-class families who sought her teachings and ritual expertise and made extensive offerings to her, including land and previously existing temples around Mindröling and extremely fine-quality horses and equestrian equipment.[19] With Mindröling under restoration and her reputation as a Great Perfection master established, they requested that she conduct wrathful rituals, as her family members had often been asked to do in the past. In a meeting with the Seventh Dalai Lama, Mingyur Peldrön expressed resistance to conducting such rituals on behalf of wealthy patrons against their rivals.[20] It is unclear whether she expected the Dalai Lama himself to ask this of her or just hoped he would support her in her refusal to conduct these rituals more generally. The Dalai Lama reportedly assured her that as a nun, she would not be expected to engage in that kind of ritual. The biography mentions that the next day her brother the senior chair was invited to meet with the Dalai Lama, but the subject of their meeting is not disclosed.

Mingyur Peldrön may also have been motivated to present Mindröling as beyond any conceivable reproach, thereby making the monastery less vulnerable to attack. We can find support for this possibility in accounts of her encounters with the fascinating and controversial character Lélung Jédrung Zhepay Dorjé (1697–1740).[21] This lama, who actively integrated Géluk and Nyingma traditions, was both a Geshé (*dge bshes*), the Géluk school's highest scholastic degree, and a visionary Treasure Revealer (*gter ston*), in the tradition of Terdak Lingpa.[22] This was a rare combination of qualifications, and indeed he was an exceptional figure. Further, he was extremely influential as an advisor to powerful rulers including the Khoshot Oirot Mongol Lhazang Khan (*lha bzang khan*, d. 1717) and Polhané.

Mingyur Peldrön's biography recounts several instances in which Lélung's dalliances, drunkenness, and otherwise untoward behavior scandalized her. In one instance, Polhané, effectively the king at the time, urged Mingyur Peldrön to receive Lélung at Mindröling. She was reluctant since she had recently visited Lélung's own monastery, where a group of monks, nuns, laymen and laywomen all became drunk and sang and danced together. At that time, while Mingyur Peldrön drank tea, some of the Mindröling monks traveling with her drank alcohol. She later rebuked them severely.[23] Despite her reservations, at Polhané's request, Mingyur Peldrön invited Lélung to Mindröling. He arrived with his secret consort and threw what the biographer presents as a raucous party in the main temple, attended by a large crowd of men and women disciples, both lay and ordained. Lélung went on to suggest that Mingyur Peldrön should engage in tantric sexual practices with him. Her biographer stresses that she flatly refused and promptly left the main monastery area for her nearby retreat place, Samtentsé, in order to avoid further contact with Lélung. From another perspective, all these activities might be interpreted as part of his esoteric tantric practice.[24] From the perspective of her pious biographer, he was a foil for Mingyur Peldrön, representing the types of behavior from which she wished to distance Mindröling.

Mingyur Peldrön's strong ethical convictions and her ability to transmit her father's complete teachings combined with her connection to Polhané to make possible Mindröling's revival. Her biography shows her regularly conducting rituals and offering teachings to men and women of the ruling class, as her father had so often done. But while she collaborated with those in political power to reestablish Mindröling, as her father had collaborated with the Fifth Dalai Lama and Desi Sangyé Gyatso, she is not recorded to have given the same kind of highly pragmatic advice her father so often offered his students with careers in government, especially later in his life.[25] Instead, her biography portrays an extremely disciplined monastic who encouraged the strictest monastic discipline from members of the Mindröling community. This might explain why members encouraged her to leave the central monastery for the Tibetan region of Kongpo, essentially entering a second period of exile. In contrast to her exile in Sikkim where the royal family hosted her, in Kongpo she spent her time doing manual labor.[26]

There are a number of explanations for Mingyur Peldrön's rejection of some characteristics commonly associated with the Nyingma school. In addition to needing to protect Mindröling from anti-Nyingma antagonism, they likely included her gendered experience and the particular details of her education. Crucially, her biographer recounts that she was not trained in the worldly fields of knowledge because her father wanted her to focus on absorbing his Buddhist teachings.[27] This is in stark contrast to the standard Mindröling curriculum, which encouraged the most capable students to learn as much as they could about the traditionally defined worldly subjects. In keeping with this omission, her biography suggests that as an adult she was suspicious of the value of the "conventional" fields of arts and science, favoring a more intensive study of Buddhist doctrine.[28] Mingyur Peldrön's biography also shows a strong undercurrent of criticizing the hypocrisy of tantric practitioners who use the appearance of engaging in esoteric ritual as an excuse for debauchery and unethical behavior. In this way, she marked a shift toward the cautious side of the tradition already established. In Mingyur Peldrön's time there was good reason to lean toward formality and discipline, since the monastery had just been destroyed by supporters of the Géluk school and the Qing government continued to mistrust and repress Nyingma institutions.

In reading accounts of Mingyur Peldrön's life it is difficult, if not impossible to separate the perspective of the biographer from that of the subject. It could be that the writer, a monk who was a devoted disciple and studied Great Perfection practices with her, was more scandalized by the events of Mingyur Peldrön's life than she was, even if she approved of the biography and shared its general perspective. In any case, the biography presents a portrait of Mingyur Peldrön as a highly disciplined nun who disapproved of wrathful rites, sexual yoga, or imbibing alcohol. Since members of today's Mindröling tradition identify her as a main character in the institution's second generation, her persona as expressed in the biography represents a slight shift in Mindröling's institutional focus toward a more programmatic monasticism, which was already an aspect of the tradition as demonstrated by the monastic constitution. How this shift played out in the following generations was complex, but it again draws our attention to the multiple sides of Mindröling. These include a focus on bridging the Buddhist and the worldly, Great Perfection practices and the study of arts and sciences, renunciation, and attention to material culture and aesthetics.

The Ongoing Work of Cultural Production

In this second generation of Mindröling's early history, the first step was to rebuild the physical location of the monastery as the material support for its traditions of artistic and ritual practices and the future site of offerings from sponsors engaged in merit-generating activities. The importance of the physical monastery and the many objects it contained, meticulously documented in the Mindröling catalogues, underscores the importance of aesthetics and cultural production at Mindröling and in Buddhist culture more generally.

As described in chapter 5, the presence of lay students from Tibet's most powerful families was a significant factor during Mindröling's founding and in subsequent generations, as former students like Polhané took up positions of political and cultural authority and became sponsors and champions of Mindröling, making donations that became inscribed in the monastery's history and enshrined in its buildings.

Future Generations of Women at Mindröling

Many of the characteristics discernible in the first generation continued to be markers of Mindröling in the second generation and beyond. An important point of continuity is the relatively strong presence of women teachers in the Mindröling lineage. In the nineteenth century Mindröling Jetsun Trinlé Chödron (d.u.) attracted fame as a practitioner and in particular for her close teacher-student relationship with Jamyang Khyentsé Wangpo (1820–1892).[29] Like Mingyur Peldrön, Trinlé Chödron is depicted in Mindröling's lineage trees, which are painted on the monastery walls in Tibet and India. Jamyang Khyentsé Wangpo was also a member of the Nyö clan on his father's side, reiterating the force of family ties in Tibetan Buddhist networks.

In the twentieth century, as predicted at the time of Terdak Lingpa's death in 1714, his reincarnation was discovered in the Kham region of Nyarong, where Rinchen Namgyal had sought refuge during the Zungar invasion. In that generation, there was no male heir to take over the Mindröling throne, so the boy recognized as a reincarnation was brought to Mindröling in Central Tibet and married the previous senior chair's daughter, allowing the lineage to continue unbroken. Recognizing the strong patriarchal tendencies of Tibetan Buddhism, it is critical to note that the Mindröling tradition allowed women to carry the line forward in this way. This approach springs in part from the impartial current in Mindröling history. There are both practical and philosophical motivations for paying heed to the nonduality of gender, just as there are both practical and religious reasons to transcend sectarian biases.

Conclusion

Concurrent with the spread of Mindröling's aura across the Buddhist world, the central monastery undertook a very focused project to revive and transmit the central teachings of the Nyingma school. In this way the founders were given place in a line of revitalizers that included Vairocana, Nub Sangyé Yeshé, Pema Lingpa, Ratna Lingpa, and Dorjé Lingpa. Their successors would in turn include the rimé or "nonsectarian" champions of nineteenth- and twentieth-century Eastern Tibet.

As an illustration of the bridging of Buddhist and worldly concerns, most relevant is Mindröling's role as a training ground for elite laypeople, such as the literati and statesmen Dokharwa and Polhané. Mindröling was attractive to lay students for four main reasons. First, the monastery was founded under the direct auspices of the powerful Fifth Dalai Lama and had a special position in relation to his new central government, so its students were well situated for positions of authority. Second, the Nyö clan, whose members founded and ran Mindröling through a hereditary system of succession, embodied both Buddhist tantric mastery and expertise in the arts and sciences. Third, the people who held the senior chair of Mindröling were not fully ordained, celibate monks but tantric adepts who married and had children; therefore laypeople could hold them as direct exemplars without renouncing worldly engagements with family. The senior chair always worked in concert with the abbot and other ordained monastic authorities. And fourth, the curriculum developed at Mindröling spanned religious and worldly subjects through the connective tissue of aesthetics.

During the tenures of the Fifth Dalai Lama and his regent, Sangyé Gyatso, the distribution of power in Central Tibet underwent a massive reorganization. Out of the near chaos of the preceding decades, during which various parties vied for dominance in Tibetan Buddhist regions, the Lhasa-based Géluk establishment emerged as a locus of political power under the auspices of the Khoshot Mongols. This did not end the competition for influence among other loci of power.

The Fifth Dalai Lama and Sangyé Gyatso had close involvement with Terdak Lingpa and Lochen Dharmaśrī. The Dalai Lama oversaw Mindröling's founding and named Terdak Lingpa as his imperial preceptor, in a move that honored Terdak Lingpa as a great teacher and the Dalai Lama as an imperial ruler. This role later allowed Terdak Lingpa to act as a close advisor and confidant to Sangyé Gyatso during the years when he hid the Dalai Lama's death from the public.

Subsequent Tibetan leaders were educated at Mindröling and remained closely involved in the monastery's reconstruction and preservation. Monk administrators and scholars from Lhasa's three major Géluk monasteries attended Mindröling when they needed to learn literary skills. And teachers from Mindröling regularly taught poetry, grammar, composition, and calligraphy at the government schools in Lhasa. In addition to these connections with dominant Géluk institutions, Mindröling was a hub of large-scale public Nyingma ritual practice and was recognized as the site of the fundamental revamping and reinvigoration of Nyingma teachings after a long period of perceived decline. The institution of Mindröling writ large is an entity that stretches beyond the main monastery to numerous branches and affiliates, and further includes the countless individuals and families who associate themselves with the monastery. At the same time as Mindröling developed as a place of distinctly Nyingma teachings and practices, it took up a pedagogical role similar to that of a liberal arts college.

There is no definitive record of how many and which aristocratic families sent their children to Mindröling. Many more studied under Mindröling-trained teachers in Lhasa schools. In my field research, oral histories reflected that this phenomenon continued until the 1950s. At least until that time, aristocratic students were in a small minority, but they were an important element in Mindröling's support base and extended community, including the official schools in Lhasa to which Mindröling supplied teachers for language arts, particularly poetry. Mindröling's role as a center for literary arts had a strong impact on Tibetan high culture. And its influence on writing and the education of the ruling class was as crucial in establishing its authority in early modern aesthetics as the ritual cycles the monks regularly conducted were in establishing Mindröling's relationship to the early modern Tibetan polity.

Both despite and because of the significance of Mindröling's traditions—including visual arts, dance, monastic music, incense, and writing—its history has not been without obstacles, and the founders' familial and lineal descendants had to develop strategies for survival and success even as they carried on their ancestors' artfully designed practices. Today Mindröling's history as a nexus of Tibetan cultural production makes the Central Tibetan location near Lhasa a target for surveillance and suppression. Nevertheless, its aesthetic influence was clearly maintained through institutional ties, extending first to important eighteenth- to twentieth-century centers of intellectual and cultural production and ritual activity such as Degé in Kham and Rebkong in Amdo. These ties are still active in both monastic and lay communities.

Mindröling remained a vital center for large-scale ritual performances and Great Perfection practice, and is known today for the visionary Treasures and scholarship of Terdak Lingpa, the artistry and scholarship of Lochen Dharmaśrī, and the relative prominence of women teachers starting with Mingyur Peldrön. The founders worked to clarify and consolidate the Nyingma school while diplomatically cultivating connections to other Tibetan Buddhist schools through an applied impartial philosophy shaped by the Great Perfection. Mindröling is still known for rituals intended to support the long life of the Dalai Lama and the stability of the Tibetan government, and for excellence in the fields of arts and sciences, especially the literary arts. The legacy of rituals focused on worldly goals has also proved long lasting. Through the generations, the relatively high number of extraordinary women masters at Mindröling has continued. For example, today Jetsün Khandro Rinpoche is a globally respected teacher. Her sister Jetsün Dechen Paldrön maintains a low profile but is known within the Mindröling community as an outstanding translator and scholar. Her young son should eventually take up role of the twelfth Mindröling throneholder or senior chair.

The shaping of worldviews through aesthetics and cultural production happens on the individual, institutional, and wider social levels. The presence of famous laypeople as students or supporters of the monastery and the institution's prestige were mutually reinforced. The greater the number of influential people who were trained there, the more noble families were eager to send their offspring. Likewise, Buddhist scholars and practitioners were drawn to the monastery by its reputation as a reliable place to learn the Nyingma tradition, and in turn their reputation as masters reinforced Mindröling's renown. Respect and prestige grew for the students and for the monastery. Through this cycle, Mindröling was a powerful generator of cultural production and cohesion. As such, the phenomenon of Mindröling enfolds and reflects a remarkable array of facets of Tibetan Buddhist history.

Abbreviations

DL *Letters* Ngag dbang blo bzang rgya mtsho. *Rgya bod hor sog gi mchog dman bar pa rnams la 'phrin yig snyan ngag tu bkod pa rab snyan rgyud mang zhes bya ba bzhugs* [The Fifth Dalai Lama's collected letters]. Thimpu: Kunsang Tobgay, 1975.

Lamp of Teachings Cat. Bstan pa'i sgron me. *O rgyan smin grol gling gi dkar chag* [Monastic catalogue containing seventeenth- and eighteenth-century and twentieth-century documents]. Xining: Krung go'i bod kyi shes rig dpe skrun khang, 1992.

M. Guidelines Bstan pa'i sgron me. "smin gling 'dus sde'i bca' yig ma bu" [Mindröling monastic guidelines]. In *O rgyan smin grol gling gi dkar chag.* Xining: Krung go'i bod kyi shes rig dpe skrun khang, 1992.

Mirror of Memory Cat. *'Og min O rgyan smin grol gling gi dkar chag dran pa'i me long.* [Monastic catalogue composed in the twentieth century]. o rgyan smin grol gling gi dkar chag. TBRC W1KG15236. 1 vol. s.l.: s.n., n.d. http://tbrc.org/link ?RID=W1KG15236.

Miwang *Bio.* Mdo mkhar zhabs drung tshe ring dbang rgyal. *Dpal mi'i dbang po'i rtogs pa brjod pa 'jig rten du dga' ba'i gtam zhes bya ba bzhugs so* [Biography of Miwang]. Chengdu: Si khron Mi rigs dpe skrun khang, 2002.

MP *Bio.* Khyung po ras pa 'gyur med 'od gsal. *rje btsun mi 'gyur dpal gyi sgron ma'i rnam thar dad pa'i gdung sel* [Mingyur Peldrön's biography]. Thimpu, Bhutan: National Library of Bhutan, 1984.

Temple Wall Cat. Gter bdag gling pa 'gyur med rdo rje. "Sgo 'phyor gyi lho ngos ldebs ris su 'khod pa'i gtsug lag khang gi dkar chag" [Catalogue composed on the southern wall of the porch of the main temple]. In *O rgyan smin grol gling gi dkar chag.* Xining: Krung go'i bod kyi shes rig dpe skrun khang, 1992.

TL *Inner Bio.* Lochen Dharmashri. "Gter bdag gling pa'i nang gi rnam thar." In *Gsung 'bum* [Terdak Lingpa's inner biography, in collected works]. TBRC W9140. Dehradun: D. G. Khochen Tulku, 1999.

TL *Letters* Gter bdag gling pa 'gyur med rdo rje. *Collected Religious Instructions and Letters of Gter-bdag-gling-pa 'gyur med rdo rje.* Dehradun: Khochen Tulku, 1977.

TL *Outer Bio.* Lochen Dharmaśrī. "gter bdag gling pa'i phyi yi rnam thar." In *Gsung 'bum* [Terdak Lingpa's "outer" biography, in collected works]. BDRC W9140. Dehradun: D. G. Khochen Tulku, 1999.

YLYD *Bio. Yum chen lha 'dzin dbyangs can sgrol ma'i rnam thar.* In *Gsung 'bum* [Biography of Yumchen Lhadzin Yangchen Drölma in collected works]. BDRC W9140. Dehradun: D. G. Khochen Tulku, 1999.

Notes

Introduction

1. On the consolidation of the Nyingma school during this period, in part thanks to the efforts of Mindröling's founders, see Jake P. Dalton, *The Gathering of Intentions: The History of a Tibetan Buddhist Tantra* (New York: Columbia University Press, 2016), 97–113. For an excellent summary and contextualization of Dalton's broader argument, see Sam van Shaik's review in *Buddhist Studies Review* 35, nos. 1–2 (2018): 308–9.

2. On the designation "early modern" in Tibet, see Janet Gyatso, *Being Human in a Buddhist World: The Intellectual History of Medicine in Early Modern Tibet* (New York: Columbia University Press, 2015), 409. Further sources include: Kurtis R. Schaeffer, "New Scholarship in Tibet 1650–1700," in *Forms of Knowledge in Early Modern Asia: Explorations in the Intellectual History of India and Tibet 1500–1800*, ed. Sheldon Pollock (Durham, NC: Duke University Press, 2011), 291–310; Janet Gyatso, "Experience, Empiricism, and the Fortunes of Authority: Tibetan Medicine and Buddhism on the Eve of Modernity," in *Forms of Knowledge in Early Modern Asia: Explorations in the Intellectual History of India and Tibet, 1500–1800*, ed. Sheldon Pollock (Chapel Hill, NC: Duke University Press, 2011), 311–35; and Matthew Kapstein, "Just Where on Jambudvīpa Are We? New Geographical Knowledge and Old Cosmological Schemes in Eighteenth-Century Tibet," in *Forms of Knowledge in Early Modern Asia: Explorations in the Intellectual History of India and Tibet 1500–1800*, ed. Sheldon Pollock (Durham, NC: Duke University Press, 2011), 336–64.

3. For a concise explanation of cosmopolitanism in the Qing context, see Johan Elverskog, "Wutai Shan, Qing Cosmopolitanism, and the Mongols," *Journal of the International Association of Tibetan Studies* 6 (December 2011): 243–74. For an art historical perspective on Qing cosmopolitanism, see Patricia Berger, *Empire of*

Emptiness: Buddhist Art and Political Authority in Qing China (Honolulu: University of Hawai'i Press, 2003); and Wen-shing Chou, "Maps of Wutai Shan: Individuating the Sacred Landscape Through Color," *Journal of the International Association of Tibetan Studies* 6 (December 2011): 372–86.

4. Toni Huber traces this closure to Qing-imposed restrictions on travel, especially to India, following the Gorkha-Tibetan war in 1792. See Huber, *The Holy Land Reborn: Pilgrimage and the Tibetan Reinvention of Tibetan Buddhism* (Chicago: University of Chicago Press, 2008), 233.

5. I generally use the term "worldly" to convey the Tibetan term *srid*. In some instances it is appropriate to translate the Tibetan term as "secular," "civil," "societal," "political," or "temporal." I believe "worldly" is the best way to convey these related meanings. It also invokes the theme of cultivating a "worldview" or mentality linked to a particular aesthetic sensibility.

6. Dungkar Losang Khrinely, *Mkhas dbang dung dkar blo bzang 'phrin las mchog gis mdzad pa'i bod rig pa'i tshig mdzod chen mo shes bya rab gsal zhes bya ba bzhugs so* [Dungkar Tibetological great dictionary] (Beijing: Krung go'i bod rig pa dpe skrun khang [China Tibetology Publishing House], 2002), 1900–1901.

7. I have considered many possibilities for the right term to describe the methods they used. I am following Dalton's lead in using "inclusive," which very nicely conveys their approach. See Dalton, *Gathering of Intentions*, 98.

8. On the prominence of the family's previous seat of Dargyé Choling for Great Perfection study and practice, see Bryan J. Cuevas, *The Hidden History of the Tibetan Book of the Dead* (Oxford: Oxford University Press, 2003), 57–68.

9. On the effectiveness of these large-scale rituals in spreading Mindröling's system of ritual practice, see Dalton, *Gathering of Intentions*, 98–101.

10. While this is the first book-length study of Mindröling in a language other than Tibetan, previous works that involve Mindröling have been important to my research. In particular: Jacob P. Dalton, "The Uses of the Dgongs pa 'dus pa'i mdo in the Development of the Rnying-ma School of Tibetan Buddhism" (PhD diss., University of Michigan, 2002); Dalton, "Recreating the Rnyingma School: the Mdo dbang Tradition of Smin grol gling," in *Power, Politics, and the Reinvention of Tradition: Tibet in the 17th and 18th Centuries, Proceedings of the 10th Seminar of the International Association for Tibetan Studies*, ed. Bryan Cuevas and Kurtis Schaeffer, Oxford, 2003 (Leiden: Brill, 2006), 91–101; Bryan Cuevas, "Preliminary Remarks on the History of Mindröling: The Founding and Organization of a Tibetan Monastery in the Seventeenth Century," in *Places of Practice: Monasteries and Monasticism in Asian Religions*, ed. James Benn et al. (Honolulu: University of Hawaii Press, forthcoming). There are also several helpful references to Mindröling in Gene Smith, *Among Tibetan Texts: History and Literature of the Himalayan Plateau* (Boston: Wisdom, 2001), 17, 18, 20, 230, 248, 330. Since Mindröling is known for its musical liturgy, ethnomusicologists also have conducted valuable research on Mindröling tradition. See n21.

11. See Janet Gyatso, "Image as Presence: The Place of the Work of Art in Tibetan Religious Thinking," in *The Newark Museum Tibetan Collection III. Sculpture and Painting*, ed. Valrae Reynolds, Amy Heller, and Janet Gyatso (Newark, NJ: Newark Museum, 1986), 30–35. Beyond the Tibetan context, on the role of images in

INTRODUCTION

Japanese Buddhism, see *Living Images: Japanese Buddhist Icons in Context*, ed. Robert H. Sharf and Elizabeth Horton Sharf (Stanford, CA: Stanford University Press, 2002). The complex place of images in South Asian Buddhism is addressed in Robert DeCaroli, *Image Problems: The Origin and Development of Buddha's Image in Early South Asia* (Seattle: University of Washington Press, 2015).

12. *Lamp of Teachings Catalogue*, 277.

13. Tulku Thondop Rinpoche, *Hidden Teachings of Tibet: An Explanation of the Terma Tradition of Tibetan Buddhism*, ed. Harold Talbott (Boston: Wisdom, 1997), 41.

14. A helpful meditation on the theme of "mentality" and its applications is Michel Vovelle, *Ideologies and Mentalities,* trans. Eamon O'Flaherty (Chicago: University of Chicago Press, 1990). In his introduction to this useful collection of essays Vovelle describes mentality as "visions of the world," a definition he attributes to Robert Mandrou, 5. In this study I also use "worldview."

15. Gillian Brock and Harry Brighouse, *The Political Philosophy of Cosmopolitanism* (New York: Cambridge University Press, 2005), 4.

16. A relevant study of cosmopolitanism and its complex relationship to nationalism is Craig Calhoun, *Nations Matter: Culture, History, and the Cosmopolitan Dream* (New York: Routledge, 2007), 24–26, 7–8, 13–14.

17. According to the *Oxford English Dictionary* (*OED*), https://www.oed.com/, "aesthetic" is defined as: A. "Of or pertaining to things perceptible to the senses, things material" and further, "1. Of or pertaining to the sensuous perceptions, received by the senses. 2. Of or pertaining to the appreciation or criticism of the beautiful. 3. Having or showing an appreciation of the beautiful or pleasing; tasteful and refined of taste. Of things: In accordance with the principles of good taste (or what is conventionally regarded as such)."And "aesthetics" is defined as: B. "The science which treats the conditions of the sensuous perceptions."

18. This book takes part in a broader turn in the study of religion toward materiality, affect, and aesthetics. See for example Webb Keane, "The Evidence of the Senses and the Materiality of Religion," Special issue: The Objects of Evidence: Anthropological Approaches to the Production of Knowledge, *Journal of the Royal Anthropological Institute* 14 (2008): 110–27; Brigit Meyers, ed., *Aesthetic Formations: Media, Religion, and the Senses* (London: Palgrave Macmillan, 2009); Melissa Gregg et al., eds., *The Affect Theory Reader* (London and Durham, NC: Duke University Press, 2010); Tim Hutchings and Joanne McKenzie, eds., *Materiality and the Study of Religion: The Stuff of the Sacred* (New York: Routledge, 2017); Inken Prohl, "Aesthetics," in *Key Terms in Material Religion*, ed. S. Brent Plate, 9–16 (New York: Bloomsbury Academic, 2015); Sally M. Promey, ed., *Sensational Religion: Sensory Cultures in Material Practice* (New Haven, CT, and London: Yale University Press, 2014).

19. Zehou Li, *Four Essays on Aesthetics, Towards a Global View,* trans. Jane Cauvel (Lanham, MD: Lexington Books, 2006), 22.

20. DL *Letters*, 500.3–6.

21. Michael Monhart notes that in writing about ritual music, Terdak Lingpa used *snyan pa* (pleasant or inspiring to hear), *yid 'phrog* (charming, alluring or ravishing to the mind), and *yid 'ong* (beautiful, charming, attractive). See Michael

Monhart, "Listening with the Gods: Offering, Beauty and Being in Tibetan Ritual Music," *Revue D'Etudes Tibétaines: Studies in the Tibetan Performing Arts* 40 (July 2017): 92–102. For more on Mindröling's musical tradition, see Daniel Scheidegger, "Tibetan Ritual Music: A General Survey with Special Reference to the Mindröling Tradition," in *Opuscula Tibetana*, fasc. 19 (Rikon: Tibet Institute, 1988); and Terry Ellingson, "The Mandala of Sound: Concepts and Sound Structures in Tibetan Ritual Music" (PhD diss., University of Wisconsin, 1979). More generally, Mireille Helffer has demonstrated how Tibetans applied their own distinct musical aesthetics to the Buddhist Indic traditions. See Mireille Helffer, *Mchod-rol: Les instruments de la musique tibetaine* (Paris: CNRS Editions, 1994), 9.

22. On ritual efficacy in regard to exorcism rites to expel Mongol armies, see James Gentry, "Representations of Efficacy: The Ritual Expulsion of Mongol Armies in the Consolidation and Expansion of the Tsang (Gtsang) Dynasty," in *Tibetan Ritual*, ed. José Ignacio Cabezón (New York: Oxford University Press, 2010), 131–64.

23. Many tantric Buddhist images appear violent. Such images traditionally are interpreted as "liberating," but the significance of symbolic violence and the occasional examples of physical violence associated with wrathful tantric images is also important to consider. On violence in the Tibetan context, see Jacob Dalton, *The Taming of the Demons: Violence and Liberation in Tibetan Buddhism* (New Haven, CT: Yale University Press, 2011). On Japanese examples, see Bernard Faure, "Buddhism and Violence," in *The Cambridge Companion to Religious Studies*, ed. Robert A. Orsi (Cambridge: Cambridge University Press, 2012), 255–72.

24. The historical relationship between these related terms and their usage since Tibetan Imperial times is a subject for further research. Fernanda Pirie traces the history of the term *khrims gnyis* in "Which 'Two Laws'? The Concept of trimnyi (khrims gnyis) in Medieval Tibet," *Cahiers d'Extrême-Asie, Droit et Bouddhisme. Principe et pratique dans le Tibet prémoderne/Law and Buddhism. Principle and Practice in Pre-modern Tibet* 26 (2017): 41–60.

25. As an introduction to this term, see David Seyfort Ruegg, "Introductory Remarks on the Spiritual and Temporal Orders," in *The Relationship Between Religion and State (chos srid zung 'brel) in Traditional Tibet*, ed. Chistoph Cüppers (Lumbini, Nepal: Lumbini International Research Institute, 2004), 9–14. This book is an excellent collection of empirical studies on the dynamics of *chos srid zung 'brel* based on a specific cases from the tenth to eighteenth centuries in China, Tibet, and Inner Asia.

26. In 2011, the Fourteenth Dalai Lama, Tenzin Gyatso, officially resigned as a political leader, ceding his position's authority to a democratically elected official. Global media outlets covered this event widely. For an overview, see John Hudson, "What the Dalai Lama's Political Resignation Means for Tibet," *Atlantic*, March 10, 2011, https://www.theatlantic.com/international/archive/2011/03/what-dalai-lamas-retirement-means-tibetan-freedom-movement/348726/. For a study of the contemporary engagement with democracy in the Tibetan exile community, see Trine Brox, *Tibetan Democracy: Governance, Leadership and Conflict in Exile* (London: I. B. Tauris, 2016).

27. *The Illusive Play: The Autobiography of the Fifth Dalai Lama*, trans. Samten Karmay (Chicago: Serindia, 2014) 17.

28. For an example of this tension in the Fifth Dalai Lama's writing, see *Illusive Play*, trans. Karmay, 73. On the ambivalence about worldly subjects of learning during this period more generally, see Dominique Townsend, "Buddhism's Worldly Other: Secular Subjects of Tibetan Learning," *Himalaya: The Journal for the Association of Nepal and Himalayan Studies* 36, no. 1 (May 2016): article 15.

29. *Lamp of Teachings Cat.*, 343–44. I address this passage in detail in chapter 2.

30. Gene Smith discusses the Terma (*gter ma*) of Terdak Lingpa in this 2005 interview: https://www.khandrorinpoche.org/teachings/video/gene-smith-on-the-mindrolling-lineage/ (accessed January 17, 2020).

31. On the history and significance of the Treasure tradition, see Janet Gyatso, "Drawn from the Tibetan Treasury: The gTer ma Literature," in *Tibetan Literature: Studies in Genre*, ed. José Ignacio Cabezón and Roger R. Jackson (Ithaca, NY: Snow Lion, 1996), 147–69; "The Logic of Legitimation in Tibetan Treasure Tradition," *History of Religions* 33, no. 2 (1993): 97–134; *Apparitions of the Self: The Secret Biography of a Tibetan Visionary* (Princeton, NJ: Princeton University Press, 1988); Tulku Thondop Rinpoche, *Hidden Teachings of Tibet* (Somerville, MA: Wisdom, 1997); Michael Aris, *Hidden Treasures and Secret Lives: A Study of Pemalingpa, 1450–1521, and the Sixth Dalai Lama, 1683–1706* (London and New York: Kegan Paul International, 1989); Andreas Doctor, *Tibetan Treasure Literature: Revelation, Tradition and Accomplishment in Visionary Buddhism* (Ithaca, NY: Snow Lion, 2005); Antonio Terrone, "Anything Is an Appropriate Treasure Teaching! Authentic Treasure Revealers and the Moral Implications of Noncelibate Tantric Practice," in *Tibetan Studies: An Anthology. Proceedings of the Eleventh Seminar of the International Association of Tibetan Studies, 2006*. ed. Peter Schwieger and Saadet Arslan (Halle: International Institute for Tibetan and Buddhist Studies, 2009), 458–86; Daniel Hirschberg, *Padmasambhava in the History of Tibet's Golden Age* (Somerville, MA: Wisdom, 2016); and Robert Mayer, "Rethinking Treasure (part one)," *Revue d'Études Tibetaines* 52 (October 2019): 119–84.

32. Tulku Thondop Rinpoche, *Hidden Teachings of Tibet*, 71.

33. In this regard, Pierre Bourdieu's work on taste, education, social status, and authority is useful in analyzing these factors at Mindröling. See Bourdieu, *Distinction: A Social Critique of the Judgment of Taste*, trans. Richard Nice (Cambridge, MA: Harvard University Press, 1984); Bourdieu, *Homo Academicus*, trans. Peter Collier (Paris: Editions de Minuit, 1988); Pierre Bourdieu and Jean-Claude Passeron, *Reproduction in Education, Society and Culture* (London: Sage, 1990); and Bourdieu with Monique de Saint Martin, *The State Nobility: Elite Schools in the Field of Power*, trans. Lauretta Clough (Cambridge: Polity Press, 1996).

34. For a brief history of ritual or "magical" warfare, see Bryan Cuevas, "The Politics of Magical Warfare," in *Faith and Empire: Art and Politics in Tibetan Buddhism*, ed. Karl Debreczeny (New York: Rubin Museum of Art, 2019), 171–89.

35. Beth Hinderliter et al., *Communities of Sense: Rethinking Aesthetics and Politics* (Durham, NC: Duke University Press, 2009), 19.

36. Jacques Rancière, "Contemporary Art and the Politics of Aesthetics," in *Communities of Sense: Rethinking Aesthetics and Politics*, ed. Beth Hinderliter et al. (Durham, NC: Duke University Press, 2009), 31.

37. On the author of these two seminal works, see Lauran Hartley, "Self as a Faithful Public Servant in the Autobiography by mDo khar Tse ring dbang rgyal," in *Mapping the Modern in Tibet, PIATS 2006: Proceedings of the Eleventh Seminar of the International Association for Tibetan Studies*, ed. Gray Tuttle (Andiast, Switzerland: International Association for Tibetan and Buddhist Studies, 2011), 45–73.

38. William Clark's work is especially relevant in regard to Mindröling's similarities to a university. Most notably, he wrote a study of the origins of the modern research university in the West, *Academic Charisma and the Origins of the Research University* (Chicago: University of Chicago Press, 2007).

39. While these questions are new to the field of Tibetan studies, several scholars of Buddhism more generally have approached similar topics. John Kieschnick's work on Chinese Buddhist material culture, for example, has helped fill in the backdrop of this study. See Kieschnick, *The Impact of Buddhism on Chinese Material Culture* (Princeton, NJ: Princeton University Press, 2003), 1–23 and 116–38. Another helpful study for comparison to the Tibetan case is Eiko Ikegami's sociological work on Tokugawa Japan, *Bonds of Civility: Aesthetic Networks and the Political Origins of Japanese Culture* (New York: Cambridge University Press, 2005), 286–359.

40. Alison Melnick's unpublished dissertation, "The Life and Times of Mingyur Peldrön: Female Leadership in 18th-Century Tibetan Buddhism" (University of Virginia, 2014) offers a productive reading of the biography of Terdak Lingpa's daughter.

1. Historical Background

1. I refer to the family group as a "clan" since its members traced their history to a common prehistoric ancestor.

2. The common spelling for the clan's name is *"gnyos,"* but the biographies of Terdak Lingpa and the Sixth Dalai Lama both spell the name *"smyos"* in this origin story.

3. TL *Outer Bio.*, 1–207, f. 20a. This passage is found in Terdak Lingpa's "outer" biography *(phyi yi rnam thar)* written in 1689, as opposed to his "inner" biography or account of his spiritual experiences *(nang gyi rtogs pa brjod pa)* written in 1713. I consult both in this chapter. See also TL *Inner Bio.*

4. For an in-depth study of this period see Ronald Davidson, *Tibetan Renaissance: Tantric Buddhism in the Rebirth of Tibetan Culture* (New York: Columbia University Press, 2005).

5. On this historical context, see Rolf A. Stein, *Tibetan Civilization* (Stanford, CA: Stanford University Press, 1972), 81–89.

6. Luciano Petech, *China and Tibet in the Early 18th Century* (Leiden: E. J. Brill, 1972), 32–50.

7. For more on the relationship of Imperial Tibet to the development of a sense of Tibetan nation, see Georges Dreyfus, "Cherished Memories, Cherished Communities: Proto-nationalism in Tibet," in *The History of Tibet: Volume 2 The Medieval Period: c. AD 850-1895, the Development of Buddhist Paramountcy* (New York: Routledge, 2003).

8. Janet Gyatso provides a persuasive description of the move toward a "scientific sensibility." See Gyatso, *Being Human in a Buddhist World: An Intellectual History of Medicine in Early Modern Tibet* (New York: Columbia University Press, 2015), 5.

9. On early modernity in Tibet, see Kurtis R. Schaeffer, "New Scholarship in Tibet 1650–1700," in *Forms of Knowledge in Early Modern Asia: Explorations in the Intellectual History of India and Tibet 1500–1800*, ed. Sheldon Pollock (Durham, NC: Duke University Press, 2011), 291–310; Janet Gyatso, "Experience, Empiricism, and the Fortunes of Authority: Tibetan Medicine and Buddhism on the Eve of Modernity," in *Forms of Knowledge in Early Modern Asia: Explorations in the Intellectual History of India and Tibet, 1500–1800*, ed. Sheldon Pollock (Durham, NC: Duke University Press, 2011), 311–35; and Matthew Kapstein, "Just Where on Jambudvīpa Are We? New Geographical Knowledge and Old Cosmological Schemes in Eighteenth-Century Tibet," in *Forms of Knowledge in Early Modern Asia: Explorations in the Intellectual History of India and Tibet 1500–1800*, ed. Sheldon Pollock (Durham, NC: Duke University Press, 2011), 336–64.

10. For a brief version of this tale, see TL *Outer Bio.*, 19b–20b. A more elaborate version is told in the Sixth Dalai Lama's biography of the Sixth Dalai Lama. See Sangs rgyas rgya mtsho, *Tshangs dbyangs rgya mtsho'i rnam thar* [Biography of Tsangyang Gyatso], TBRC W1KG9087, 2 vols. (Gangtok, Sikkim: Chhentse labrang, 1980), 106–7. The story is followed by a lengthy explanation of the family line, 106–12. See also Per K. Sørensen and Guntram Hazod in cooperation with Tsering Gyalpo, *Rulers on the Celestial Plain: Ecclesiastic and Secular Hegemony in Medieval Tibet: A Study of Tshal Gung-thang* (Vienna: Osterreichische Akademie der Wissenschaften, 2007), 415.

11. TL *Outer Bio.*, 20a–20b.

12. On "crazy wisdom" in Tibet and Buddhism, see David DiValerio, *The Holy Madmen of Tibet* (New York: Oxford University Press, 2015). DiValerio prefers "holy madness" to "crazy yogin," 3.

13. David Jackson, *Tantric Treasures: The Collections of Mystical Verse from Buddhist India* (New York: Oxford University Press, 2004), 3–52.

14. For example, see Han-Shan, *The Collected Songs of Cold Mountain*, trans. Bill Porter (Port Townsend, WA: Copper Canyon Press, 2000).

15. TL *Outer Bio.*, 19b.

16. As Pierre Bourdieu persuasively argued, the defining links between high social standing, education, and cultural and political authority are common across diverse societies. See Bourdieu, *Distinction: A Social Critique of the Judgment of Taste*, trans. Richard Nice (Cambridge, MA: Harvard University Press, 1984); Bourdieu, *Homo Academicus*, trans. Peter Collier (Paris: Editions de Minuit, 1988); Bourdieu and Jean-Claude Passeron, *Reproduction in Education, Society, and Culture*, trans. Richard Nice (London: Sage, 1990); Bourdieu and Monique de Saint Martin, *The State Nobility: Elite Schools in the Field of Power*, trans. Loretta C. Clough (Cambridge: Polity Press, 1996). Concerning Mindröling's historical background, Bourdieu's concept of the "fields of power" can apply to Mindröling and its relationship to the early modern Tibetan government. According to this model, the dominant poles of power are typically the political or economic power base on one side and the intellectual or artistic power base on the other. The Fifth Dalai

Lama's Ganden Podrang government and the founders of Mindröling made up the dominant poles of one field of power. The Lhasa-based Géluk government occupied the dominant political pole, and Mindröling an intellectual and artistic pole generating cultural production. This frame will help illuminate the distribution of power and influence that took place around the founding of Mindröling as a distinctly Nyingma institution with immense cultural capital and crucial connections to the Géluk establishment. Mindröling was not by any means the only occupant of the cultural pole in its time and place, but it was one dominant agent in this field of power and helps illustrate how monasteries and other religious institutions fulfill such roles.

17. Per K. Sørensen, "Control Over the lHa-sa Mandala Zone: Geo-political Schemes, Notional Monuments, Flood Control Politics and Ideological Battlefield," in *Rulers of the Celestial Plan: Ecclesiastic and Secular Hegemony in Medieval Tibet: A Study of Tshal Gung-thang* (Vienna: Osterreichische Akademie der Wissenschaften, 2007), vol. 2, 381.

18. For a brief overview of differing accounts of their travels to India and Nepal, see Davidson, *Tibetan Renaissance*, 143.

19. There are excellent English translations of Marpa and Milarepa's life stories. See Chogyam Trungpa, trans., *The Life of Marpa the Translator: Seeing Accomplishes All* (Boston: Shambhala, 1982); and Andrew Quintman, trans., *The Life of Milarepa* (New York: Penguin, 2010).

20. Sørensen and Hazod, *Rulers on the Celestial Plains*, 382.

21. Sørensen and Hazod, *Rulers on the Celestial Plains*, 384–85.

22. Sørensen and Hazod, *Rulers on the Celestial Plains*, 382.

23. Sørensen and Hazod, *Rulers on the Celestial Plains*, 353.

24. Sørensen and Hazod, *Rulers on the Celestial Plains*, 413. The first examples of the "chos srid" merger took place in Western Tibet, for instance in the kingdom of Gugé (*Gu ge*). On Lama Zhang, see Carl Yamamoto, *Vision and Violence: Lama Zhang and the Politics of Charisma in Twelfth-Century Tibet* (Leiden: Brill, 2012)

25. For a detailed history of the particular transmission of Great Perfection active at Dargyé Chöling and Mindröling, see Bryan J. Cuevas, *The Hidden History of the Tibetan Book of the Dead* (Oxford: Oxford University Press, 2003), 57–68.

26. For example, on gender and class in seventeenth-century China and in particular elite women's culture in seventeenth-century Jiangnan, China, see Dorothy Ko, *Teachers of the Inner Chamber: Women and Culture in Seventeenth-Century China* (Stanford, CA: Stanford University Press, 1994).

27. There are three main types of lineage in Tibetan Buddhism: (1) lineages that pass from teacher to student; (2) lineages based on identification of the reincarnation of the lineage head after his or her death and supposed rebirth; (3) family lineages.

28. In Sam van Schaik's introduction to *Approaching the Great Perfection* (Somerville, MA: Wisdom, 2004), he supplies a translation of one such early text, 4.

29. Van Schaik has a helpful overview of critiques of Great Perfection based on perceived similarities with Chinese Buddhism, which Tibetan sources claim was rejected during Tibet's imperial period (*Approaching the Great Perfection*, 15).

30. Jacob P. Dalton, *The Gathering of Intentions: The History of a Tibetan Buddhist Tantra* (New York: Columbia University Press, 2016). Dalton cites Dharmaśrī as distinguishing between Garap Dorjé's holding of all nine vehicles and Déwa Seldzé's gathering of the vehicles into the first Sutra Initiation ritual manuals, 105–6.
31. Dalton, *Gathering of Intentions*, 97–113.
32. In his historical study, *The Great Perfection (rDzogs chen): A Philosophical and Meditative Teaching*, Samten Gyaltsen Karmay summarizes the system as "a syncretism of the Mahayoga tantric teachings on the one hand, the theories of 'Primal Spontaneity' and 'Primal Purity' on the other" (Karmay, *Great Perfection* [Leiden: Brill, 2007], 11).
33. Van Schaik, *Approaching the Great Perfection*, 5.
34. For an introduction to the preliminaries of Great Perfection practice, see The Third Dzogchen Rinpoche, *The Great Perfection: Outer and Inner Preliminaries*, trans. Cortland Dahl (Boston: Shambhala, 2008).
35. On the history of the term *ris med* in the context of Great Perfection philosophy and practice, see Marc-Henri Deroche, "On Being 'Impartial' (*ris med*): From Non-Sectarianism to the Great Perfection," *Revue d'Etudes Tibétaines* 44 (2018): 129–58.
36. Ian Baker and Thomas Laird, *The Dalai Lama's Secret Temple: Tantric Wall Paintings from Tibet* (London: Thames and Hudson, 2000); Ian Baker, "Embodying Enlightenment: Physical Culture in Dzogchen as Revealed in Tibet's Lukhang Murals," *Asian Medicine* 7 (2012): 225–64.
37. On the Bön tradition of Great Perfection, see Dylan Esler, "The Origins and Early History of rDzogs Chen," *Tibet Journal* 30, no. 3 (Autumn 2005): 33–62.
38. For an overview of Longchenpa's work, see the translators' introduction in *Finding Rest in the Nature of the Mind: The Trilogy of Rest*, Volume 1, translated by Padmakara Translation Group (Boulder, CO: Shambhala, 2017), xix–xlvii.
39. Bryan Cuevas, "The Politics of Magical Warfare," in *Faith and Empire: Art and Politics in Tibetan Buddhism*, ed. Karl Debreczeny (New York: Rubin Museum of Art, 2019), 172–74.
40. Jam dbyangs rdo rje, Nyoshul Khenpo (Smyo shul Mkhan po), *A Marvelous Garland of Rare Gems: Biographies of Masters of Awareness in the Dzogchen Lineage: A Spiritual History of the History of the Teachings on Natural Great Perfection*, trans. Richard Barron (Junction City, CA: Padma Publishing, 2005), 179.
41. TL *Inner Bio*, 31.
42. YLYD *Bio.*, 347b. This copy of the biography is incomplete and the number of folios missing is unknown at this time.
43. YLYD *Bio.*, 348b.
44. There are several excellent recent works in English on women who are the subjects of biographies and autobiographies. See Kurtis Schaeffer, *Himalayan Hermitess: The Life of a Tibetan Buddhist Nun* (New York: Oxford University Press, 2004); Hildegard Diemberger, *When a Woman Becomes a Religious Dynasty: The Samding Dorje Phagmo of Tibet* (New York: Columbia University Press, 2007); Sarah Jacoby, *Love and Liberation: Autobiographical Writings of the Tibetan Buddhist Visionary Sera Khandro* (New York: Columbia University Press, 2015); Suzanne Bessenger, *Echoes*

of Enlightenment: The Life and Legacy of the Tibetan Saint Sönam Peldren (New York: Oxford University Press, 2016); Holly Gayley, *Love Letters from Golok: A Tantric Couple in Modern Tibet* (New York: Columbia University Press, 2017).

45. Mindrolling Jetsün Khandro Rinpoche and Mindrolling Jetsün Dechen Paldrön, "The Mindrolling History Project" (Stanley, VA: Dharmashri Group, Pema Gatsal, 2015), https://www.lotusgardens.org/dharmashri/mindrolling-history/ (accessed March 23, 2020), 12.

46. YLYD *Bio.*, 348a.

47. YLYD *Bio.*, 348b.

48. YLYD *Bio.*, 349b.

49. YLYD *Bio.*, 349b.

50. YLYD *Bio.*, 349b.

51. YLYD *Bio.*, 346a.

52. YLYD *Bio.*, 346b.

53. Gdung Rin po che, *'Og min O rgyan smin grol gling gi dkar chag dran pa'i me long.* Tashi Tsering of the Amnye Machen Institute generously shared this manuscript with me in 2010. The text has been made available on TBRC: *o rgyan smin grol gling gi dkar chag*, TBRC W1KG15236, 1 vol., s.l.: s.n., n.d., http://tbrc.org/link?RID=W1KG15236, 18 (hereafter cited as *Mirror of Memory Cat.*), 69–73.

54. For example, the Fifth Dalai Lama uses the phrase *sgyu thabs* to describe Terdak Lingpa's activities in the consort letter. See DL *Letters*, 509.

55. TL *Outer Bio.*, 28b–29a.

56. TL *Outer Bio.*, 28b–29a.

57. Dudjom Rinpoché, Jikdrel Yeshe Dorje, *The Nyingma School of Tibetan Buddhism: Its Fundamentals and History*, trans. Gyurmé Dorjé, ed. Matthew Kapstein (Boston: Wisdom, 1991), 80n1119.

58. Two early meetings are described in TL *Inner Bio*, 116–18.

59. Dudjom Rinpoché summarizes these two episodes. See *The Nyingma School of Tibetan Buddhism*, 826.

60. See Yumiko Ishihama, "On the Dissemination of the Belief in the Dalai Lama as a Manifestation of the Bodhisattva Avalokiteśvara," *Acta Asiatica: Bulletin of the Institute of Eastern Culture, Tokyo: The Toho Gakkai* [The Institute of Eastern Culture] 64 (1993): 38–56. In this article on the cult of Avalokiteśvara in Tibet, Yumiko Ishihama demonstrates how public rituals were used to bolster the Dalai Lama's legitimacy.

61. Dudjom Rinpoché, *The Nyingma School of Tibetan Buddhism*, 728.

62. See Dilgo Khyentsé, "Lo chen d+harma shrwi'i gsung 'bum par bskrun dsal bshad," [Introduction to Dharmaśrī's Gsung 'bum], 1–35 in Dharma shrI, Gsung 'bum/_d+harma shrI, TBRC W9140, 20 vols. (Dehradun: D. G. Khochen Tulku, 1999), http://tbrc.org/link?RID=W9140, 18.

63. Heather Stoddard, "The Style and Artistic Context," in *Secret Visions of the Fifth Dalai Lama: The Gold Manuscript in the Fournier Collection Musee Guimet, Paris*, ed. Samten Karmay (London: Serindia, 1991), 11. Stoddard does not provide the Tibetan reference.

64. This association is asserted widely. For example, see TL *Inner Bio*, 18.

65. TL *Letters*.

66. Samten G. Karmay, *Secret Visions of the Fifth Dalai Lama: The Gold Manuscript in the Fournier Collection Musee Guimet* (Paris, London: Serindia, 1988), 8–9.

67. "Mindrolling History Project," https://www.lotusgardens.org/documents /mindrolling-history.pdf (accessed January 22, 2020), 16.

68. TL *Inner Bio*, 130.

69. TL *Inner Bio*, 123; Tulku Thondop Rinpoche, *Hidden Teachings of Tibet: An Explanation of the Terma Tradition of Tibetan Buddhism*, ed. Harold Talbott (Boston: Wisdom, 1997), 73–74.

70. Tulku Thondup, *Hidden Teachings of Tibet*, 78. This passage is found in TL *Inner Bio*, 130.

71. His Treasure collections are: The *Knowledge Holder's Heart Essence* (rig 'dzin thugs thigs), *The Lord of Death Who Destroys Arrogance* (gshin rje dregs 'joms), *The Vajrasattva Atiyoga Cycle* (rdor sems ati skor), and the *Doctrinal Cycle of the Great Compassionate One as the Gathering of All the Sugatas* (thugs rje chen po bde gshegs kun dus kyi chos skor). Accounts of his Treasure revelations are found in TL *Inner Bio*, 123, 140, 157.

72. TL *Inner Bio*, 157.

73. See Richard J. Kohn, *Lord of Dance: The Mani Rimdu Festival in Tibet and Nepal* (New York: SUNY Series in Buddhist Studies, 2001), 49. For an overview of the Lord of Dance ritual's origins at Mindröling and the influence Mindröling exerted over monastic dance traditions more generally, see 49–55.

74. On the Mindröling founders' successful establishment of rituals for large public audiences, see Dalton, *Gathering of Intentions*, chap. 6.

75. I benefited from discussing this passage of the biography with Riga Shakya, who generously shared his alternate translation with me. Miwang *Bio.*, 100.

76. Miwang *Bio.*, 101.

77. Miwang *Bio.*, 100.

2. A Pleasure Grove for the Buddhist Senses

1. Gter bdag gling pa 'gyur med rdo rje, *sgo 'phyor gyi lho ngos ldebs ris su 'khod pa'i gtsug lag khang gi dkar chag* [Catalogue displayed on the wall painting of the southern porch of the main temple] (hereafter cited as *Temple Wall Cat.*), in Bstan pa'i sgron me, *O rgyan smin grol gling gi dkar chag* (Xining: krung go'i bod kyi shes rig dpe skrun khang, 1992), 340–53. *Temple Wall Cat.*, 344.

2. *Lamp of Teachings Cat.*, 12–14.

3. There is abundant evidence of this perspective in the writings of Mindröling authors. One case in point is a letter Terdak Lingpa composed to the Sixth Dalai Lama in which he bemoans the paucity of expertise in Nyingma practices and entreats the Dalai Lama for support and protection, with a focus on the importance of Mahāmudrā and Dzogchen. TL *Letters*, 345–57.

4. Gyurmé Dorjé, "Guyhagharba Tantra: An Introduction," 45–46, http://hankop .blogspot.com/2017/07/an-introduction-to-guhyagarbha-tantra.html (accessed March 10, 2020). (This document appears to be a summary of Gyurmé Dorjé's

introduction, but the only authorship information provided attributes the document to Gyurmé Dorjé himself.) For a brief history of the Guyhagharba Tantra in Tibet, see Sam van Schaik, "In Search of the Guyhagharba Tantra," https://earlytibet.com/2007/08/27/in-search-of-the-guhyagarbha-tantra/ (accessed March 23, 2020).

5. Here I adapt the definition provided by Annabella Pitkin, "Lineage, Authority and Innovation: The Biography of Ku Nu Bla Ma Bstan 'Dzin Rgyal Mtshan," in *Mapping the Modern in Tibet*, PIATS 2006: *Proceedings of the Eleventh Seminar of the International Association for Tibetan Studies*, ed. Gray Tuttle (Andiast, Switzerland: International Association for Tibetan and Buddhist Studies, 2011), 174.

6. On what has been dubbed the "string of pearls fallacy," and more generally the importance of lineage histories in the Chan context, see John McRae, *Seeing Through Zen: Encounter, Transformation, and Genealogy in Chinese Chan Buddhism* (Berkeley: University of California Press, 2003).

7. Other major women teachers include Jetsün Trinlé Chödron (rje btsun ma 'phrin las chos sgron), who was the Great Perfection teacher of nineteenth-century masters such as Jamyang Khyentsé Wangpo (1820–1892) and Jamgön Kongtrul Lodrö Tayé (1813–1899); the twentieth-century female practitioner Jetsün Tséwang Lhamo (d. 1995); and Jetsün Tsering Paldrön, better known as Khandro Rinpoche, a world-renowned Buddhist master today. Her sister, Jetsün Dechen Paldrön, maintains a low profile but is an accomplished scholar, historian, and translator.

8. A Mindröling lineage prayer, which is attributed to Mingyur Peldrön, can be found here: https://www.lotsawahouse.org/tibetan-masters/jetsun-mingyur -paldron/lineage-prayer (accessed February 1, 2020).

9. Such a prediction is recorded in Mingyur Peldrön's biography: Khyung po ras pa 'gyur med 'od gsal, *rje btsun mi 'gyur dpal gyi sgron ma'i rnam thar dad pa'i gdung sel* (Thimpu, Bhutan: National Library of Bhutan, 1984) (hereafter cited as MP *Bio.*), 63.

10. Two recent works that reveal the complexity of the social roles of tantric consort are: Sarah Jacoby, *Love and Liberation: Autobiographical Writings of the Tibetan Buddhist Visionary Sera Khandro* (New York: Columbia University Press, 2016); and Holly Gayley, "Revisiting the 'Secret Consort' (*gsang yum*) in Tibetan Buddhism," *Religions* 9, no. 6 (June 2018): 179/1–21.

11. For a comparable case study, see Dorothy Ko, *Teachers of the Inner Chamber: Women and Culture in Seventeenth-Century China* (Stanford, CA: Stanford University Press, 1994).

12. For instance, Jetsün Kunga Tenpé Nyima (*rje btsun kun dga bstan pa'i nyi ma*, 1704–1760) was a prominent female Sakya teacher. Accordingly, she was also the subject of a biography. See Gene Smith, *sa skya'i bla ma 'ga' yi rnam thar phyogs bsgrigs* [Collected Sakya Biographies], TBRC W1KG9245.2.

13. In addition to the biographies of women composed during this period already cited. See also the Treasure rediscovery of Yeshé Tsogyel's biography: Nus ldan rdo rje (b. 1655), "Mkhar chen bza' mkha' 'gro ye shes mtsho rgyal gyi rnam thar" [Biography of Yeshé Tsogyel], in *bka' thang dri ma med pa'i rgyan* (Lhasa: Bod ljongs mi dmangs dpe skrun khang, 2006), 154–91. TBRC W1PD83974.

14. *Lamp of Teachings Cat.*, 126–28. This section outlines the basic information about the first three throne holders. An account of the full list of throne holders until the twentieth century is available in *Lamp of Teachings Cat.*, 126–30.
15. For more on the first abbot, see *Lamp of Teachings Cat.*, 130 and 377. For a full list of the abbots until the middle of the twentieth century, see *Lamp of Teachings Cat.*, 130–133. Tenpé Nyima's training is described briefly in Mindrolling Jetsün Khandro Rinpoche and Mindrolling Jetsün Dechen Paldrön, "The Mindrolling History Project," (Stanley, VA: Dharmashri Group, Pema Gatsal, 2015), https://www.lotusgardens.org/dharmashri/mindrolling-history/, 23.
16. On the role of ideals of sacred kingship in "proto-nationalism" in Tibet, see George Dreyfus, "Cherished Memories, Cherished Communities: Proto-nationalism in Tibet," in *The History of Tibet: Volume 2 The Medieval Period: c. AD 850-1895, the Development of Buddhist Paramountcy,* ed. Alex McKay (New York: Routledge, 2003), 492–522.
17. For an invaluable and in-depth analysis of the history of education at one such monastery, see José Cabezón and Penpa Dorjee, *Sera Monastery* (Boston: Wisdom, 2019), 147–302.
18. Bryan J. Cuevas, *The Hidden History of the Tibetan Book of the Dead* (New York: Oxford University Press, 2003), 67.
19. The year was the fire snake year, 1676. TL *Outer Bio.*, 93b.
20. TL *Outer Bio.*, 94a.
21. TL *Outer Bio.*, 94a.
22. TL *Outer Bio.*, 94a.
23. Berthe Jansen's work drew my attention to this important feature of the Mindröling monastic guidelines. See Jansen, *The Monastery Rules: Buddhist Monastic Organization in Premodern Tibet* (Oakland: University of California Press, 2018), 124–25, 132. (Due to a typo the date of the *bca' yig* is misprinted in Jansen's book as 1698; it should be 1689.) I am indebted to her for sharing her archive of notes on the Mindröling *bca' yig* with me.
24. These figures also appear in TL *Outer Bio.*, 94a.
25. TL *Inner Bio.*, 140.
26. *Lamp of Teachings Cat.*, 12.
27. *Lamp of Teachings Cat.*, 2.
28. The status of these monks as opposed to those who are staying at Mindröling temporarily for training is expanded on in *Lamp of Teachings Cat.*, 155–59.
29. Desi Sangyé Gyatso, *Vaidurya Serpo* (Ziling: Krung go bod kyi shes rig dpe skrun khang, 1989), 468.
30. The inhabitants are referred to as servants of the temple or "serfs" (*lha 'bangs*), implying that the people would become subjects of the monastic estate (*Lamp of Teachings Cat.*, 12).
31. TL *Outer Bio.*, 124a–125b.
32. On monastic economy, see Jansen, *Monastery Rules*, chap. 5.
33. *Mirror of Memory Cat.*, 134–36.
34. *Lamp of Teachings Cat.*, 6.
35. For an overview of these events and the community response, see *Lamp of Teachings Cat.*, 4–7.

36. MP *Bio.*, 80.1–80.3.
37. Tsepon Wangchuk Deden Shakabpa, *One Hundred Thousand Moons: An Advanced History of Tibet*, Volume 1, trans. Derek F. Maher (Leiden: Brill, 2010), 421.
38. See Jansen, *Monastery Rules*, 132.
39. *Mirror of Memory Cat.*, 1.
40. On the history of the Gar (*mgar*) clan and its members' role as imperial Tibetan ministers, see Hugh Richardson, *High Peaks, Rare Earth: Collected Writings on Tibetan History and Culture* (London: Serindia, 2005), 57–73.
41. On this period in general, see Ronald M. Davidson, *Tibetan Renaissance: Tantric Buddhism in the Rebirth of Tibetan Culture* (New York: Columbia University Press, 2005).
42. *Lamp of Teachings Cat.*, 2.
43. *Mirror of Memory Cat.*, 1–5.
44. *Temple Wall Cat.*, 348.
45. This refers to the part of the shrine with the most important images.
46. These are the "three wheels" of reading, hearing, and contemplation.
47. *Temple Wall Cat.*, 343–44.
48. Pema Bhum photographed a section of what appears to be the *Temple Wall Catalogue* (*dkar chag*) during a visit to Mindröling in the late 2000s. A monk guide told him the wall painting had been whitewashed during the Cultural Revolution and subsequently scrubbed clean. Pema Bhum said he was struck by the outstanding quality of the calligraphy and noted that two monks present at the monastery during his visit were practicing to emulate the seventeenth-century style preserved on the wall (personal communication, November 2019).
49. *Lamp of Teachings Cat.*, 353.
50. An excellent overview of the history of the concept is found in Marc-Henri Deroche, "On Being 'Impartial' (*Ris Med*): From Non-Sectarianism to the Great Perfection," *Revue d'Etudes Tibétaines* 44 (2018): 129–58.
51. E. Gene Smith, "Jam mgon kong sprul and the Nonsectarian Movement," in *Among Tibetan Texts: History and Literature of the Himalayan Plateau,* ed. Kurtis Schaeffer (Boston: Wisdom, 2001), 235–72.
52. E. Gene Smith, "Mipham and the Philosophical Controversies of the Nineteenth Century," in *Among Tibetan Texts: History and Literature of the Himalayan Plateau,* ed. Kurtis Schaeffer (Boston: Wisdom, 2001), 227–34. A useful study of Mipham's life is found in Douglas Duckworth, *Jamgön Mipham: His Life and Teachings* (Boston: Shambhala, 2011).
53. See for instance the statement attributed to Mipham Jamyang Namgyal Gyatso on Mindröling's early days as a golden age for benefiting beings through the Buddhist Dharma. Jikdrel Yeshe Dorje Dudjom Rinpoché, *The Nyingma School of Tibetan Buddhism: Its Fundamentals and History,* trans. Gyurmé Dorjé, ed. Matthew Kapstein (Boston: Wisdom, 1991), 879.
54. Alexander Gardner critiqued the term "nonsectarian movement" as a fabrication inadvertently mischaracterized by Gene Smith. See Gardner, "The Twenty-five Great Sites of Khams: Religious Geography, Revelation, and Nonsectarianism in Nineteenth-Century Eastern Tibet" (PhD diss., University of Michigan,

2006), 112–17. Amy Holmes-Tagchungpa further developed Gardner's initial critique, suggesting that "pansectarian" would be a more appropriate rendering of "ris med" than "nonsectarian." See Holmes-Tagchungpa, *The Social Life of Tibetan Biography: Textuality, Community, and Authority in the Lineage of Tokden Shakya Shri* (Lanham, MD: Lexington Books, 2014), 44–52.

55. The italics are to highlight the Tibetan term *ris med*, here translated as "unbiased." TL *Inner Bio.*, 2.

56. TL *Letters*, 12, 13, 50, 54.

57. TL *Letters*, 84.

58. TL *Letters*, 81.

59. Pema Bhum confirmed this range of meanings, which I recognize is broader than generally understood. Personal communication, April 2020.

60. See YLYD *Bio.*

61. *Lamp of Teachings Cat.*, 185.

62. Education in the worldly subjects of *rig gnas* (*tha snyad kyi gnas*) was a point of pride in Terdak Lingpa's family history. Expertise in both religious practice and the conventional fields of knowledge are documented. For instance, see TL *Outer Bio.*, 21–21a.

63. A useful overview of these traditional fields of learning is found in Sangye Tender Naga, "Aspects of Traditional Tibetan Learning," *Tibet Journal* 31, no. 3 (2006): 3–16, http://www.jstor.org/stable/43300980 (accessed April 1, 2020).

64. Georges B.J. Dreyfus, *The Sound of Two Hands Clapping: The Education of a Tibetan Buddhist Monk* (Berkeley and Los Angeles: University of California Press, 2003), 120–23.

65. Jacob P. Dalton, "Recreating the Rnyingma School: The Mdo dbang Tradition of Smin grol gling," in *Power, Politics, and the Reinvention of Tradition: Tibet in the 17th and 18th Centuries, PIATS 2003: Tibetan Studies: Proceedings of the 10th Seminar of the International Association for Tibetan Studies, Oxford, 2003*, Vol. 10/3, ed. Bryan J. Cuevas and Kurtis R. Schaeffer (Leiden; Boston: Brill, 2006), 93n3, quoting Richard J. Kohn, *Lord of Dance: The Mani Rimdu Festival in Tibet and Nepal* (New York: SUNY Series in Buddhist Studies, 2001), 49–50.

66. There are six mother monasteries (*ma dgon drug*), which are principal centers for Nyingma practice. They were all founded (or in one case expanded and reconceived) during the seventeenth century. In Central Tibet they include Mindröling, founded in 1676, and the nearby Dorjé Drak (*rdo rje brag*), founded in 1610. In Eastern Tibet, the mother monasteries are Kathok (*kaHthog*), founded in 1159 and reestablished in 1656; Palyul (*dpal yul*), founded in 1665; Dzogchen (*rdzogs chen*), founded in 1675; and Shechen (*zhe chen*), founded in 1695. I have not encountered the term "mother monastery" in Mindröling documents written during the first few decades of the monastery's existence. The term is used in the sections of the *Lamp of Teachings Cat.* composed in the twentieth century, for instance, *Lamp of Teachings Cat.*, 154.

67. On alterations to the institutional identity and the curriculum at Kathok, one of the Nyingma mother monasteries, beginning in the seventeenth century, and on the influence of Mindröling's traditions in this process, see Jann Ronis,

"Celibacy, Revelations, and Reincarnated Lamas: Contestation and Synthesis in the Growth of Monasticism at Katok Monastery from the 17th through 19th Centuries" (PhD diss., University of Virginia, 2009), chap. 4.

68. On *ngakpa* (*sngags pa*) practice in Eastern Tibet, see: Yangdon Dhondup, Geoffrey Samuel, and Ulrich Pagel, eds., *Monastic and Lay Traditions in North-Eastern Tibet* (Leiden: Brill, 2013).

69. This is according to the monk who guided me through the monastery during a research trip to Lumora, in 2007. He said that the monastic guidelines (*bca' yig*) were also based on those of Mindröling, but he did not have a copy on hand to show me. Personal communication, June 2007.

70. Yangdon Dhondup, "Rules and Regulations of the Reb kong Tantric Community," in *Monastic and Lay Traditions in North-Eastern Tibet*, ed. Yangdon Dhondup, Geoffrey Samuel, and Ulrich Pagel (Leiden: Brill, 2013), 117–40.

71. On the relationship between branch monasteries (*gzhi dgon*) and large monastic educational centers in the Géluk school (*gdan sa*), see José Cabezón and Penpa Dorjee, *Sera Monastery*, 8–9. Berthe Jansen addresses the significance of interregional and international monastic networks that stretched across the Himalayas and neighboring regions in premodern Tibetan societies: Jansen, *Monastery Rules*, 47–48.

72. The list also includes: Nyendo (*snyen mdo*), Metok Kul Pema Gon (*me tog khul padma dgon*), Powo Dungkar Gon (*spo bo dung dkar dgon*), Tsona Khongkar Teng Gon (*mtsho sna khongs skar steng dgon*), Tashi Tongmon Gon (*bkra shis mthong smon dgon*), Jemo Gon (*bye mo dgon*), Lhuntse Kongjor (*lhun rtse khongs sbyor ra so rnying lha khang*), Drakpo Tselegon (*drags po rtse le dgon*), Tsang rong du ri lung buk (*gtsang rong du ri lung sbug*), Gojo tserong draknak gon (*go 'jo rtse rong brag nag dgon*), Gochen gon (*mgo chen dgon*), Gongkar tsechu drubdé (*gong dkar tshes bcu sgrub sde*), and Yartod Karmé Lhakhang (*yar stod dkar me lha khang*). *Lamp of Teachings Cat.*, 153–54.

73. *Lamp of Teachings Cat.*, 154.

74. *Lamp of Teachings Cat.*, 154.

75. *Lamp of Teachings Cat.*, 154. Other monasteries on this list include Ö yug gö ngon lakang (*'od yug gos sngon lha khang*); Rong Örgyan Chöter Ling (*rong O rgyan chos gter gling*); Gyaltsé Ling Bu (*rgyal rtse gling bu dgon*); Panna Palri (*pa sna dpal ri dgon*); and Tödza Rongpu (*stod rdza rong phu*). Given that the list represents just a small number of monasteries that fit within this category of affiliates, it appears these particular sites were chosen as significant examples.

76. In regard to Mindröling's connections to Pemayangtsé monastery, see Saul Mullard, *Opening the Hidden Land: State Formation and the Construction of Sikkimese History*, Brill's Tibetan Studies Library Series (Leiden; Boston: Brill, 2011), 166–70.

77. This period is described in *Lamp of Teachings Cat.*, 3–7. The *Lamp of Teachings* gives the dates of Mingyur Peldrön's exile in Sikkim as 1718–1720. Mullard gives the dates 1720–1722. See Mullard, *Opening the Hidden Land*, 168, 170.

78. *Mirror of Memory*'s list also mentions: Tsang Chödé Ling (*gtsang chos sde gling*); Drösa Orgyen Dzong (*drod sa o rgyan rdzong*); Gurü Tukyi Drupné Tsang Zapulung (*gu ru'i thugs kyi sgrub gnas gtsang zab phu lung*); Nyeljor Ragön (*g.nyal sbyor ra*

dgon); and Nyaklé Densa Kelzang Gön (*nyag bla'i gdan sa skal bzang dgon*) (*Mirror of Memory Cat.*, 133–34).

79. Nicolas Sihlé, "Assessing and Rituals That Reproduce Collectivity: The Large-Scale Rituals of the Repkong Tantrists in Tibet," *Religion and Society* 9, no. 1 (2018): 165–70.

80. *Mirror of Memory Cat.*, 134–36.

81. The history of how these monasteries and other sites became incorporated in the Mindröling fold over the centuries since the monastery was founded is worthy of a book in its own right. More broadly, the institutional relationship of Tibetan monasteries to each other through interregional and international networks warrants further study.

82. *Lamp of Teachings Cat.*, 267. The spelling in the catalogue is "*ti shir*" rather than "*ti shri.*" Dudjom Rinpoché also notes the Dalai Lama's conferral of the title "*Ti-Shih*" on Terdak Lingpa: *The Nyingma School*, 830. Both sources directly connect the conferral of the title with Terdak Lingpa's teaching the Dalai Lama the "Collected Tantras of the Ancients" (*snga 'gyur rgyud 'bum*).

83. Shakabpa, *One Hundred Thousand Moons*, 384.

84. This fraught period is documented in Sangyé Gyatso's account of the period between the death of the Fifth Dalai Lama and the announcement of the Sixth Dalai Lama. See Sangs rgyas rgya mtsho, *Sku lnga pa drug par 'phos pa'i gtam rna ba'i bcun len 'bring bsdud sgrogs sbyangs kyis gsang rgya khrom bsgrags gnang skor* [Account of the interim between the Fifth and Sixth Dalai Lamas] (Lhasa: bod ljongs mis dmangs dpe skrun khang, 1989), 84–87.

85. Desi Sangyé Gyatso, *Life of the Fifth Dalai Lama*. Vol. IV, Part I, trans. Zahiruddin Ahmad (New Delhi: International Academy of Indian Culture and Aditya Prakashan, 1999), 264.

86. Desi Sangyé Gyatso, *Life of the Fifth Dalai Lama*, trans. Zahiruddin Ahmad, 11, 249, 265, 266.

3. Plucking the Strings

1. For historical context focused on diplomatic letters between Mongol rulers and Tibetan hierarchs, see Dieter Schuh, *Erlasse und Sendschreiben mongolischer Herrscher für tibetische Geistliche. Ein Beitrag zur Kenntniss der Urkunden des tibetischen Mittelalters und ihrer Diplomatik* [Regulations and letter exchanges from the Mongol rulers to Tibetan monks: contributing to the understanding of medieval Tibet and its diplomacy] (Monumenta Tibetican Historica. Abt III: Diplomata et Epistolae, Bd. 1.) (St. Augustin: VGH, Wissenschaftsverlag, 1977), xxvii.

2. On the complexities of the position of the secret consort as a social role, see Holly Gayley, "Revisiting the 'Secret Consort' (*gsang yum*) in Tibetan Buddhism," *Religions* 9, no. 6 (June 2018): 179/1–21, DOI: 10.3390/rel9060179.

3. According to Hugh Richardson, in a footnote to his translation of the Dalai Lama's 1679 decree appointing Sangyé Gyatso to the post of regent, the designation "Greater Tibet" included "all of Tibet comprising the three *skor* of Mnga'-ris

(west Tibet), the four *ru* of Dbus and Gtsang and the six *sgang* of Mdo-khams (east Tibet)." Hugh Richardson, *High Peaks, Rare Earth: Collected Writings on Tibetan History and Culture* (London: Serindia, 1998), 458n4.

4. On epistolary forms, see Christina Kilby, "Bowing with Words: Paper, Ink, and Bodies in Tibetan Buddhist Epistles," *Journal of the American Academy of Religion* 87, no. 1 (March 2019): 260–81, DOI: 10.1093/jaarel/lfy036.

5. Hannah Schneider, "Tibetan Epistolary Style," In *The Dalai Lamas: A Visual History*, ed. Martin Brauen (Chicago: Serindia, 2005), 258–62. Schneider's essay addresses how officials should compose letters to the Dalai Lama but not vice versa.

6. An excellent study of intimate communications in modern Tibetan letter writing can be found in Holly Gayley, *Love Letters from Golok: A Tantric Couple in Modern Tibet* (New York: Columbia University Press, 2017).

7. Riga Shakya drew my attention to the significance of the Dalai Lama's use of this drum's name, in contrast to the more usual reference to the *damaru* drum. It comes from the Sanskrit *dundubhi* and in the Tibetan context suggests a massive instrument associated with the grandeur of divinity and royalty.

8. DL *Letters*, 500.3–6.

9. On these terms' relevance to Tibetan ritual arts and "magical warfare," see Bryan Cuevas, "The Politics of Magical Warfare," in *Faith and Empire,* ed. Karl Debreczeny (New York: Rubin Museum of Art, 2019).

10. DL *Letters*, 500.6–501.2.

11. TL *Outer Bio.*, 94a.

12. DL *Letters*, 501.2–3.

13. On the various editions of the *Collected Nyingma Tantras* (*rnying ma'i rgyud 'bum*), see Cathy Cantwell and Rob Mayer, "Two Proposals for Critically Editing the Texts of the rNying ma'i rGyud 'bum," *Revue d'Études Tibétaines* (Langues et Cultures de l'Aire Tibétaines, CNRS, Paris) 10 (April 2006): 56–70. More particularly to Mindröling, see Gyurmé Dorjé, "The Guhyagharba Tantra: An Introduction," *Hankop Blogspot*, July 28, 2017, http://hankop.blogspot.com/2017/07/an-introduction-to-guhyagarbha-tantra.html (accessed February 2020), 12; on the twenty-three-volume collection from Mindröling, 15; on the variety of compilations, 18.

14. Sam van Schaik, "A Catalogue of the First Volume of the Waddell Manuscript rNying ma rgyud 'bum." *The Tibet Journal* 25, no. 1 (2000): 27–50. Accessed August 24, 2020. http://www.jstor.org/stable/43300793. 49.

15. DL *Letters*, 501.3–4.

16. DL *Letters*, 501.5.

17. On the aesthetics and cultural production associated with the listing of rebirth lineages during this period, especially as focused on the Fifth Dalai Lama, see Nancy Lin, "Recounting the Fifth Dalai Lama's Rebirth Lineage," *Revue d'Études Tibétaines* 38 (February 2017): 119–56.

18. DL *Letters*, 501.6–502.1.

19. DL *Letters*, 502.1–2.

20. TL *Outer Bio.*, 112 a.

21. In her book on the female Treasure revealer Sera Khandro, Sarah Jacoby addresses the motivations for sexual consort relations in Tibetan tantric contexts. She outlines three standard aims for sexual consort union: attaining enlightenment, revealing further Treasure, and healing illness. Sarah Jacob, *Love and Liberation: Autobiographical Writings of the Tibetan Buddhist Visionary Sera Khandro* (New York: Columbia University Press, 2014), 193–222.

22. DL *Letters*, 509–12.

23. On the influence of Indic literary aesthetics and poetics on Tibetan literary history, see Matthew Kapstein, "The Indian Literary Identity in Tibet," in *Literary Cultures in History: Reconstructions from South Asia,* ed. Sheldon Pollock (Berkeley and Los Angeles: University of California Press, 2003), 747–802; Roger R. Jackson, " 'Poetry' in Tibet: *Glu, mGur, sNyan ngag* and 'Songs of Experience,' " in *Tibetan Literature: Studies in Genre,* ed. José Ogmacop Cabezon and Roger R. Jackson (Ithaca, NY: Snow Lion, 1996), 368–92; Leonard W. J. van der Kuijp, "Tibetan Belles-Lettres: The Influence of Daṇḍin and Kṣemendra," in *Tibetan Literature: Studies in Genre,* ed. José Ogmacop Cabezon and Roger R. Jackson (Ithaca, NY: Snow Lion, 1996), 393–410. Pema Bhum and Janet Gyatso, "Condensed Tibetan Allusions: The Figure of Samōskoti in Tibetan Poetics," *Revista degli Studi Orientali* (2017): 169–82.

24. Other female terms used in the letter include *rig ma* (knowledgeable woman) and *lha mo* (goddess), but these refer to women actors in the consecration rite, not the consort herself. In Terdak Lingpa's outer biography, the consort is referred to as *rig ma*, implying she was an expert practitioner in her own right. See TL *Outer Bio.,* 110a–112b.

25. This resonates with recent research on the complex social role of "secret consorts." See Gayley, "Revisiting the 'Secret Consort' (*gsang yum*) in Tibetan Buddhism."

26. TL *Outer Bio.,* 112b.

27. Sheldon Pollock, "Sanskrit Literary Culture from the Inside Out," in *Literary Cultures in History: Reconstructions from South Asia,* ed. Sheldon Pollock (Berkeley and Los Angeles: University of California Press, 2003), 52. I'm grateful to Julie Regan for pointing out this reference.

28. The Tibetan term (provided in the letter's marginal notes) for this metrical category is *sdeb sbyor mnyam ba'i bri tha las zlum po* (DL *Letters,* 509).

29. DL *Letters,* 509.

30. TL *Outer Bio.,* 112a.

31. See TL *Outer Bio.,* 110a–110b.

32. The outer biography suggests a wedding in a more conventional social sense, rather than a union treated strictly in terms of formal tantric practice. See TL *Outer Bio.,* 110b and 112b.

33. For a detailed analysis of the justifications for actual (as opposed to visualized) tantric consort practice in the Tibetan Treasure tradition see Jacoby, *Love and Liberation,* 196–222. According to Jacoby, and in keeping with the Mindröling materials, the three main justifications are enlightenment, Treasure rediscovery, and health. All three are invoked in this case.

34. DL *Letters,* 509–10.

35. DL *Letters,* 510.

36. DL *Letters*, 510.
37. DL *Letters*, 511.
38. DL *Letters*, 510. The "sweet seed of bodhicitta" might also imply the expectation that the union would lead to the birth of children, who would carry on Terdak Lingpa's family lineage.
39. DL *Letters*, 510.
40. DL *Letters*, 510.
41. For an excellent analysis of the various life stories of Yeshé Tsogyel, see Elizabeth Angowski, "Literature and the Moral Life: Reading the Early Biography of the Tibetan Queen Yeshe Tsogyal" (PhD diss., Harvard University, Graduate School of Arts and Sciences, 2019).
42. DL *Letters*, 510.
43. DL *Letters*, 510.
44. DL *Letters*, 510–11.
45. DL *Letters*, 511.
46. DL *Letters*, 511.
47. DL *Letters*, 511.
48. DL *Letters*, 511–12.
49. Samten G. Karmay, trans., *The Illusive Play: The Autobiography of the Fifth Dalai Lama* (Chicago: Serindia, 2014), 208, 328, 376, 385, 499.
50. For more on Lozang Yönten in his role as choirmaster, see Samten G. Karmay, *Secret Visions of the Fifth Dalai Lama: The Gold Manuscript in the Fournier Collection Musee Guimet* (London: Serindia, 1988), 8 and 30.
51. DL *Letters*, 510.
52. TL *Outer Bio.*, 110a.
53. In regard to the term "*ris med*," see TL *Letters*, 12, 13, 50, 54, 81, 84.
54. One example of spontaneous writing, labeled "*gang shar*" to suggest that Terdak Lingpa naturally wrote whatever came to mind, is addressed to no one in particular. See TL *Letters*, 26.
55. TL *Letters*, 345–57.
56. TL *Letters*, 250–57; 299–308.
57. TL *Letters*, 149–151.
58. A letter to Sakya Dakchen (*sa skya bdag chen*) begins on TL *Letters*, 413.
59. An example of a letter to a Bön master begins on TL *Letters*, 480.
60. For two examples, see TL *Letters*, 12, 86.
61. TL *Letters*, 299–308.
62. TL *Letters*, 338.
63. TL *Letters*, 250–57.
64. TL *Letters*, 257. Here Terdak Lingpa quotes several sources, including the Tibetan chronicle, *Bazhé* (*sba bzhed*). I have not located other historical references to such an event.
65. For instance, see TL *Letters*, 487.
66. TL *Letters*, 470.
67. An extensive letter on making mandalas is found in TL *Letters*, 416–21.
68. TL *Letters*, 285.
69. TL *Letters*, 210.

70. TL *Letters*, 397.
71. TL *Letters*, 400.
72. TL *Letters*, 206–9.
73. TL *Letters*, 399.
74. TL *Letters*, 408.
75. For an analysis of the spectrum of attitudes toward the feminine in Buddhism, see Alan Sponberg, "Attitudes Toward Women and the Feminine in Early Buddhism," in *Buddhism, Sexuality, and Gender*, ed. José Cabezón (Albany: State University of New York Press, 1992), 3–36.
76. In an effort to address this problem, recently the Karmapa Lama collaborated with a group of nuns to make it possible for Tibetan nuns to be ordained. They conducted the initial ordination ritual in Bodhgaya, India. https://kagyuoffice .org/history-in-the-making-the-first-step-toward-full-ordination-for-tibetan -buddhist-nuns/ (accessed April 28, 2020). On the history and contemporary situation of women's ordination in Buddhist societies, see *Dignity and Discipline: Reviving Full Ordination for Buddhist Nuns*, ed. Thea Mohr and Ven. Jampa Tsedroen (Boston: Wisdom, 2010).
77. On women's relationship to suffering in Himalayan Buddhist contexts, see Kurtis Schaeffer, *Himalayan Hermitess: The Life of a Tibetan Buddhist Nun* (New York: Oxford University Press, 2004), 91–104.
78. TL *Letters*, 81.
79. TL *Letters*, 12.
80. TL *Letters*, 87, 123.
81. I profited from reading through these verses with Lama Jabb in 2019 and Pema Bhum in 2020. In those personal communications, they both confirmed that the meter is not consistent but hesitated to make a determination on whether that was a flaw.
82. TL *Letters*, 85–87.
83. TL *Letters*, 144–45.
84. See a range of definitions and glosses for "*rten 'brel*" in the online *THL* dictionary, http://ttt.thlib.org/org.thdl.tib.scanner.OnLineScannerFilter (accessed January 2020); *Dung dkar tshig mdzod chen mo*, 989–90.
85. The Tibetan people are referred to in the Dalai Lama's two letters to Terdak Lingpa as "*bod chen 'gro rnams*" (people of greater Tibet), "*bod yul skye rgu*" (people of the land of Tibet), and "*gangs can skye rgu*" (people of the Snowland).

4. Training the Senses

1. On the genre of monastic constitutions as a source for Tibetan social histories, see Berthe Jansen, *The Monastery Rules: Buddhist Organization in Premodern Tibet: Buddhist Monastic Organization in Pre-Modern Tibet* (Oakland: University of California Press, 2018).
2. The section I refer to as the "curriculum" is not designated as such in the Tibetan, but stands out as a distinct section of the 1689 constitutional

guidelines in which Terdak Lingpa provides the basic overview of what students should study, how examinations should be administered, pedagogical advice for teachers, and so forth (*M. Guidelines*, 287–89).

3. Sam van Schaik sums up the history of the Nyingma school succinctly in his review of *The Gathering of Intentions: The History of a Tibetan Buddhist Tantra*, by Jacob P. Dalton (New York: Columbia University Press, 2016). He notes that Dalton's book demonstrates how the founders of Mindröling helped "shape the Nyingma school into a coherent tradition." *Buddhist Studies Review* 35, nos. 1–2 (2018): 308–9 in a Special Issue: Buddhist Path, Buddhist Teachings: Studies in Memory of L. S. Cousins, https://journals.equinoxpub.com/BSR/article/view/37894/35464.

4. Samten G. Karmay, trans., *The Illusive Play: The Autobiography of the Fifth Dalai Lama* (Chicago: Serindia, 2014), 150.

5. Jann Ronis, "Celibacy, Revelations, and Reincarnated Lamas: Contestation and Synthesis in the Growth of Monasticism at Katok Monastery from the 17th through 19th Centuries" (PhD diss., University of Virginia, 2009).

6. Marc-Henri Deroche notes that a previous list of the six main Nyingma monasteries included Palri (*dpal ri*), which was later replaced by Shechen (*zhe chen*). See Deroche, "History of the Forgotten Mother Monastery of the Ancients' School: The dPal ri Monastery in the Valley of the Tibetan Emperors," *Bulletin of Tibetology* 49, no. 1 (2013): 79–80. An overview of the six main Nyingma monasteries is found in Nyoshul Khenpo Jamyang Dorjé, *A Marvelous Garland of Rare Gems: Biographies of Masters of Awareness in the Dzogchen Lineage*, trans., Richard Barron (Junction City, CA: Padma Publishing, 2005), 549–54.

7. Ronis, "Celibacy, Revelations, and Reincarnated Lamas," 138.

8. Ronis, "Celibacy, Revelations, and Reincarnated Lamas," 163–96; on the adoption of these practices at Dzogchen monastery in particular, 193.

9. On the increased focus on literary arts at Nyingma monasteries in Degé, Eastern Tibet, see Ronis, "Celibacy, Revelations, and Reincarnated Lamas," 2, 161–62.

10. Jansen, *The Monastery Rules*, 54 and 200n79; *Lamp of Teachings Cat.*, 313.

11. Ter Ellingson points out the centrality of the "field of merit" in "Tibetan Monastic Constitutions: The Bca' Yig," in *Reflections on Tibetan Culture: Essays in Memory of Turrell V. Wylie*, ed. Lawrence Epstein and R. F. Shelburne, Studies in Asian Thought and Religion 12 (Lewiston, NY: Edwin Mellon Press, 1990), 205–29.

12. Berthe Jansen refers to the Mindröling *bca' yig* in every chapter of *The Monastery Rules*. In a personal communication in December 2019, she confirmed that Terdak Lingpa's text stood out among the many examples she studied, for its comprehensiveness and vivid details.

13. For an excellent summary of the history of the suspicion of Nyingma practitioners due to their association with literal interpretations of sexual tantra and ritual violence, see Holly Gayley, "Revisiting the 'Secret Consort' (*gsang yum*) in Tibetan Buddhism," *Religions* 9, no. 6 (June 2018): 4–5, DOI: 10.3390/rel9060179.

14. George Dreyfus, *The Sound of Two Hands Clapping: The Education of a Tibetan Buddhist Monk* (Berkeley and Los Angeles: University of California Press, 2003), 114; José Cabezón, "Monks," http://www.thlib.org/#!essay=/cabezon/sera/people/monks/s/b4; Jansen, *Monastery Rules*, 18.
15. Personal communication with Khenpo Tséyang, Dehradun, India, June 2017.
16. Berthe Jansen, "Monastic Guidelines (bCa' yig): Tibetan Social History from a Buddhist Studies Perspective," in *Social Regulation: Case Studies from Tibetan History*, ed. Jeannine Bischoff and Saul Mullard (Leiden: Brill, 2016), 82; and Dominic Sur, "Constituting Canon and Community in Eleventh-Century Tibet: The Extant Writings of Rongzom and His *Charter of Mantrins (sngags pa'i bca' yig),*" *Religions* 8, no. 3 (2017): 40/1–29, 14.
17. Jansen, "Monastic Guidelines," 83.
18. I have not found a clear record of the Mindröling guidelines (*bca' yig*) having been displayed on a monastery wall. However, Mindröling's first written monastic history or catalogue (*dkar chag*), which Terdak Lingpa and the Fifth Dalai Lama jointly composed, was displayed on the monastery's wall. This document , which I refer to as the *Temple Wall Cat.*, is reproduced in *Lamp of Teachings Cat.*, 340–53.
19. Jansen, "Monastic Guidelines," 32.
20. *M. Guidelines*, 279.
21. *M. Guidelines*, 282–83.
22. *M. Guidelines*, 280.
23. Jansen, *Monastery Rules*, 78; *Lamp of Teachings Cat.*, 309–10.
24. Jansen, *Monastery Rules*, 124–25.
25. *M. Guidelines*, 311.
26. This gloss of the guidelines is drawn from *M. Guidelines*, 279–84.
27. This metaphor seems to suggest that students and teachers should be compelled to study and practice just as ants are attracted to honey.
28. This passage is ambiguous in the Tibetan. It could refer to the student's age being fifteen years, but the context and phrasing suggest it refers to fifteen years of study.
29. "Young people's work" includes manual labor such as fetching water.
30. A *porkang* is a measure of weight for the butter that fills an offering lamp.
31. *M. Guidelines*, in *Lamp of Teachings Cat.*, 287–89.
32. On the significance of the public rituals see Dalton, *Gathering of Intentions*, chap. 6.
33. Janet Gyatso, *Being Human in a Buddhist World: An Intellectual History of Medicine in Early Modern Tibet* (New York: Columbia University Press, 2015). On the regent's approach to Buddhism and statecraft, see Ian MacCormack, "Buddhism and State in Seventeenth-Century Tibet: Cosmology and Theology in the Works of Sangyé Gyatso" (PhD diss., Harvard University, 2018).
34. Jacques Rancière, "Contemporary Art and the Politics of Aesthetics," in *Communities of Sense: Rethinking Aesthetics and Politics*, ed. Beth Hinderliter et al. (Durham, NC: Duke University Press, 2009), 31.
35. *M. Guidelines*, 287.
36. *M. Guidelines*, 287.

37. *M. Guidelines*, 287.
38. *M. Guidelines*, 288.
39. *M. Guidelines*, 288.
40. *M. Guidelines*, 288.
41. *M. Guidelines*, 288
42. *M. Guidelines*, 288.
43. In a personal communication during a meeting in Clementown, India, June 2017, Khenpo Tséyang told me that Mindröling's ritual traditions are special because they are based on Terdak Lingpa's pure insight in revealing them, not the perceived "beauty" of the ritual offerings.
44. *M. Guidelines*, 288.
45. *M. Guidelines*, 288.
46. *M. Guidelines*, 288.
47. Dominique Townsend, "Buddhism's Worldly Other: Secular Subjects of Tibetan Learning," *Himalaya: The Journal for the Association of Nepal and Himalayan Studies* 36, no. 1 (May 2016): article 15.
48. *M. Guidelines*, 288.
49. *M. Guidelines*, 289.
50. *M. Guidelines*, 289.
51. *M. Guidelines*, 289.
52. Jansen, *Monastery Rules*, 155; *M. Guidelines*, 283.
53. *M. Guidelines*, 289.
54. *M. Guidelines*, 289.
55. Jansen provides detailed descriptions of several related monastic roles. See "Monastic Education," in *Monastery Rules*, chap. 4, 57–94.
56. *M. Guidelines*, 287.
57. On the repression of writing in Central Tibetan Géluk monasteries, see Dreyfus, *The Sound of Two Hands Clapping*, 111, 120–21.
58. Dreyfus, *The Sound of Two Hands Clapping*, 121.
59. José Ignacio Cabezón and Penpa Dorjee, *Sera Monastery* (Boston: Wisdom, 2019), 223–24.
60. Cabezón and Penpa Dorjee, *Sera Monastery*, 214–20.
61. Cabezón and Penpa Dorjee, *Sera Monastery*, 224.
62. Jonathan C. Gold, *The Dharma's Gatekeepers: Sakya Pandita on Buddhist Scholarship in Tibet* (Albany: State University of New York Press, 2008), 155.
63. *Lamp of Teachings Cat.*, 175–76.
64. *Lamp of Teachings Cat.*, 175.
65. The scripts mentioned are: Tibetan cursive and block printing (*bod yig dbu med* and *dbu chen*), Landza, Wartu, and Mongolian (*hor yig*). *Lamp of Teachings Cat.*, 175.
66. *'byung rtsis zla ba'i 'od zer* [A treatise on the principles of Tibetan astrology] and *rtsis gzhung nyin byed snang ba'i sngon 'gro* [An introductory astrology textbook].
67. Paul Hackett, "The Sman rtsis khang: A Survey of Pedagogical and Reference Literature," in *Tibetan and Himalayan Healing: An Anthology for Anthony Aris*, ed. Charles Ramble and Ulrike Roesler (Kathmandu: Vajra Publications, 2015), 292.
68. *Lamp of Teachings Cat.*, 176.
69. *Lamp of Teachings Cat.*, 175 (*dag yig ngag sgron* [Verse orthological dictionary]).

70. *Lamp of Teachings Cat.*, 175 (*legs bshad ljon dbang* [A collection of eloquent phrases]), (*dka' gnad gsal ba'i me long* [Elucidation of difficult points]).
71. *Lamp of Teachings Cat.*, 161–62.

5. Taming the Aristocrats

1. An overview of the standard course of study of literary arts, and ornate poetry (*snyan ngag*) in particular, is found in *Lamp of Teachings Cat.*, 176.
2. This is expressed in Beth Newman's introduction to Mdo mkhar Tshe ring dbang rgyal, *The Tale of the Incomparable Prince*, trans. Beth Newman (New York: HarperCollins, 1996), xv.
3. Lochen Dharmaśrī's writings on vows include: Dharmaśrī, "snga 'gyur sdom rgyun gyi mkhan brgyud kyi rnam thar nyung gsal sgron me," and "'dul ba'i las chog," in *Gsung 'bum* (Dehradun: D. G. Khochen Tulku, 1999), 318–45; 551–636.
4. William Clark, *Academic Charisma and the Origins of the Research University* (Chicago: University of Chicago Press, 2007), 15.
5. I analyze the Mindröling constitutional guidelines (*bca' yig*) in detail in chapter 4. The full guidelines are reproduced in *Lamp of Teachings Cat.*, 272–316.
6. Yale University, "The Yale Corporation: Charter and Legislation," https://www.yale.edu/sites/default/files/files/University-Charter.pdf (accessed January 2020).
7. Harvard University, "Harvard University Archives: The Harvard Charter of 1650," https://library.harvard.edu/university-archives/using-the-collections/online-resources/charter-of-1650 (accessed January 2020). The document is held in the Harvard Archive (UAI 15.100). Although it is beyond the scope of this study to address this issue, I want to draw attention to the inclusion of "Indian youth," reflecting the authors' intentions to disseminate the colonists' values and aesthetics to the indigenous population.
8. On this period, see Tsepon Wangchuk Dedun Shakabpa, *One Hundred Thousand Moons: An Advanced Political History of Tibet*, Volume 1, trans. Derek F. Maher (Leiden; Boston: Brill, 2010), 321–482.
9. For an excellent study of Dokharwa's autobiographical writing, see Lauran Hartley, "Self as a Faithful Public Servant: The Autobiography of Mdo khar ba Tshe ring dbang rgyal (1697–1763)," in *Mapping the Modern in Tibet*, PIATS 2006: *Proceedings of the Eleventh Seminar of the International Association for Tibetan Studies*, ed. Gray Tuttle (Andiast, Switzerland: International Association for Tibetan and Buddhist Studies, 2011), 45–73.
10. Leonard van der Kuijp's book review of *The Biography of Miwang* provides valuable details on Dokharwa's work. See Leonard W. J. van der Kujip, "Untitled Review of *Mi-dbang rtogs-brjod* by Mdo-mkhar Tshe-ring by Zhuang Ting," *Journal of the American Oriental Society* 105, no. 2 (April–June, 1985): 321–22.
11. See Mdo mkhar Tshe ring dbang rgyal, *The Tale of the Incomparable Prince*.
12. Van der Kuijp, "Untitled Review of Mi-dbang rtogs-brjod," 321.
13. Doring Tenzin Paljor's autobiography is available on BDRC: rdo ring pa bstan 'dzin dpal 'byor. *rdo ring paN+Di ta'i rnam thar* [Biography of Doring Pandita]. TBRC

W1PD96348, 2 vols. (Chengdu: Si khron mi rigs dpe skrun khang, 1987), http://tbrc.org/link?RID=W1PD96348. Another illuminating example of lay autobiography from this period (although not associated with a Mindröling graduate) is *Song of the Bee*, an autobiography of Surkhang Sichö Tseten (Zur khang sri gcod rtse brtan, 1766–1820), a Tibetan minister. See Riga Tsegyal Shakya and Chokro Yundrung Gyurme, eds., *Bka'i gung blon gyi 'khur 'dzin pa'i rtogs brjod bung ba'i mgrin glu* (Bod ljongs mi dmangs dpe skrun khang, 2019).

14. This fact was also noted by Gene Smith, *Among Tibetan Texts: History and Literature of the Himalayan Plateau* (Boston: Wisdom, 2001), 20.

15. Mdo mkhar Tshe ring dbang rgyal, *Autobiography of a Cabinet Minister* (*bka' blon rtogs brjod*), trans. Riga Shakya, 6. Riga Shakya generously shared his unpublished translation of this section of the biography with me. I slightly revised his translation for style.

16. Pema Bhum and Janet Gyatso, "Condensed Tibetan Allusions," *Rivisti degli Studi Orientali* (2017): 169–82. Rome: Fabrizio Serra, 169.

17. Mdo mkhar Tshe ring dbang rgyal, *Autobiography of a Cabinet Minister* (*bka' blon rtogs brjod*), trans. Riga Shakya, 6–7.

18. Mdo mkhar Tshe ring dbang rgyal, *Autobiography of a Cabinet Minister* (*bka' blon rtogs brjod*), trans. Riga Shakya, 7.

19. *Lamp of Teachings Cat.*, 175–76; Paul G. Hackett, "The sman rtsis khang: A Survey of Pedagogical and Reference Literature," in *Tibetan and Himalayan Healing: An Anthology for Anthony Aris*, ed. Charles Ramble and Ulrike Roesler (Kathmandu: Vajra Publications, 2015), 292.

20. Mdo mkhar Tshe ring dbang rgyal, *Autobiography of a Cabinet Minister* (*bka' blon rtogs brjod*), trans. Riga Shakya, 7.

21. Mdo mkhar Tshe ring dbang rgyal, *Autobiography of a Cabinet Minister* (*bka' blon rtogs brjod*), trans. Riga Shakya, 7–8.

22. Mdo mkhar Tshe ring dbang rgyal, *Autobiography of a Cabinet Minister* (*bka' blon rtogs brjod*), trans. Riga Shakya, 7–8.

23. Mdo mkhar Tshe ring dbang rgyal, *Autobiography of a Cabinet Minister* (*bka' blon rtogs brjod*), trans. Riga Shakya, 8.

24. Mdo mkhar Tshe ring dbang rgyal, *Autobiography of a Cabinet Minister* (*bka' blon rtogs brjod*), trans. Riga Shakya, 8–9.

25. Miwang *Bio.*, 92–115.

26. Miwang *Bio.*, 100.

27. Miwang *Bio.*, 101. This is an interesting parallel to Chan and Zen anecdotes in which teachers often hold or strike students with fly whisks.

28. Miwang *Bio.*, 100.

29. Miwang *Bio.*, 102.

30. Miwang *Bio.*, 103.

31. Miwang *Bio.*, 102–104.

32. Miwang *Bio.*, 92.

33. Miwang *Bio.*, 96–99.

34. Some of Dokharwa's erotic imagery is reminiscent of Daṇḍin's *Daśakumāracarita*. See Daṇḍin, *What Ten Young Men Did*, trans. Isabelle Onians (New York: New York University Press, J. J. C. Foundation, 2005).

35. Benjamin Bogin, *The Illustrated Life of the Great Yolmowa* (London: Serindia, U.K. Editions, 2013), 148, 234.
36. Van der Kuijp, "Untitled Review of Mi-dbang rtogs-brjod," 322.
37. Riga Shakya is currently conducting dissertation research on the four extant lay biographies from the eighteenth century entitled, "Writing Lives, Writing Empire: The Poetics of Polity." His work examines the role of life writing and poetry in eighteenth-century Sino-Tibetan relations.
38. Lama Jabb illuminates the connection between oral and written literatures across historical periods as a crucial aspect of Tibetan identity. See Lama Jabb, *Oral and Literary Continuities in Modern Tibetan Literature: The Inescapable Nation* (New York: Lexington Books, 2015).
39. See David S. Ruegg, *Ordre Spirituel and Ordre Temporal dans la pensée boudhique de l'Inde et du Tibet* [Spiritual order and temporal order in the Buddhist thought of India and Tibet] (Paris: Collège de France, 1995), 132–38; and an English summary, 153–55.
40. On Sakya Paṇḍita's significant influence on the intellectual history of Tibet, and in particular his treatment of the five sciences or *rikné*, see Jonathan C. Gold, *The Dharma's Gatekeepers: Sakya Pandita on Buddhist Scholarship in Tibet* (Albany: State University of New York Press, 2008), 11–16, 20–24, 31, 139, 155–56.
41. On these lists, and for more on the other versions attributed to the Kālacakra (*dus 'khor*), the Vinaya (*'dul ba lung*), and other sources, as well as more on the category of *rikné* (*rig gnas*), see Dungkar Losang Khrinley, *Bod rig pa'i tshig mdzod chen mo shes bya rab gsal zhes bya ba bzhugs so* [Dungkar Tibetological dictionary] (Beijing: krung go'i bod rig dpe skrun khang [China Tibetology Publishing House], 2002), 1900–1901.
42. Miwang *Bio.*, 482. This detail was brought to my attention by Hanung Kim. The relevant passage is translated in his unpublished paper, "Two Different Narratives on Early Eighteenth-Century Tibet" (Columbia University, 2009), 9.
43. On the place of Pemayangtsé in Sikkimese history and its intricate ties to Mindröling through the activities of Jigmé Pabo (*'jigs med dpa' bo*), see Saul Mullard, *Opening the Hidden Land: State Formation and the Construction of Sikkimese History*, Brill's Tibetan Studies Library Series (Leiden; Boston: Brill, 2011).
44. L. Austine Waddell, *Buddhism of Tibet or Lamaism* (Cambridge: W. Heffer and Sons Ltd, [1894]; repr., Whitefish: Kessinger Publishing, 2003), 175.
45. Waddell, *Buddhism of Tibet or Lamaism*, 174.
46. Waddell, *Buddhism of Tibet or Lamaism*, 73.
47. An example can be found as far away as Nyarong (*nyag rong*), in the Kham region of Eastern Tibet, in Sichuan province. At Lumora monastery the monk caretaker told me they follow the Mindröling curriculum and constitution (personal communication, July 2007).
48. George Dreyfus, *The Sound of Two Hands Clapping: The Education of a Tibetan Buddhist Monk* (Berkeley and Los Angeles: University of California Press, 2003), 121.
49. On "consecration" in regard to class status and education beyond Tibet, see Pierre Bourdieu and Jean-Claude Passeron, *Reproduction in Education, Society, and Culture*, trans. Richard Nice (London: Sage, 1990), 37–40, 42.

50. Bourdieu and Passeron. *Reproduction in Education*, 31–32; Pierre Bourdieu and Monique de Saint Martin, *The State Nobility: Elite Schools in the Field of Power*, trans. Loretta C. Clough (Cambridge: Polity Press, 1996), 2–3.

51. Jacques Derrida, *Of Grammatology*, trans. Gayatri Spivak (Baltimore: Johns Hopkins University Press, 1997), 119.

52. Roland Barthes, "Zazie and Literature," in *Critical Essays*, ed. Roland Barthes (Evanston, IL: University of Chicago Press, 1972), 119.

53. Melvyn Goldstein and Gelek Rinpoché, *A History of Modern Tibet 1913-1951: The Demise of the Lamaist State* (Berkeley: University of California Press, 1989), 7.

54. On the repression of writing at Central Tibet's Géluk centers, see Dreyfus, *The Sound of Two Hands Clapping*; and José Cabezón and Penpa Dorjee, *Sera Monastery* (Boston: Wisdom, 2019).

55. Dreyfus, *The Sound of Two Hands Clapping*, 133.

56. In his study of the modern research university, William Clark devotes a good deal of attention to related aspects of material history, such as the "chair" as "crystallized charisma." See Clark, *Academic Charisma*, 15, 17–18, 72, 286–87.

57. *Lamp of Teachings Cat.*, 286. Contemporary teachers in the Mindröling tradition claim that Terdak Lingpa was highly attentive to social and gender equality. While this is not explicit in his writing, throughout the documents of the catalogue he remarks on treating various social classes equally, in reference to donors, women visiting the monastery on pilgrimage, or poor monks who fall ill and need to be cared for; his letters also display a relatively egalitarian rapport with his women disciples, as is documented in more detail in chapter 3.

58. Some of these images have been photographed and reproduced and were displayed at the Rubin Museum of Art in New York City in 2011, making the details far more accessible than they are in the original temple in Lhasa. See Ian Baker and Thomas Laird, *The Dalai Lama's Secret Temple: Tantric Wall Paintings from Tibet* (London: Thames and Hudson, 2000). See also Thomas Laird, *Murals of Tibet* (London: Taschen, 2018).

59. Janet Gyatso has demonstrated the significance of generic representations of people and deities in Tibetan medical paintings produced under the direction of Sangyé Gyatso during this period. Her observations drew my attention to the anonymity of the people represented here. See Janet Gyatso, *Being Human in a Buddhist World: An Intellectual History of Medicine in Early Modern Tibet* (New York: Columbia University Press, 2015), 51–55 (in relation to scientific representation), 70–73 (regarding religious figures and deities).

60. For more general information on the Tibetan aristocracy see Luciano Petech, "Aristocracy and Government in Tibet 1728-1959," in *Selected Papers on Tibetan History*, Seriale Orientale Roma 60 (Rome: Istituto Italiano per il Medio ed Estremo Oriente, 1988); and Tsering Yangdzom, *The Aristocratic Families in Tibetan History, 1900-1951* (Beijing: China Intercontinental Press, 2006). Although both these works focus on periods after Mindröling was founded, they shed light on related issues. See also Peter Prince of Greece's work on this subject: Peter Prince of Greece, *The Aristocracy of Central Tibet: A Provisional List of the Names of the Noble Houses of U-Tsang* (Kalimpong: G. Tharchin, Melong Press, 1954).

61. Ruohong Li mentions a short work on the education of Tibetan aristocrats written in Chinese. Qian'eba duojieouzhu and Zhuomatai, "Xizang SuguanXuexiao—Zikang Jianshu" [A Tibetan school for lay officials—A brief introduction to *rtsi khang*], *Zhongguo zangxue* [China Tibetology] 4 (1990): 90–92. See Ruohong Li, "A Tibetan Aristocratic Clan in Eighteenth-century Tibet: A Study of Qing-Tibetan Contact" (PhD diss., Harvard University, 2002), 109.

62. Gene Smith also noted Mindröling's fame for higher learning and for the literary arts in particular, mentioning that Mindröling "provided poetry teachers to the official government schools in Lhasa." See Smith, *Among Tibetan Texts*, 19. He likely referred to the Tsé Lobdra (*rtse slob grwa*) and the Tsikhang (*rtsi khang*). Li mentions the latter as "an official training school for young aristocrats before they entered government service." See Li, "A Tibetan Aristocratic Family in Eighteenth-century Tibet," 108. Mindröling's connection to Tsé Lobdra is supported in Dungkar Losang Khrinley, *Bod rig pa'i tshig mdzod chen mo shes bya rab gsal zhes bya ba bzhugs so* [Dungkar Tibetological dictionary] (Beijing: krung go'i bod rig p dpe skrun khang, 2002), 1681.

63. José Cabezón, "The Regulations of a Monastery," in *Religions of Tibet in Practice*, ed. Donald Lopez Jr. (Princeton, NJ: Princeton University Press, 1997), 335–51.

64. On lay donors receiving training at the Jé college of Sera monastery, see Cabezón, "The Regulations of a Monastery," 346. This marks the contrast between Géluk institutions and Mindröling.

65. Michel Foucault, "Of Other Spaces: Heterotopias," trans. Jay Miskowiec (Paris: Architecture, Mouvement, Continuité, 1984), 46–49. Foucault first presented his ideas on the concept of heterotopia in a 1967 lecture.

66. For example, see *Lamp of Teachings Cat.*, 287. Terdak Lingpa often uses the phrase *blo reng mi 'gro*, which suggests "open minded" to describe a student who is making good progress.

Epilogue: Destruction and Revival

1. *Lamp of Teachings Cat.*, 129–30. The full list of senior chairs and abbots is found in *Lamp of Teachings Cat.*, 126–33.

2. Mindrolling Jetsün Khandro Rinpoche and Mindrolling Jetsün Dechen Paldrön, "Mindrolling History Project," https://www.lotusgardens.org/documents /mindrolling-history.pdf (accessed January 22, 2020), 6.

3. On the philosophical scholarship of Pema Gyurmé Gyatso, see Matthew T. Kapstein, "Zhentong Traces in the Nyingma Tradition: Two Texts from Mindroling," in *The Other Emptiness: Rethinking the Zhentong Buddhist Discourse in Tibet*, ed. Michael R. Sheehy and Klaus Dieter-Mathes (Albany: State University of New York Press, 2019), 235–56. (Kapstein's chapter also addresses the work of Dharmaśrī.)

4. On the significance of hair in Tibetan tantric practice, see Benjamin Bogin, "The Dreadlocks Treatise: On Tantric Hairstyles in Tibetan Buddhism," *History of Religions* 48, no. 2 (2008): 85–109.

5. This episode is recounted in "Mindrolling History Project," 34–35.

6. This is titled: "snyan ngag me long gi 'grel pa gzhung don rab gsal snang ba zhes bya ba bzhugs so," in *Smin gling khri rabs gnyis pa Padma 'gyur med rgya mtsho'i gsung 'bum* [The collected works of the Second Minling Throneholder, Pema Gyurmé Gyatso], ed. Khanpo Pema Tashi (Dehra Dun, Uttarakhand, India: Mindrolling Ngagyur Nyingma College, 2019), Vol. 1, 141–479. Pema Gyurmé Gyatso's and Mingyur Peldrön's collected works were recently made available in India. I am indebted to Sean Price for sharing a copy of the collections with me.

7. Dharmaśrī, "rgyal sras pad+ma 'gyur med rgya mtsho'i gsol 'debs" [Prayer for Pema Gyurmé Gyatso], in *dharma shrī. gsung 'bum/_d+harma shrī*. TBRC W9140, 20 vols. (Dehra Dun: D. G. Khochen Tulku, 1999), http://tbrc.org/link ?RID=W9140, 259.

8. *Smin gling khri rabs gnyis pa Padma 'gyur med rgya mtsho'i gsung 'bum*, Vol. 2.

9. "Mindrolling History Project," 35–36.

10. Norbu Sampel (nor bu bsam 'phel), *Sde pa gzhung gi lo rgyus nyin byed snang ba* [History of the Tibetan government] (Beijing: mi rigs dpe skun khang, 2017), 935. I am grateful to Pema Bhum for this reference. This account is corroborated in *Lamp of Teachings Cat.*, 3.

11. Norbu Sampel (nor bu bsam 'phel), *Sde pa gzhung gi lo rgyus nyin byed snang ba*, 936.

12. For more on the Zungar sacking of Lhasa see Luciano Petech, *China and Tibet in the Early 18th Century* (Leiden: E. J. Brill, 1972), 53–57. The events at Mindröling are documented in more detail in a history of the Nyingma school composed in 1731 by Orgyan Chökyi Drakpa (b. 1676), who was Terdak Lingpa's brother. *O rgyan chos kyi grags pa. Chos 'byung bstan pa'i nyi ma* [A history of the Nyingma school]. TBRC W21492, Vol. 2, 260–90.

13. For an overview of the biography, see Alison Melnick, "The Life and Times of Mingyur Peldrön: Female Leadership in 18th-Century Tibetan Buddhism" (PhD diss., University of Virginia, 2014). My reading of Mingyur Peldrön's biography was enriched by an unpublished translation by the late Marilyn Silverstone. My thanks to Hubert Decleer and Julie Regan for sharing the translation with me.

14. *Lamp of Teachings Cat.*, 5. This story is also mentioned in MP *Bio.*, 77–79.

15. MP *Bio.*, 93.

16. Saul Mullard documents this period in detail. He traces the ramifications of Mingyur Peldrön's stay in Sikkim, with a focus on establishing Pemayangtsé monastery as the most important site for rituals associated with the Sikkimese royal government. See Saul Mullard, *Opening the Hidden Land: State Formation and the Construction of Sikkimese History* (Leiden; Boston: Brill, 2011), 161–88. The list of Mindröling branches and affiliates in *Lamp of Teachings Cat.* includes Pemayangtsé (see *Lamp of Teachings Cat.*, 154).

17. Mullard, *Opening the Hidden Land*, 170.

18. MP *Bio.*, 63.

19. MP *Bio.*, 114. Horses appear to have been a regular offering from Polhané to Mingyur Peldrön. On the collection of ornaments and equestrian equipment at Mindröling, including gold and silver saddles, see *Mirror of Memory Cat.*, 3.

20. MP *Bio.*, 179.

21. On the life and work of Zhepay Dorjé, see Cameron Bailey, "A Feast for Scholars: The Life and Works of Sle lung Bzhad pa'i rdo rje" (PhD diss., Faculty of Oriental Studies, Wolfson College, Oxford University, 2017).
22. On Lélung's *ris med* characteristics, see Bailey, "A Feast for Scholars," 3–7. In personal communications, Gene Smith frequently stressed Lélung Zhépay Dorjé's close connections to Mindröling. In particular, he pointed out the common literary aesthetic apparent between Lélung and Mindröling graduates.
23. These events are described in MP *Bio.*, 120–23.
24. See Bailey, "A Feast for Scholars," 2–3. From Bailey's more sympathetic perspective these occasions look very different from how they are described in Mingyur Peldrön's biography.
25. On this aspect of Terdak Lingpa's engagement with his disciples and sponsors, see chapter 3.
26. Melnick, "Life and Times of Mingyur Peldrön," 28, 97–98.
27. MP *Bio.*, 66.
28. MP *Bio.*, 17.
29. Jetsun Trinlé Chödron is named as a root teacher of Jamyang Khyentsé Wangpo in (Dilgo Khyentsé Rinpoche) bkra shis dpal 'byor. "'jam dbyangs mkhyen brtse'i dbang po'i snying thig ma bu'i sngon 'gro'i bla ma'i rnal 'byor gyi gsol 'debs kha skong/." In gsung 'bum/_rab gsal zla ba. TBRC W21809. 3: 248–249. Delhi: Shechen Publications, 1994. http://tbrc.org/link?RID=O2DB57601|O2DB576012DB58065$W 21809.

Bibliography

Tibetan Language Sources

Bstan pa'i sgron me. *O rgyan smin grol gling gi dkar chag* [Mindröling monastic catalogue]. Xining: Krung go'i bod kyi shes rig dpe skrun khang, 1992.

Dilgo Khyentsé. "Lo chen d+harma shrī'i gsung 'bum par bskrun dsal bshad" [Introduction to Dharmaśrī's Gsung 'bum]. In *Dharma shrī, Gsung 'bum/_ d+harma shrī*, 1–35. TBRC W9140. 20 vols. Dehradun: D. G. Khochen Tulku, 1999. http://tbrc.org/link?RID=W9140.

Dungkar Losang Khrinley. *Mkhas dbang dung dkar blo bzang 'phrin las mchog gis mdzad pa'i bod rig pa'i tshig mdzod chen mo shes bya rab gsal zhes bya ba bzhugs so* [Dungkar Tibetological dictionary]. Beijing: Krung go'i bod rig dpe skrun khang, 2002.

Gter bdag gling pa (1646–1714). *Collected Religious Instructions and Letters of Gter-bdag-glin-pa-'gyur-med-rdo-rje*. Dehradun: D. G. Khochen Tulku, 1977.

——. *The Collected Works (gsu bum) of Smin-lin gTerchen Rigdzin gyurmed rdorje*. 16 vols. Dehradun: D. G. Khochen Tulku, 1998.

——. *Record of Teachings Received: The gsan yig of Gterbdag gli-pa Gyurme rdo-rje of smin-grolling*. New Delhi: Sanje Dorje, 1974.

——. "sgo 'phyor gyi lho ngos ldebs ris su 'khod pa'i gtsug lag khang gi dkar chag" [Catalogue composed on the southern wall of the porch of the main temple]. In Bstan pa'i sgron me, *o rgyan smin grol gling gi dkar chag*. Xining: Krung go'i bod kyi shes rig dpe skrun khang, 1992.

——. "smin gling 'dus sde'i bca' yig ma bu." In Bstan pa'i sgron me, *o rgyan smin grol gling gi dkar chag* [Mindröling monastic guidelines]. Xining: Krung go'i bod kyi shes rig dpe skrun khang, 1992.

Khyung po ras pa 'gyur med 'od gsal (b. 1715). *Rje btsun mi 'gyur dpal gyi sgron ma'i rnam thar dad pa'i gdung sel* [Mingyur Peldrön's biography]. Thimpu, Bhutan: National Library of Bhutan, 1984.

Lochen Dharmashri (1654–1717). *The Collected Works* (gsung 'bum) *of Smin-gling Lochen Dharma-sri.* 19 vols. Dehradun: D. G. Khochen Tulku, 1977.

——. "'dul ba'i las chog." In *Gsung 'bum*. Dehradun: D. G. Khochen Tulku, 1999.

——. "gter bdag gling pa'i nang gi rnam thar." In *Gsung 'bum* [Terdak Lingpa's inner biography]. TBRC W9140. Dehradun: D. G. Khochen Tulku, 1999.

——. "gter bdag gling pa'i phyi yi rnam thar." In *Gsung 'bum* [Terdak Lingpa's outer biography]. BDRC W9140. Dehradun: D. G. Khochen Tulku, 1999.

——. "rdor sems rmi khrid" [Instructions on Vajrasattva dream yoga]. In *Gsung 'bum* [Collected works]. Dehradun: D. G. Khochen Tulku, 1999.

——. *Rje btsun bla ma dam pa gter chen chos kyi rgyal po'i nang gi rtogs pa yon tan mtha' yas rnam par bkod pa'i rol mo* [Account of the spiritual experiences of the Dharma King Terdak Lingpa]. Dehradun: D. G. Khochen Tulku, 1975.

——. "rgyal sras pad+ma 'gyur med rgya mtsho'i gsol 'debs" [Supplication prayer for Pema Gyurmé Gyatso]. In *Gsung 'bum*, 695–722. BDRC W9140. Dehradun: D. G. Khochen Tulku, 1999.

——. "snga 'gyur sdom rgyun gyi mkhan brgyud kyi rnam thar nyung gsal sgron me" [Brief biographies of the Nyingma lineage]. In *Gsung 'bum*. Dehradun: D. G. Khochen Tulku, 1999.

——. "yum chen lha 'dzin dbyangs can sgrol ma'i rnam thar" [Yumchen Lhadzin Yangchen Dolma's biography]. In *Gsung 'bum*, 695–722. BDRC W9140. Dehradun: D. G. Khochen Tulku, 1999.

Mdo mkhar zhabs drung tshe ring dbang rgyal (1697-1763). *Bka' blon rtogs brjod.* [The autobiography of a cabinet minister]. Chengdu: Si khron mi rigs dpe skrun khang, 1981.

——. *Dpal mi'i dbang po'i rtogs pa brjod pa 'jig rten kun tu dga' ba'i gtam Zhes bya ba bzhugs so* [Biography of Miwang]. Chengdu: Si khron mi rigs dpe skrun khang, 2002.

Mi 'gyur dpal sgron (1699-1769). *Smin gling rje btsun mi 'gyur dpal sgron gsung 'bum* [The collected works of Minling Jetsun Mingyur Peldrön]. Ed. Khanpo Pema Tashi. Dehra Dun, Uttarakhand: Mindrolling Ngagyur Nyingma College, 2019.

Ngag dbang blo bzang rgya mtsho (1617–1682). *The Collected Works* (gsung 'bum) *of the Fifth Dalai Lama Ngag dbang blo bzang rgya mtsho.* Gangtok: Sikkim Institute of Tibetology, 1995.

——. *Rgya bod hor sog gi mchog dman bar pa rnams la 'phrin yig snyan ngag tu bkod pa rab snyan rgyud mang* [Letters to various notables of China, Tibet, and Mongolia written by the Fifth Dalai Lama]. Thimpu: Kunsang Tobgay, 1975.

Norbu Sampel (nor bu bsam 'phel). *Sde pa gzhung gi lo rgyus nyin byed snang ba* [History of the Tibetan government]. Beijing: mi rigs dpe skun khang, 2017.

Nus ldan rdo rje (b.1655). "Mkhar chen bza' mkha' 'gro ye shes mtsho rgyal gyi rnam thar" [Biography of Yeshé Tsogyel]. In *bka' thang dri ma med pa'i rgyan*, 154–91. Lhasa: Bod ljongs mi dmangs dpe skrun khang, 2006.

'Og min O rgyan smin grol gling gi dkar chag dran pa'i me long [Monastic catalogue of Mindröling monastery]. o rgyan smin grol gling gi dkar chag. TBRC W1KG15236. 1 vol. s.l.: s.n., n.d. http://tbrc.org/link?RID=W1KG15236.

O rgyan chos kyi grags pa (b. 1676). *Chos 'byung bstan pa'i nyi ma* [A history of the Nyingma school]. TBRC W21492.

Pad+ma 'gyur med rgya mtsho (1686–1717). *Smin gling khri rabs gnyis pa Pad+ma 'gyur med rgya mtsho'i gsung 'bum* [The collected works of the Second Minling Throne-holder, Pema Gyurmé Gyatso]. Ed. Khanpo Pema Tashi. Dehra Dun, Uttarakhand, India: Mindrolling Ngagyur Nyingma College, 2019.

Rdo ring pa bstan 'dzin dpal 'byor (b. 1760). *rdo ring paN+Di ta'i rnam thar* [Biography of Doring Pandita]. TBRC W1PD96348. 2 vols. Chengdu: Si khron mi rigs dpe skrun khang, 1987. http://tbrc.org/link?RID=W1PD96348.

Riga Tsegyal Shakya and Chokro Yundrung Gyurme, eds. *Bka'i gung blon gyi 'khur 'dzin pa'i rtogs brjod bung ba'i mgrin glu* [Song of the Bee]. Bod ljongs mi dmangs dpe skrun khang, 2019.

Sde srid sangs rgyas rgya mtsho (1653–1705). *Sku lnga pa drug par 'phos pa'i gtam rna ba'i bcun len 'bring bsdud sgrogs sbyangs kyis gsang rgya khrom bsgrags gnang skor* [Account of the interim between the Fifth and Sixth Dalai Lamas]. Lhasa: Bod ljongs mis dmangs dpe skrun khang, 1989.

——.*Tshangs dbyangs rgya mtsho'i rnam thar* [Biography of Tsangyang Gyatso] (lha sa par ma), 106–7. TBRC W1KG9087. 2 vols. Gangtok, Sikkim: Chhentse labrang, 1980. http://tbrc.org/link?RID=W1KG9087.

——. *Vaidurya Serpo*. Xining: Krung go bod kyi shes rig dpe skrun khang, 1989.

Smith, Gene. *Sa skya'i bla ma 'ga' yi rnam thar phyogs bsgrigs* [Collected Sakya biographies]. TBRC W1KG9245.2.

Non-Tibetan Language Sources

Abé, Ryuichi. *The Weaving of Mantra: Kukai and the Construction of Esoteric Buddhist Discourse*. New York: Columbia University Press, 1999.

Ahmad, Zahiruddin. *A History of Tibet by the Fifth Dalai Lama*. Indiana University Oriental Series 7. Bloomington: Indiana University Research Institute for Inner Asian Studies, 1995.

Ahmed, Sara. "Affective Economies." *Social Text* 22, no. 2 (2004): 117–39.

——. "Happy Objects." In *The Affect Theory Reader*, ed. Melissa Gregg and Gregory J. Seigworth, 29–51. Durham, NC: Duke University Press, 2010.

Anderson, Benedict. *Imagined Communities: Reflections on the Origin and Spread of Nationalism*. London and New York: Verso, 1991.

Angowski, Elizabeth. "Literature and the Moral Life: Reading the Early Biography of the Tibetan Queen Yeshe Tsogyal." PhD diss., Harvard University, Graduate School of Arts and Sciences, 2019.

Aris, Michael. *Hidden Treasures and Secret Lives: A Study of Pemalingpa, 1450–1521, and the Sixth Dalai Lama, 1683–1706*. London and New York: Kegan Paul International, 1989.

Aśvaghoṣa. *Life of Buddha*. Trans. Patrick Olivelle. New York: New York University Press, 2008.

Bailey, Amanda, and Mario DiGangi. *Affect Theory and Early Modern Texts: Politics, Ecologies, and Form*. New York: Palgrave Macmillan, 2017.

Bailey, Cameron. "A Feast for Scholars: The Life and Works of Sle lung Bzhad pa'i rdo rje." PhD diss., Faculty of Oriental Studies, Wolfson College, Oxford University, 2017.

Baker, Ian. "Embodying Enlightenment: Physical Culture in Dzogchen as Revealed in Tibet's Lukhang Murals." *Asian Medicine* 7 (2012): 225–64.

Baker, Ian, and Thomas Laird. *The Dalai Lama's Secret Temple: Tantric Wall Paintings from Tibet.* London: Thames and Hudson, 2000.

Barthes, Roland. "Zazie and Literature." In *Critical Essays*, ed. Roland Barthes. Evanston, IL: University of Chicago Press, 1972.

Beckwith, Christopher. "The Tibetans in the Ordos and North China: Considerations on the Role of the Tibetan Empire in World History." In *Silver on Lapis*, ed. Christopher Beckwith. Bloomington, IN: Tibet Society, 1987.

Berger, Patricia. *Empire of Emptiness: Buddhist Art and Political Authority in Qing China.* Honolulu: University of Hawai'i Press, 2003.

Bessenger, Suzanne. *Echoes of Enlightenment: The Life and Legacy of the Tibetan Saint Sonam Peldren.* New York: Oxford University Press, 2016.

Bhum, Pema, and Janet Gyatso. "Condensed Tibetan Allusions." *Rivista degli Studi Orientali* (2017): 169–82. Rome: Fabrizio Serra.

Bogin, Benjamin. "The Dreadlocks Treatise: On Tantric Hairstyles in Tibetan Buddhism." *History of Religions* 48, no. 2 (2008): 85–109.

——. *The Illustrated Life of the Great Yolmowa.* London: Serindia, UK Editions, 2013.

——. "The Life of Yol mo Bstan 'dzin nor bu: A Critical Edition, Translation, and Study of the Memoirs of a Seventeenth-century Tibetan Buddhist Lama." PhD diss., University of Michigan, 2005.

Boulnois, Luce. "Gold, Wool and Musk: Trade in Lhasa in the Seventeenth Century." In *Lhasa in the Seventeenth Century: The Capital of the Dalai Lamas*, ed. Francoise Pommaret. Leiden, Boston, Koln: Brill Academic, 2003.

Bourdieu, Pierre. *Distinction: A Social Critique of the Judgment of Taste.* Trans. Richard Nice. Cambridge, MA: Harvard University Press, 1984.

——. *Homo Academicus.* Trans. Peter Collier. Paris: Editions de Minuit, 1988.

Bourdieu, Pierre, and Jean-Claude Passeron. *Reproduction in Education, Society, and Culture.* Trans. Richard Nice. London: Sage, 1990.

Bourdieu, Pierre, with Monique de Saint Martin. *The State Nobility: Elite Schools in the Field of Power.* Trans. Loretta C. Clough. Cambridge: Polity Press, 1996.

Brennan, Teresa. *The Transmission of Affect.* Ithaca: Cornell University Press, 2004.

Brook, Timothy. "Institution." In *Critical Terms for the Study of Buddhism*, ed. Donald Lopez, 143–61. Chicago: University of Chicago Press, 2005.

——. *Praying for Power: Buddhism and the Formation of Gentry Society in Late-Ming China.* Cambridge, MA: Harvard University Press, 1993.

Brox, Trine. *Tibetan Democracy: Governance, Leadership and Conflict in Exile.* London: I. B. Tauris, 2016.

Bull, M., and J. P. Mitchell. Introduction. In *Ritual, Performance and the Senses.* London: Bloomsbury, 2015.

Cabezón, José Ignacio. "Monks." http://www.thlib.org/#!essay=/cabezon/sera/people/monks/s/b4.

——. "The Regulations of a Monastery." In *Religions of Tibet in Practice*, ed. Donald Lopez Jr., 335–51. Princeton, NJ: Princeton University Press, 1997.

Cabezón, José Ignacio, and Penpa Dorjee. *Sera Monastery*. Boston: Wisdom, 2019.

Cabezón, José Ignacio, and Roger R. Jackson, eds. *Tibetan Literature: Studies in Genre*. Ithaca, NY: Snow Lion, 1996.

Calhoun, Craig. *Nations Matter: Culture, History, and the Cosmopolitan Dream*. New York: Routledge, 2007.

Calhoun, Craig, Edward LiPuma, and Postone Moishe, eds. *Bourdieu: Critical Perspectives*. Cambridge: Polity Press, 1993.

Cantwell, Cathy, and Rob Mayer. "Two Proposals for Critically Editing the Texts of the rNying ma'i rGyud 'bum." *Revue d'Études Tibétaines* (Langues et Cultures de l'Aire Tibétaines, CNRS, Paris) 10 (April 2006): 56–70.

Caple, Jane. *Morality and Monastic Revival in Post-Mao Tibet*. Honolulu: University of Hawai'i Press, 2019.

Chogyam Trungpa, trans. *The Life of Marpa the Translator: Seeing Accomplishes All*. Boston: Shambhala, 1982.

Chou, Wen-shing. "Maps of Wutai Shan: Individuating the Sacred Landscape Through Color." *Journal of the International Association of Tibetan Studies* 6 (December 2011): 372–86.

Clark, William. *Academic Charisma and the Origins of the Research University*. Chicago: University of Chicago Press, 2007.

Clough, Patricia Ticineto et al., eds. *The Affective Turn: Theorizing the Social*. London and Durham, NC: Duke University Press, 2007.

Clunas, Craig. *Art in China*. New York: Oxford University Press, 1997.

——. *Superfluous Things: Material Culture and Social Status in Early Modern China*. Honolulu: University of Hawai'i Press, 1997.

Cuevas, Bryan J. *The Hidden History of the Tibetan Book of the Dead*. Oxford: Oxford University Press, 2003.

——. "The Politics of Magical Warfare." In *Faith and Empire: Art and Politics in Tibetan Buddhism*, ed. Karl Debreczeny, 171–89. New York: Rubin Museum of Art, 2019.

——. "Preliminary Remarks on the History of Mindrölling: The Founding and Organization of a Tibetan Monastery in the Seventeenth Century." In *Places of Practice: Monasteries and Monasticism in Asian Religions*, ed. James Benn, Lori Meeks, and James Robson. Honolulu: University of Hawaii Press (forthcoming).

Cüppers, Christoph. "A Letter by the Fifth Dalai Lama to the King of Bhaktapur." Ed. Franz Steiner, JNRC. Nepal Research Centre Publications, 1977.

——. *The Relationship Between Religion and State* (chos srid zung 'brel) *in Traditional Tibet*. Lumbini: Lumbini International Research Center, 2004.

Dalton, Jacob P. *The Gathering of Intentions: The History of a Tibetan Buddhist Tantra*. New York: Columbia University Press, 2016.

——. "Recreating the Rnyingma School: the Mdo dbang tradition of Smin grol gling." In *Power, Politics, and the Reinvention of Tradition: Tibet in the 17th and 18th Centuries. PIATS 2003: Tibetan Studies: Proceedings of the 10th Seminar of the International Association for Tibetan Studies, Oxford, 2003*, vol. 10/3, ed. Bryan J. Cuevas and Kurtis R. Schaeffer. Leiden; Boston: Brill, 2006.

———. *The Taming of the Demons: Violence and Liberation in Tibetan Buddhism*. New Haven, CT: Yale University Press, 2011.

———. "The Uses of the Dgongs pa 'dus pa'i mdo in the Development of the Rning-ma School of Tibetan Buddhism." PhD diss., University of Michigan, 2002.

Daṇḍin. *What Ten Young Men Did*. Trans. Isabelle Onians. New York: New York University Press, J. J. C. Foundation, 2005.

Davidson, Ronald. *Indian Esoteric Buddhism: A Social History of the Tantric Period*. New York: Columbia University Press, 2002.

———. *Tibetan Renaissance: Tantric Buddhism in the Rebirth of Tibetan Culture*. New York: Columbia University Press, 2005.

DeCaroli, Robert. *Image Problems: The Origin and Development of Buddha's Image in Early South Asia*. Seattle: University of Washington Press, 2015.

Deroche, Marc-Henri. "History of the Forgotten Mother Monastery of the Ancients' School: The dPal ri Monastery in the Valley of the Tibetan Emperors." *Bulletin of Tibetology* (Gangtok: Namgyal Institute of Tibetology) 49, no. 1 (2013): 77–112.

———. "On Being 'Impartial' (*ris med*): From Non-Sectarianism to the Great Perfection." *Revue d'Etudes Tibétaines* 44 (2018): 129–58.

Derrida, Jacques. *Of Grammatology*. Trans. Gayatri Spivak. Baltimore: Johns Hopkins University Press, 1997.

Desideri, Ippolito, and Michael Sweet, trans. *Mission to Tibet: The Extraordinary Eighteenth-Century Account of Father Ippolito Desideri S.J.* Ed. Leonard Zwilling. Boston: Wisdom, 2010.

Diemberger, Hildegard. *When a Woman Becomes a Religious Dynasty: The Samding Dorje Phagmo of Tibet*. New York: Columbia University Press, 2007.

DiValerio, David. *The Holy Madmen of Tibet*. New York: Oxford University Press, 2015.

Doctor, Andreas. *Tibetan Treasure Literature: Revelation, Tradition and Accomplishment in Visionary Buddhism*. Ithaca, NY: Snow Lion, 2005.

Dorje, Gyurme. "The Guhyagharba Tantra: An Introduction." *Hankop Blogspot*. July 28, 2017. http://hankop.blogspot.com/2017/07/an-introduction-to-guhyagar bha-tantra.html (accessed February 2020).

Dreyfus, George. "Cherished Memories, Cherished Communities: Proto-nationalism in Tibet." In *The History of Tibet: Volume 2 The Medieval Period: c. AD 850-1895, the Development of Buddhist Paramountcy*, ed. Alex McKay, 492-522. New York: Routledge, 2003.

———. *The Sound of Two Hands Clapping: The Education of a Tibetan Buddhist Monk*. Berkeley and Los Angeles: University of California Press, 2003.

Duckworth, Douglas. *Jamgön Mipham: His Life and Teachings*. Boston: Shambhala, 2011.

Dudjom Rinpoché, Jikdrel Yeshe Dorje. *The Nyingma School of Tibetan Buddhism: Its Fundamentals and History*. Trans. Gyurmé Dorjé. Ed. Matthew Kapstein. Boston: Wisdom, 1991.

Ellingson, Ter. "The Mandala of Sound." PhD diss., University of Wisconsin-Madison, 1979.

———. "Tibetan Monastic Constitutions: The Bca' Yig." In *Reflections on Tibetan Culture: Essays in Memory of Turrell V. Wylie*, ed. Lawrence Epstein and R. F. Shelburne, 205–29. Lewistown, NY: Edwin Mellon Press, 1990.

Elverskog, Johan. "Wutai Shan, Qing Cosmopolitanism, and the Mongols." *Journal of the International Association of Tibetan Studies* 6 (December 2011): 243–74.

Esler, Dylan. "The Origins and Early History of rDzogs Chen." *Tibet Journal* 30, no. 3 (Autumn 2005): 33–62.

Faure, Bernard. "Buddhism and Violence." In *The Cambridge Companion to Religious Studies*, ed. Robert A. Orsi, 255–72. Cambridge: Cambridge University Press, 2012.

——. *Visions of Power: Imagining Medieval Japanese Buddhism.* Trans. Phyllis Brooks. Princeton, NJ: Princeton University Press, 2000.

Foucault, Michel. "Of Other Spaces: Heterotopias." Trans. Jay Miskowiec. Paris: Architecture, Mouvement, Continuité, 1984.

——. *Religion and Culture.* Selected and ed. by Jeremy R. Carrette. New York: Routledge, 1999.

Gamble, Ruth. "'Cosmic Onomatopoeia' or the Source of the Waterfall of Youth: Chögyam Trungpa and Döndrup Gyal's Parallel Histories of Tibetan mGur." In *Tibetan Literary Genres, Texts, and Text Types*, ed. Jim Rheingans, 110–37. Leiden: Brill, 2015.

Gardner, Alexander. "The Twenty-five Great Sites of Khams: Religious Geography, Revelation, and Nonsectarianism in Nineteenth-Century Eastern Tibet." PhD diss., University of Michigan, 2006.

Gayley, Holly. *Love Letters from Golok: A Tantric Couple in Modern Tibet.* New York: Columbia University Press, 2017.

——. "Revisiting the 'Secret Consort' (*gsang yum*) in Tibetan Buddhism," *Religions* 9, no. 6 (June 2018): 179/1–21. DOI: 10.3390/rel9060179.

Gell, Alfred. *Art and Agency: An Anthropological Theory.* Oxford: Oxford University Press, 1998.

——. "The Technology of Enchantment and the Enchantment of Technology." In *Anthropology, Art, and Aesthetics*, ed. Jeremy Coote and Anthony Shelton, 40–66. New York: Oxford University Press, 1992.

Gentry, James. "Representations of Efficacy: The Ritual Expulsion of Mongol Armies in the Consolidation and Expansion of the Tsang (Gtsang) Dynasty." In *Tibetan Ritual*, ed. José Ignacio Cabezón, 131–64. New York: Oxford University Press, 2010.

Gold, Jonathan C. *The Dharma's Gatekeepers: Sakya Pandita on Buddhist Scholarship in Tibet.* Albany: State University of New York Press, 2008.

Goldstein, Melvyn. "Lhasa Street Songs: Political and Social Satire in Traditional Tibet." *Tibet Journal* 7 (1982): 56–66.

Goldstein, Melvyn, and Gelek Rinpoché. *A History of Modern Tibet 1913-1951: The Demise of the Lamaist State.* Berkeley: University of California Press, 1989.

Goodman, Nelson. *Languages of Art: An Approach to a Theory of Symbols.* Indianapolis, IN: Hackett, 1976.

——. *Ways of Worldmaking.* Indianapolis, IN: Hackett, 1978.

Goodman, Nelson, and Catherine Elgin. *Reconceptions in Philosophy and Other Arts and Sciences.* Indianapolis, IN: Hackett, 1988.

Graham, Patricia J. *Faith and Power in Japanese Buddhist Art, 1600-2005.* Honolulu: University of Hawai'i Press, 2007.

Gregg, Melissa, et al., eds. *The Affect Theory Reader*. London and Durham, NC: Duke University Press, 2010.

Gyatrul Rinpoché. *Meditation, Transformation and Dream Yoga*. Trans. B. Alan Wallace and Sangyé Khandro. Ithaca, NY: Snow Lion, 2002.

Gyatso, Janet. *Apparitions of the Self: The Secret Biography of a Tibetan Visionary*. Princeton, NJ: Princeton University Press, 1988.

——. *Being Human in a Buddhist World: An Intellectual History of Medicine in Early Modern Tibet*. New York: Columbia University Press, 2015.

——. "Down with the Demoness: Reflections on a Feminine Ground in Tibet." *Tibet Journal* 21, no. 4 (1987): 33–51.

——. "Drawn from the Tibetan Treasury: the gTer ma Literature." In *Tibetan Literature: Studies in Genre*, ed. José Ignacio Cabezón and Roger R. Jackson, 147–69. Ithaca, NY: Snow Lion, 1996.

——. "Experience, Empiricism, and the Fortunes of Authority: Tibetan Medicine and Buddhism on the Eve of Modernity." In *Forms of Knowledge in Early Modern Asia: Explorations in the Intellectual History of India and Tibet, 1500–1800*, ed. Sheldon Pollock, 311–35. Durham, NC: Duke University Press, 2011.

——. "Image as Presence." In *From the Sacred Realm: Treasures of Tibetan Art from the Newark Museum*, ed. Valrae Reynolds, 171–79. Munich, London, New York: Prestel, 1999.

——. "The Logic of Legitimation in Tibetan Treasure Tradition." *History of Religions* 33, no. 2 (1993): 97–134.

Hackett, Paul. "The Sman rtsis khang: A Survey of Pedagogical and Reference Literature." In *Tibetan and Himalayan Healing: An Anthology for Anthony Aris*, ed. Charles Ramble and Ulrike Roesler, 291–98. Kathmandu: Vajra Publications, 2015.

Hallisey, Charles. "Works and Persons in Sinhala Literary Culture." In *Literary Cultures in History: Reconstructions from South Asia*, ed. Sheldon Pollock, 689–746. Berkeley: University of California Press, 2003.

Hansen, Anne. *How to Behave: Buddhism and Modernity in Colonial Cambodia 1860–1930*. Honolulu: University of Hawai'i Press, 2007.

Han-Shan. *The Collected Songs of Cold Mountain*. Trans. Bill Porter. Port Townsend, WA: Copper Canyon Press, 2000.

Hartley, Lauren. "Self as a Faithful Public Servant: The Autobiography of Mdo khar ba Tshe ring dbang rgyal (1697–1763)." In *Mapping the Modern in Tibet*, PIATS 2006: *Proceedings of the Eleventh Seminar of the International Association for Tibetan Studies*, ed. Gray Tuttle, 45–73. Andiast, Switzerland: International Association for Tibetan and Buddhist Studies, 2011.

Harvard University. "Harvard University Archives: The Harvard Charter of 1650." https://library.harvard.edu/university-archives/using-the-collections/online -resources/charter-of-1650 (accessed January 2020).

——. "Welcome to Library.Harvard." *Harvard Library*. 2020. http://hul.harvard.edu /huarc/charter.html.

Helffer, Mireille. *Mchod-rol: Les instruments de la musique tibetaine* [The instruments of Tibetan music]. Paris: CNRS Editions, 1994.

Henss, Michael. *The Cultural Monuments of Tibet*. New York: Prestel, 2014.

Hinderleter, Beth. Introduction, In *Communities of Sense: Rethinking Aesthetics and Politics*, ed. Beth Hinderleter et al. Durham, NC: Duke University Press, 2009.

Hinderliter, Beth, William Kaizen, Vered Maimon, Jaleh Mansoor, and Seth McCormick, eds. *Communities of Sense: Rethinking Aesthetics and Politics*. Durham, NC: Duke University Press, 2009.

Hirschberg, Daniel. *Padmasambhava in the History of Tibet's Golden Age*. Somerville, MA: Wisdom, 2016.

Holly, Michael Ann, and Keith Moxey, eds. *Art History, Aesthetics, Visual Studies*. Williamstown, MA: Sterling and Francine Clark Art Institute, 2002.

Holmes-Tagchungdarpa, Amy. *The Social Life of Tibetan Biography: Textuality, Community, and Authority in the Lineage of Tokden Shakya Shri*. Lanham, MD: Lexington Books, 2014.

Hutchings, Tim, and Joanne McKenzie, eds. *Materiality and the Study of Religion: The Stuff of the Sacred*. New York: Routledge, 2017.

Ikegami, Eiko. *Bonds of Civility: Aesthetic Networks and the Political Origins of Japanese Culture*. New York: Cambridge University Press, 2005.

Ishihama, Yumiko. "An Aspect of the Tibet, Mongol and China Relationship in the Late 17th Century from the View of Tibetan Letter Format—based on the Letters of the Fifth Dalai Lama, the Regent Sangs-rgyas-rgya-mtsho and the Mongolian Prince Galden." *Journal of Asian and African Studies* 55 (1988): 165–89.

——. "On the Dissemination of the Belief in the Dalai Lama as a Manifestation of the Bodhisattva Avalokiteśvara." *Acta Asiatica: Bulletin of the Institute of Eastern Culture*, Tokyo: The Toho Gakkai [The Institute of Eastern Culture] 64 (1993): 38–56.

Jackson, David. *History of Tibetan Painting: The Great Tibetan Painters and Their Traditions*. Vienna: Verlag der Osterreichischen Akadamie der Wissenschaften, 1996.

Jackson, David, and Janice Jackson. *Tibetan Thangka Painting: Methods and Materials*. Ithaca, NY: Snow Lion, 2006.

Jackson, Roger R. "'Poetry' in Tibet: *Glu, mGur, sNyan ngag* and 'Songs of Experience.'" In *Tibetan Literature: Studies in Genre*, ed. Jos Ignacio Cabezon and Roger R. Jackson, 368–92. Ithaca, NY: Snow Lion, 1996.

——. *Tantric Treasures: Three Collections of Mystical Verse from Buddhist India*. Oxford: Oxford University Press, 2004.

Jacoby, Sarah. "Consorts and Revelation in Eastern Tibet: The Autobiographical Writings of the Treasure Revealer Sera Khandro (1892–1940)." PhD Diss., University of Virginia, 2007.

——. *Love and Liberation: Autobiographical Writings of the Tibetan Buddhist Visionary Sera Khandro*. New York: Columbia University Press, 2014.

Jamyang Dorjé, Nyöshul Khenpo (Smyo shul Mkhan po). *A Marvelous Garland of Rare Gems: Biographies of Masters of Awareness in the Dzogchen Lineage: A Spiritual History of the Teachings on Natural Great Perfection*. Trans. Richard Barron. Junction City, CA: Padma Publishing, 2005.

Jansen, Berthe. "The Monastery Rules: Buddhist Monastic Organization in Pre-Modern Tibet." PhD diss., Leiden University, 2015.

——. *The Monastery Rules: Buddhist Monastic Organization in Pre-Modern Tibet*. Oakland: University of California Press, 2018.

——. "Monastic Guidelines (bCa' yig): Tibetan Social History from a Buddhist Studies Perspective." In *Social Regulation: Case Studies from Tibetan History*, ed. Jeannine Bischoff and Saul Mullard. Leiden: Brill, 2016.

Kapstein, Matthew T. "The Indian Literary Identity in Tibet." In *Literary Cultures in History: Reconstructions from South Asia*, ed. Sheldon Pollock, 747–802. Oakland: University of California Press, 2003.

——. "Just Where on Jambudvīpa Are We? New Geographical Knowledge and Old Cosmological Schemes in Eighteenth-Century Tibet." In *Forms of Knowledge in Early Modern Asia: Explorations in the Intellectual History of India and Tibet 1500–1800*, ed. Sheldon Pollock, 336–64. Durham, NC: Duke University Press, 2011.

——. "Zhentong Traces in the Nyingma Tradition: Two Texts from Mindroling." In *The Other Emptiness: Rethinking the Zhentong Buddhist Discourse in Tibet*, ed. Michael R. Sheehy and Klaus Dieter-Mathes, 235–56. Albany: State University of New York Press, 2019.

Karmay, Samten G. *The Arrow and the Spindle: Studies in History, Myths, Rituals, and Beliefs in Tibet*. Kathmandu: Mandala Book Point, 1998.

——. *The Great Perfection (rDzogs Chen): A Philosophical and Meditative Teaching*. Leiden: Brill Academic Publishers, 2007.

——, trans. *The Illusive Play: The Autobiography of the Fifth Dalai Lama*. Chicago: Serindia, 2014.

——. "The Ordinance of lHa Bla-ma Ye-shes-'od." In *The Arrow and the Spindle*, 3–16. Kathmandu: Mandala, 1988.

——. "The Rituals and Their Origins in the Visionary Accounts of the Fifth Dalai Lama." In *Religion and Secular Culture in Tibet, Tibetan Studies: Proceedings of the Ninth Seminar of the International Association for Tibetan Studies*, ed. Henk Blezer. Leiden: Brill Academic Publishers, 2002.

——. *Secret Visions of the Fifth Dalai Lama: The Gold Manuscript in the Fournier Collection Musee Guimet*. Paris; London: Serindia, 1988.

Keane, Webb. "The Evidence of the Senses and the Materiality of Religion." Special Issue: The Objects of Evidence: Anthropological Approaches to the Production of Knowledge. *Journal of the Royal Anthropological Institute* 14 (2008): 110–27.

Kieschnick, John. *The Impact of Buddhism on Chinese Material Culture*. Princeton, NJ: Princeton University Press, 2003.

Kilby, Christina. "Bowing with Words: Paper, Ink, and Bodies in Tibetan Buddhist Epistles." *Journal of the American Academy of Religion* 87, no. 1 (March 2019): 260–81. DOI: 10.1093/jaarel/lfy036/.

Kim, Hanung."Renaissance Man from Amdo: The Life and Scholarship of the Eighteenth-Century Amdo Scholar Sum pa Mkhan po Ye shes dpal 'byor (1704–1788)." PhD diss., Harvard University, 2018.

Ko, Dorothy. *Teachers of the Inner Chambers: Women and Culture in Seventeenth-Century China*. Stanford, CA: Stanford University Press, 1994.

Kohn, Richard J. *Lord of Dance: The Mani Rimdu Festival in Tibet and Nepal*. New York: SUNY Series in Buddhist Studies, 2001.

Lama Jabb. *Oral and Literary Continuities in Modern Tibetan Literature: The Inescapable Nation*. Lanham, MD: Lexington Books, 2015.

Li, Ruohong. "A Tibetan Aristocratic Family in Eighteenth-Century Tibet: A Study of Qing- Tibetan Contact." PhD diss., Harvard University, 2002.

Li, Zehou. *The Chinese Aesthetic Tradition*. Trans. Maija Bell Samei. Honolulu: University of Hawai'i Press, 2010.

——. *Four Essays on Aesthetics Toward a Global View*. Trans. Jane Cauvel, Landham: Lexington Books, 2006.

Lin, Nancy Grace. "Adapting the Buddha's Biographies: A Cultural History of the Wish-Fulfilling Vine in Tibet, Seventeenth to Eighteenth Centuries." PhD diss., University of California, Berkeley, 2011.

——. "Recounting the Fifth Dalai Lama's Rebirth Lineage." *Revue d'Études Tibétaines* 38 (February 2017): 119–56.

Linrothe, Rob. "'Utterly False, Utterly Undeniable' Visual Strategies in the Akaniṣṭha Shrine Murals of Takden Phuntsokling Monastery." *Archives of Asian Art* 67, no. 2 (2017): 143–87.

Longchenpa. *Finding Rest in the Nature of the Mind: The Trilogy of Rest*. Vol. 1. Trans. Padmakara Translation Group. Boulder, CO: Shambhala, 2017.

Lopez, Donald. *Prisoners of Shangri-la: Tibetan Buddhism and the West*. Chicago: University of Chicago Press, 1998.

MacCormack, Ian. "Buddhism and State in Seventeenth-Century Tibet: Cosmology and Theology in the Works of Sangyé Gyatso." PhD diss., Harvard University, 2018.

MacDonald, Ariene, with Dvags-po Rinpoché and Yon-tan rgya-mtso. "Un Portrait du Cinquieme Dalai Lama" [A portrait of the Fifth Dalai Lama]. In *Essais sur L'Art du Tibet*, ed. Ariene MacDonald and Yoshira Imaeda, 119–56. Paris: Librairie d'Amerique et d'Orient, 1977.

Mauss, Marcel. *The Gift: Forms and Functions of Exchange in Archaic Societies*. London: Cohen and West, 1966.

Mayer, Robert. "Rethinking Treasure (part one)." *Revue d'Études Tibetaines* 52 (October 2019): 119–84.

McRae, John. *Seeing Through Zen: Encounter, Transformation, and Genealogy in Chinese Chan Buddhism*. Berkeley: University of California Press, 2003.

Mdo mkhar Tshe ring dbang rgyal. *The Tale of the Incomparable Prince*. Trans. Beth Newman. New York: HarperCollins, 1996.

Melnick, Alison. "The Life and Times of Mingyur Peldrön: Female Leadership in 18th-Century Tibetan Buddhism." PhD diss., University of Virginia, 2014.

Meyer, Birgit. *Aesthetic Formations: Media, Religion, and the Senses*. London: Palgrave Macmillan, 2009.

——. "Religious Sensations: Why Media, Aesthetics, and Power Matter in the Study of Contemporary Religion." In *Religion: Beyond a Concept*, ed. Hent de Vries, 704–23. New York: Fordham University Press, 2008.

Mills, Martin A. *Identity, Ritual, and State in Tibetan Buddhism: The Foundations of Authority in Gelukpa Monasticism*. London and New York: Routledge, 2003.

Mindrolling Jetsün Khandro Rinpoche and Mindrolling Jetsün Dechen Paldrön. "The Mindrolling History Project." Stanley, VA: Dharmashri Group, Pema Gatsal, 2015. https://www.lotusgardens.org/dharmashri/mindrolling-history/ (accessed March 23, 2020).

Mohr, Thea, and Ven. Jampa Tsedroen. *Dignity and Discipline: The Evolving Role of Women in Buddhism.* Boston: Wisdom, 2010.

Monhart, Michael. "Listening with the Gods: Offering, Beauty and Being in Tibetan Ritual Music." *Revue D'Etudes Tibétaines: Studies in the Tibetan Performing Arts* 40 (July 2017): 92–102.

Mullard, Saul. *Opening the Hidden Land: State Formation and the Construction of Sikkimese History.* Brill's Tibetan Studies Library Series. Leiden; Boston: Brill, 2011.

——. "The 'Tibetan' Formation of Sikkim: Religion, Politics, and the Construction of a Coronation Myth." *Bulletin of Tibetology* 41, no. 2 (2005): 31–48.

Naga, Sangye Tender. "Aspects of Traditional Tibetan Learning." *Tibet Journal* 31, no. 3 (2006): 3–16. http://www.jstor.org/stable/43300980 (accessed April 1, 2020).

Nardi, Isabella. *Theory of Citrasutras in Indian Painting: A Critical Reevaluation of Their Uses and Interpretations.* London and New York: Routledge, 2006.

Newman, Beth. "The Tibetan Novel and Its Sources." In *Tibetan Literature: Studies in Genre,* ed. José Ogmacop Cabezon and Roger R. Jackson, 411–21. Ithaca, NY: Snow Lion, 1996.

Oxford English Dictionary (OED). https://www.oed.com/.

Pasang Wangdu and Hildegard Diemberger. *dBa' bzhad: The Royal Narrative Concerning the Bridging of the Buddha's Doctrine to Tibet.* Vienna: Verlag de Osterreichischen Akademie der Wissenschaften, 2000.

Petech, Luciano. "Aristocracy and Government in Tibet 1728–1959." In *Selected Papers on Tibetan History.* Seriale Orientale Roma 60. Rome: Istituto Italiano per il Medio ed Estremo Oriente, 1988.

——. *Central Tibet and the Mongols: The Yuan Sa-Skya Period of Tibetan History.* Rome: Instituto Italiano per il Medio ed Estremo Oriente, 1990.

——. *China and Tibet in the Early 18th Century.* Leiden: E. J. Brill, 1972.

Peter Prince of Greece. *The Aristocracy of Central Tibet: A Provisional List of the Names of the Noble Houses of U-Tsang.* Kalimpong: G. Tharchin, Melong Press, 1954.

Pinney, Christopher, and Nicholas Thomas, eds. *Beyond Aesthetics: Art and the Technologies of Enchantment.* Oxford and New York: Berg, 2001.

Pirie, Fernanda. "Which 'Two Laws'? The Concept of trimnyi (khrims gnyis) in Medieval Tibet." *Cahiers d'Extrême-Asie, Droit et Bouddhisme. Principe et pratique dans le Tibet prémoderne/Law and Buddhism. Principle and Practice in Pre-modern Tibet* 26 (2017): 41-60.

Pitkin, Annabella. "Lineage, Authority and Innovation: The Biography of Ku Nu Bla Ma Bstan 'Dzin Rgyal Mtshan." In *Mapping the Modern in Tibet,* PIATS 2006: *Proceedings of the Eleventh Seminar of the International Association for Tibetan Studies,* ed. Gray Tuttle, 173–204. Andiast, Switzerland: International Association for Tibetan and Buddhist Studies, 2011.

Pollock, Sheldon, ed. *Forms of Knowledge in Early Modern Asia: Explorations in the Intellectual History of India and Tibet 1500-1800.* Durham, NC: Duke University Press, 2011.

——. *A Rasa Reader: Classical Indian Aesthetics.* New York: Columbia University Press, 2016.

Pommaret, Françoise, ed. *Lhasa in the Seventeenth Century: The Capital of the Dalai Lamas.* Trans. Howard Solverson. Leiden: Brill Academic Publishers, 2003.

Pomplun, Trent. *Jesuit on the Roof of the World: Ippolito Desideri's Mission to Tibet.* New York: Oxford University Press, 2010.

Prohl, Inken. "Aesthetics." In *Key Terms in Material Religion,* ed. S. Brent Plate, 9–16. New York: Bloomsbury Academic, 2015.

Promey, Sally M., ed. *Sensational Religion: Sensory Cultures in Material Practice.* New Haven, CT, and London: Yale University Press, 2014.

Qian'eba duojieouzhu, and Zhuomatai. "Xizang SuguanXuexiao—Zikang Jianshu" [A Tibetan school for lay officials—A brief introduction to *rtsi khang*]. *Zhongguo zangxue* [China Tibetology] 4 (1990): 90–92.

Quintman, Andrew, trans. *The Life of Milarepa.* New York: Penguin, 2010.

Rancière, Jacques. "Contemporary Art and the Politics of Aesthetics." In *Communities of Sense: Rethinking Aesthetics and Politics,* ed. Beth Hinderliter, William Kaizen, Vered Maimon, Jaleh Mansoor, and Seth McCormick, 31–50. Durham, NC: Duke University Press, 2009.

Rhie, Marilyn, and Robert Thurman. *Wisdom and Compassion: The Sacred Art of Tibet.* New York: Tibet House with Harry M. Abrams, 1991.

Richardson, Hugh. *High Peaks, Rare Earth: Collected Writings on Tibetan History and Culture.* London: Serindia, 1998.

Ronis, Jann. "Celibacy, Revelations, and Reincarnated Lamas: Contestation and Synthesis in the Growth of Monasticism at Katok Monastery from the 17th Through 19th Centuries." PhD diss., University of Virginia, 2009.

Rossabi, Morris, ed. *China Among Equals: The Middle Kingdom and Its Neighbors, 10th–14th Centuries.* Berkeley and Los Angeles: University of California Press, 1983.

Ruegg, David S. "Introductory Remarks on the Spiritual and Temporal Orders." In *The Relationship Between Religion and State (chos srid zung 'brel) in Traditional Tibet,* ed. Chistoph Cüppers, 9–14. Lumbini, Nepal: Lumbini International Research Institute, 2004.

——. *Ordre Spirituel and Ordre Temporal dans la pensée boudhique de l'Inde et du Tibet.* Paris: Collège de France. 1995.

——. "The Preceptor-Donor (Yon Mchod) Relation in Thirteenth Century Tibetan Society and Polity, Its Inner Asian Precursors and Indian Models." In *Tibetan Studies II: Proceedings of the 7th Seminar of the International Association for Tibetan Studies, Graz 1995,* ed. Ernst Steinkellner, II: 857–72. Vienna: Verlag der Österreichischen Akademie der Wissenschaften, 1997.

——. "Semantics of a Tibetan Religio-Social and Religio-Political Concept." In *Tibetan History and Language: Studies Dedicated to Uray Geza on His Seventieth Birthday,* ed. Ernst Steinkellner. Vienna: Arbeitskreis fur Tibetische und Buddhistische Studien Universitat, 1991.

Samei, Maija Bell. Translator's introduction. In *The Chinese Aesthetic Tradition.* Honolulu: University of Hawai'i Press, 2010.

Samuel, Geoffrey. *Civilized Shamans: Buddhism in Tibetan Societies.* Washington and London: Smithsonian Institution, 1993.

Sangs rgyas rgya mtsho. *Life of the Fifth Dalai Lama.* Vol IV, Part I. Trans. Ahmad Zahiruddin. New Delhi: International Academy of Indian Culture and Aditya Prakashan, 1999.

Schaeffer, Kurtis. "The Fifth Dalai Lama Ngawang Lobsang Gyatso." In *The Dalai Lamas: A Visual History*, ed. Martin Brauen, 64–91. Chicago: Serindia, 2005.

——. *Himalayan Hermitess: The Life of a Tibetan Buddhist Nun*. New York: Oxford University Press, 2004.

——. "New Scholarship in Tibet 1650–1700." In *Forms of Knowledge in Early Modern Asia: Explorations in the Intellectual History of India and Tibet 1500–1800*, ed. Sheldon Pollock, 291–310. Durham, NC: Duke University Press, 2011.

——. "Ritual, Festival, and Authority Under the Fifth Dalai Lama." In *Power, Politics and the Reinvention of Tradition in Seventeenth- and Eighteenth-Century Tibet: Proceedings of the International Association for Tibetan Studies, 10th Seminar, Oxford University, 2003*, ed. Bryan Cuevas and Kurtis Schaeffer, 187–202. Leiden: Brill, 2006.

Scheidegger, Daniel. "Tibetan Ritual Music: A General Survey with Special Reference to the Mindrölling Tradition." In *Opuscula Tibetana*, fasc. 19. Rikon-Zurich: Tibet-Institut, 1988.

Schneider, Hannah. "Tibetan Epistolary Style." In *The Dalai Lamas: A Visual History*, ed. Martin Brauen, 258–61. Chicago: Serindia, 2005.

Schopen, Gregory. *Buddhist Monks and Business Matters: Still More Papers on Monastic Buddhists in India*. Honolulu: University of Hawai'i Press, 2004.

Schuh, Dieter. *Erlasse und Sendschreiben mongolischer Herrscher für tibetische Geistliche: Ein Beitrag zur Kenntniss der Urkunden des tibetischen Mittelalters und ihrer Diplomatik* [Regulations and letter exchanges from the Mongol rulers to Tibetan monks: contributing to the understanding of medieval Tibet and its diplomacy] (Monumenta Tibetican Historica. Abt III: Diplomata et Epistolae, Bd. 1). St. Augustin: VGH, Wissenschaftsverlag, 1977.

Schuler, Barbara, ed. *Historicizing Emotions: Practices and Objects in India, China, and Japan*. Leiden: Brill, 2017.

Schwartz, Susan. *Rasa: Performing the Divine in India*. New York: Columbia University Press, 2004.

Schwieger, Peter. *Tibetische Handschriften und Blockdrucke* [Tibetan manuscripts and block prints]. In *Verzeichnis der Orientalischen Handischriften in Deutschland* [Catalogues of Oriental manuscripts in Germany], vol. 9, ed. Dieter Schuh and Franz Steiner. Stuggart: Verlag Wiesbaden, 1985.

Sharf, Robert H. "Prolegomenon to the Study of Japanese Buddhist Icons." In *Living Images, Japanese Buddhist Icons in Context*, ed. Robert H. Sharf and Elizabeth Horton Sharf, 1–18. Stanford, CA: Stanford University Press, 2001.

Sharf, Robert H., and Elizabeth Horton Sharf, eds. *Living Images: Japanese Buddhist Icons in Context*. Stanford, CA: Stanford University Press, 2001.

Sharma, Bhramanand. *Rasalocana: English and Sanskrit*. Jaipur: Champa Lal Ranka, 1985.

Sihlé, Nicolas. "Assessing and Rituals that Reproduce Collectivity: The Large-scale Rituals of the Repkong Tantrists in Tibet," *Religion and Society* 9, no. 1 (2018): 165–70.

Singer, Jane Casey, and Philip Denwood. *Tibetan Art: Towards a Definition of Style*. London: Laurence King with Alan Marcuson, 1997.

Sluga, Glenda, and Julia Horne. "Cosmopolitanism: Its Pasts and Practices." *Journal of World History* 21, no. 3 (2010): 369–73. http://www.jstor.org/stable/40985021.

Smith, E. Gene. *Among Tibetan Texts: History and Literature of the Himalayan Plateau*. Ed. Kurtis Schaeffer. Boston: Wisdom, 2001.

Sørensen, Per K. "Divinity Secularized: An Inquiry Into the Nature and Form of the Songs Ascribed to the Sixth Dalai Lama." PhD diss., Leipzig University, 1990.

Sørensen, Per K., and Guntram Hazod. *Rulers on the Celestial Plains: Ecclesiastic and Secular Hegemony in Medieval Tibet, A Study of Tshal Gung-thang*. Vienna: Osterreichische Akademie der Wissenschaften, 2007.

Sperling, Elliot. "Part One: Historical Facts." In *Authenticating Tibet: Answers to China's 100 Questions*, ed. Anne-Marie Blondeau and Katia Buffetille, 11–19. Berkeley and Los Angeles: University of California Press, 2008.

Stanley, Liz. "The Epistolarium: On Theorizing Letters and Correspondences." *Auto/Biography* 12, no. 3 (2004): 201–35. DOI: 10.1191/0967550704ab014oa.

Stein, Rolf A. *Tibetan Civilization*. Stanford, CA: Stanford University Press, 1972.

Stoddard, Heather. "The Style and Artistic Context." In *Secret Visions of the Fifth Dalai Lama: The Gold Manuscript in the Fournier Collection Musee Guimet, Paris*, ed. Samten Karmay, 10–13. London: Serindia, 1991.

Sur, Dominic. "Constituting Canon and Community in Eleventh-Century Tibet: The Extant Writings of Rongzom and His *Charter of Mantrins (sngags pa'i bca' yig)*." *Religions* 8, no. 3 (2017): 40/1–29.

Tambiah, Stanley. *World Conqueror and World Renouncer: A Study of Buddhism and Polity in Thailand Against a Historical Background*. New York: Cambridge University Press, 1976.

Terrone, Antonio. "Anything is an Appropriate Treasure Teaching! Authentic Treasure Revealers and the Moral Implications of Noncelibate Tantric Practice." In *Tibetan Studies: An Anthology. Proceedings of the Eleventh Seminar of the International Association of Tibetan Studies, 2006*, ed. Peter Schwieger and Saadet Arslan, 458–86. Halle: International Institute for Tibetan and Buddhist Studies, 2009.

Terrone, Antonio, and Sarah Jacoby. *Buddhism Beyond the Monastery: Tantric Practices and Their Performers in Tibet and the Himalayas. Proceedings of the Tenth Seminar of the International Association of Tibetan Studies, Oxfod 2003*. Leiden: Brill, 2008.

Thondop Rinpoche, Tulku. *Hidden Teachings of Tibet: An Explanation of the Terma Tradition of Tibetan Buddhism*. Ed. Harold Talbott. Boston: Wisdom, 1997.

Thurman, Robert. *The Speech of Gold: Reason and Enlightenment in Tibetan Buddhism*. Delhi: Motilal Banardisas Press, 1990.

Townsend, Dominique. "Buddhism's Worldly Other: Secular Subjects of Tibetan Learning." *Himalaya: The Journal for the Association of Nepal and Himalayan Studies* 36, no. 1 (May 2016): article 15.

——. "How to Constitute a Field of Merit: Structure and Flexibility in a Tibetan Buddhist Monastery's Curriculum." *Religions* 8, no. 9 (2017): 174. DOI: 10.3390/rel8090174.

Tsepon Wangchuk Deden Shakabpa. *One Hundred Thousand Moons: An Advanced History of Tibet*. Vol. 1. Trans. Derek F. Maher. Leiden; Boston: Brill, 2010.

Tuttle, Gray. *Tibetan Buddhists in the Making of Modern China*. New York: Columbia University Press, 2007.

van der Kuijp, Leonard W. J. "Tibetan Belles-Lettres: The Influence of Daṇḍin and Kṣemendra." In *Tibetan Literature: Studies in Genre*, ed. José Ogmacop Cabezon and Roger R. Jackson, 393–410. Ithaca, NY: Snow Lion, 1996.

——. "Untitled Review of Mi-dbang rtogs-brjod by Mdo-mkhar Tshe-ring by Zhuang Ting." *Journal of the American Oriental Society* 105, no. 2 (April–June, 1985): 321–22.

van Schaik, Sam. *Approaching the Great Perfection.* Somerville, MA: Wisdom, 2004.

——. Review of *The Gathering of Intentions: The History of a Tibetan Buddhist Tantra*, by Jake P. Dalton (New York: Columbia University Press, 2016). *Buddhist Studies Review* 35, nos. 1–2 (2018): 308–9.

——. "A Catalogue of the First Volume of the Waddell Manuscript RNying Ma Rgyud 'bum." *The Tibet Journal* 25, no. 1 (2000): 27–50. Accessed August 27, 2020. http://www.jstor.org/stable/43300793.

Van Vleet, Stacey. "Medicine as Impartial Knowledge: The Fifth Dalai Lama, the Tsarong School, and Debates of Tibetan Medical Orthodoxy." In *The Tenth Karmapa and Tibet's Turbulent Seventeenth Century*, ed. Karl Debreczeny and Gray Tuttle, 263–91. London: Serindia, 2016.

Vovelle, Michel. *Ideologies and Mentalities.* Trans. Eamon O'Flaherty. Chicago: University of Chicago Press, 1990.

Waddell, L. Austine. *Buddhism of Tibet or Lamaism.* Cambridge: W. Heffer and Sons Ltd, [1894]. Repr., Whitefish: Kessinger Publishing, 2003.

Yale University. "Traditions & History." *Yale.* 2020. http://www.yale.edu/about/history.html.

——. "The Yale Corporation: Charter and Legislation." https://www.yale.edu/sites/default/files/files/University-Charter.pdf (accessed January 2020).

Yamamoto, Karl. *Vision and Violence: Lama Zhang and the Politics of Charisma in Twelfth-Century Tibet.* Leiden: Brill, 2012.

Yangdon Dhondup, "Rules and Regulations of the Reb kong Tantric Community." in Monastic and Lay Traditions in North-Eastern Tibet, 117–40. Leiden: Brill, 2013.

Yangdon Dhondup, Geoffrey Samuel, and Ulrich Pagel, eds. *Monastic and Lay Traditions in North-Eastern Tibet.* Leiden: Brill, 2013.

Yangdzom Tsering. *The Aristocratic Families in Tibetan History, 1900-1951.* Beijing: China Intercontinental Press, 2006.

Yü, Chün-fang. *Kuan-yin: The Chinese Transformation of Avalokiteshvara.* New York: Columbia University Press, 2001.

Zabsdkar Tshogsdrug ranggrol (1781-1851). *The Life of Shabkar: The Autobiography of a Tibetan Yogin.* Trans. Richard Matthieu et al. Ithaca, NY: Snow Lion, 2001.

Index

Amdo (*a mdo*) (*continued*)
interpersonal connections, 107, 120;
and the Tibetan Buddhist world at
the time of Mindröling's founding,
107
Amitāyus, 61, 87f3.1, 95
Avalokiteśvara: the Dalai Lama
identified with, 45, 50, 204n61;
Kyirong Rangjung Pakba (*skyid
grong rang byng 'phags pa*), wooden
statue of, 44; Terdak Lingpa's
discovery of a Treasure related to,
16, 50

Bailey, Cameron, 225n21, 225n22,
225n24
Barthes, Roland, on the power of
writing, 169
Berger, Patricia, 195–96n3
Bhum, Pema, 208n48, 209n59,
215n81
Bhutan, 2, 65; and Mindröling's
institutional network, 79, 82.
See also Pema Lingpa
biographies (*rnam thar*): as a major
genre of Tibetan literature, 163–64;
and Tibetan letters (*chap shok* [*chab
shog*]), 89. *See also* lay people—and life
writing
Bogin, Benjamin, 223n4
Bön (*bon*) tradition, 38, 94; Terdak
Lingpa's letter to a Bön master, 107,
214n59
Bourdieu, Pierre, 199n33, 201–2n16,
222n50
Buddhism: deities. *See* Amitāyus;
Avalokiteśvara; textual system of
the Sūtra Vehicle (*mtshan nyid theg
pa'i gzhung*), 130, 135. *See also*
Abhidharmakośa (*chos mngon pa'i
mdzod*); Akaniṣṭha ('*og min*) realm;
Perfection of Wisdom (*phar phyin*);
tantric Buddhism; Two Systems of
Buddhist and worldly expertise (*lugs
gnyis* also "Two Laws" *khrims gnyis*);
Vinaya ('*dul ba lung*)

Cabezón, José, 223n64
Cabezón, José and Penpa Dorjee,
141–42, 207n17, 210n71, 222n54
Chan and Zen Buddhist traditions, 32,
206n6, 220n27
charisma: and the appearance of
madness, 32; of Nyö Lotsawa,
34–35; of the senior chairs and
abbots of Mindröling, 150; spiritual
and political topoi merged in
"academic charisma," 150, 200n38,
222n56
China (*rgya nag*): aesthetics fever just
after the Cultural Revolution, 11;
and the societies and cultures
surrounding seventeenth-century
Tibet, 33; and the three
architectural styles at Samyé and
Mindröling, 53; and the Tibetan
Buddhist world at the time of
Mindröling's founding, 2–3
chösi zungdrel (*chos srid zung 'brel*,
integration of religion and politics),
90, 198n25, 202n25; and the Fifth
Dalai Lama and Desi Sangyé Gyatso's
state-building project, 13–14; and
the Nyö clan, 33–35
Chou, Wen-shing, 196n3
Clark, William, on "academic
charisma," 150, 200n38, 222n56
cosmopolitanism: Lhasa as the
cosmopolitan capital of Greater
Tibet (*bod chen*), 2–3, 120, 190–91;
and the mentality and style
exemplified and cultivated at
Mindröling, 3, 8–9; and the Tibetan
Buddhist world at the time of
Mindröling's founding, 2, 33, 158–59.
See also Mindröling—as a center for
cultural production

Dalai Lamas: and "patron-priest"
(*mchod yon*) dynamics, 35, 119;
unification of the Tibetan polity
under the rule of the Ganden
Podrang (*dga' ldan pho brang*), 2

Doring (*rdo ring*) family: aristocratic legacy of, 168; Doring Tenzin Paljor (*rdo ring pa bstan 'dzin dpal 'byor*, 1721–1792), 152, 219–20n13; training at Mindröling of young men from, 173, 175–76

Dorjé Lingpa (*rdo rje gling pa*, 1346–1405), 43, 46, 48, 94, 104, 117, 189

Drachi (*grwa spyi*): and the Fifth Dalai Lama's gift to Terdak Lingpa of, 63–67; Gar Tongtsen's birthplace in, 68; Tharpaling monastery's location in, 62, 68, 181

Dranang (*grwa nang*) valley: Dargyé Chöling founded in, 35–36; households in the region of allotted to the support of Terdak Lingpa's wife or consort, 63

dreams (*rmi lam*): and *bardo* (*bar do*) states, 40; the Fifth Dalai Lama's dreams and visions of Mindröling's construction, 60–62; and the prophetic instructions received by Terdak Lingpa for finding his second Treasure, 49–50; and Terdak Lingpa's Vajrasattva Treasure cycle, 40; Terdak Lingpa's vision of the Fifth Dalai Lama as Avalokiteśvara, 45

Drépung monastery (*bras spungs dgon pa*), as a center for Géluk scholasticism, 30

Dreyfus, Georges B.J., 200n7, 207n16, 218n58; Géluk versus Nyingma pedagogy assessed by, 170

Dudjom Rinpoché, 211n82

Dumpopa Dondrub Wangyel (*ldum po ba don grub dbang rgyal*, d.u.), 40

Dzogchen monastery (*rdzongs chen dgon*), and the six mother monasteries (*ma dgon drug*) of the Nyingma tradition, 123, 209n66

Dzogchen (*rdzogs chen*). *See* Great Perfection

Ellingson, Ter, 216n11

Elverskog, Johan, 195n3

Europe, institutional affiliates of Mindröling located in, 11, 79

fields of knowledge. *See* rikné (*rig gnas*)

Fifth Dalai Lama. *See* Dalai Lamas—Dalai Lama V

Foucault, Michel, concept of heterotopia, 174, 223n65

Ganden monastery (*dga' ldan*), as a center for Géluk scholasticism, 30

Ganden Podrang (*dga' ldan pho brang*): and calendrical studies at Mindröling, 30, 158; and the founding of Mindröling, 28, 55, 75, 88, 122, 201–2n16; and the Khoshot Oriat Mongols, 83; and Lhasa's major Géluk monasteries, 142; material offerings granted to Mindröling to support ritual functions performed by Terdak Lingpa, 64; Pakmodru (*phag mo gru*) and Rinpungpa (*ring spungs pa*) periods contrasted with, 30; patronage of Mindröling by members of, 171; and power in Central Tibet during the tenure of the Fifth Dalai Lama and Sangyé Gyatso, 189; unification of the Tibetan polity under the rule of the Dalai Lama and the Géluk school, 2, 17, 19, 29–30, 201–2n16. *See also* Dalai Lamas; Sangyé Gyatso, *desi*

Garap Dorjé (*dga' rab rdo rje*), 56, 203n31

Gardner, Alexander, 208–9n54

Gathering of Intentions Sutra (*dgongs pa 'du pa'i mdo*): and the nine vehicles (*theg pa rim pa dgu*), 37; Nub Sangyé Yeshé's commentary on, 39; and the rituals of its *Sutra Initiation*, 37, 201n31

Gayley, Holly, 206n10, 211n2, 212n6, 213n25, 216n13

Jetsün Kunga Tenpé Nyima (*rje btsun kun dga bstan pa'i nyi ma*), 206n12
Jetsun Trinlé Chodron (*rje btsun phrin las chos sgron*, 18th–19th c.), 188, 225n29
Jikmé Pawo ('*jigs med dpa' bo*, b. 1682), 81

Kagyu (*bka' brgyud*) school: and Miwang Dokharwa, 152; ordination of nuns addressed by the current Karmapa Lama, 215n76; ritual events at the Tenth Karmapa's encampment, 41
Kālacakra (*dus 'khor*), 221n41; Terdak Lingpa's advice to Sangyé Gyatso to visualize rather than construct a physical Kālacakra maṇḍala, 108–9
Kapstein, Matthew T., 195n2, 201n9, 213n23, 223n3
Karmay, Samten G., 203n33
Kashmir (*kasmi ra*), and the societies and cultures surrounding seventeenth-century Tibet, 33
Kathok monastery (*kaHthog dgon*): and Mindröling's traditions, 123–24, 209–10n67; and the six mother monasteries (*ma dgon drug*) of the Nyingma tradition, 123, 209n6
Kāvyādarśa (*snyan ngag me long*) of Daṇḍin: and Dokharwa Tsering Wangyel studies at Mindröling, 153; Pema Gyurmé Gyatso's commentary on, 179–80; Sakya Paṇḍita's's commentary on, 162
khrims gnyis (Two Laws), 13, 90, 198n24. See also Two Systems of Buddhist and worldly expertise (*lugs gnyis* also "Two Laws" *khrims gnyis*)
Kieschnick, John, 1, 299n39
Ko, Dorothy, 58, 202n27
Kongpo (*kong po*): and the grant given to Terdak Lingpa by the Fifth Dalai Lama for Mindröling's founding, 65; Kongpo Dechen Tengon (*kong po bde chen steng dgon*), 80; and Mindröling's institutional network, 82; Mingyur

Peldrön's exile in, 186; and the Tibetan Buddhist world at the time of Mindröling's founding, 107

Lama Jabb, 215n81, 221n38
Lamp of Teachings Catalogue (*O rgyan smin grol gling gi dkar chag*): and the College of Arts and Sciences (*rig gnas slob grwa*), 143; on the first three throne holders, 207n14; funeral services from the Fifth Dalai Lama described in, 76; and Mindröling conceived as a material offering to Terdak Lingpa and his family by the Fifth Dalai Lama, 62–67; Mindröling's branch monasteries listed in, 79–80; Mindröling's first monastic history (*dkar chag*) reproduced in, 217n18; on monks and other students staying at Mindröling, 62, 207n28; and the term "mother monastery" (*ma dgon*), 209n66; and the term "*ti shir*" [*sic*] (imperial preceptor), 211n82
laypeople: donor-practitioners (*chözé* [*chos mdzad*]), 173; and the material support of monastic communities, 7, 67, 148; Mindröling's role in education for the ruling class, 4–5, 7–8, 18, 22–23, 84, 128, 146–49, 152, 158, 171–75, 188, 190; and *slob ma* (student) used as a general term by Terdak Lingpa, 147–48
—and life writing: the life of Dokharwa. See Dokharwa Tsering Wangyel (*mdo mkhar ba tshe ring dbang rgyal*); the life of Doring Tenzin Paljor (*rdo ring pa bstan 'dzin dpal 'byor*, 1721–1792), 152, 219–20n13; and the life of Polhané. See Miwang Polhané Sonam Topgyé (*mi dbang pho lha nas bsod nams stobs rgyas*); and the life of Surkhang Sichö Tseten (*zur khang sri gcod rtse brtan*, 1766–1820), 219–20n13; and Mindröling's significance as a center for culture production beyond a

Songtsen Gampo (*srong btsan sgam po*, 617–650): and the Fifth Dalai Lama, 46; and Gar Tongtsen, 68; and the Kyirong Rangjung Pakba (*skyid grong rang byng 'phags pa*), 44
Sørensen, Per K., 34
Sūtra Vehicle (*mtshan nyid theg pa'i gzhung*), textual system of, 130, 135

tantric Buddhism: interpretation of tantric Buddhist images as "liberating," 198n23; and the Nyö clan, 189; and old Tibetan stereotypes of Nyingma practitioners, 126; students of Development Stage and Complete Stage practices at Mindröling, 130, 137; Tantra Trilogy of Nyö (*gnyos kyi rgyud gsum*) transmitted by Nyö Lotsawa, 34; vows and renunciations of tantric practitioners, 8. *See also* Great Perfection practice; Guhyagharba tantra (*dpal gsang ba snying po'i*); Kālacakra (*dus 'khor*); Nyingma Gyubum (*rnying ma rgyud 'bum, Collected Tantras of the Nyingma School*); Padmasambhava; Vajrasattva Atiyoga Cycle
—consort (*yum*) practice: actual (as opposed to visualized types of), 118, 184, 213n33; and the example of Lélung Jédrung Zhépay Dorjé (*sle lung rje drung bzhad pa'i rdo rje*), 186; and the Fifth Dalai Lama's letter celebrating Terdak Lingpa's secret consort (*gsang yum*), 96–104, 204n55, 213n24; and the Fifth Dalai Lama's letter on the occasion of Terdak Lingpa's enthronement as senior chair of Mindröling, 21, 88, 90–96, 117–19; motivations for, 213n21; social roles of tantric consorts, 58, 206n10. *See also* Ngödrup Pelzom (*dngos grub dpal 'dzom*); Yeshé Tsogyel
Taoist tradition, 32

Tenpé Nyima (*bstan pa'i nyi ma*, 1648–1674), 59, 177, 207n15
Terdak Lingpa Gyurmé Dorjé (*gter bdag gling pa 'gyur med rdo rje*, 1646–1714): and early modern Central Tibet, 1; acrostic letter to aristocrat, 116; identified with Amitāyus, 87f3.1, 95
—biographical details, 54f2.1; brothers discussed in this book. *See* Dharmaśri, Lochen; Orgyan Chökyi Drakpa; Tenpé Nyima; and the catalogue (*dkar chag*) of Mindröling, 70–73; commentaries on teachings related to the *Guhyagharba* tantra compiled and edited by, 123; daughter. *See* Mingyur Peldrön (*mi 'gyur dpal sgron*); death of, 177, 188; egalitarian views of, 222n57; empowerment of Guru Chowang's *Eight Transmitted Precepts* received by, 43; father. *See* Trinlé Lhundrup (*'phrin las lhun grub*); fiery temper and magical flair of, 43–44; as first throne holder (*khri chen*) of Mindröling, 59, 96; inner or religious biography of (*gter bdag gling pa'i nang gi rnam thar*), 73–74, 200n3; letters addressed to Sonam Pelzom (possibly his sister), 75, 110–14; mother. *See* Yumchen Lhadzin Yangchen Dolma (*yum chen lha 'dzin dbyangs can sgrol ma*, 1624–?); prophecy to an officer that he would have a chance to aid Mindröling in the future, 183; public (in the "marketplace" [*khrom*]) appearances of, 50–51; sons. *See* Pema Gyurmé Gyatso; Rinchen Namgyal; wives and consorts (*yum*). *See* Ngödrup Pelzom (*dngos grub dpal 'dzom*); Yönten Dolma (*yon tan sgrol ma*). *See also* Nyö clan (*smyos*)
—Treasure revelations (*terma* [*gter ma*]): appearance at the right time and place of, 16; *The Doctrinal Cycle of the Great Compassionate One as the*

STUDIES OF THE WEATHERHEAD EAST ASIAN INSTITUTE
COLUMBIA UNIVERSITY

Selected Titles

(Complete list at: http://weai.columbia.edu/publications)

The Power of the Brush: Epistolary Practices in Chosŏn Korea, by Hwisang Cho.
University of Washington Press, 2020.

*On Our Own Strength: The Self-Reliant Literary Group and Cosmopolitan Nationalism in
Late Colonial Vietnam,* by Martina Thucnhi Nguyen. University of Hawaii Press, 2020.

A Third Way: The Origins of China's Current Economic Development Strategy,
by Lawrence Chris Reardon. Harvard University Asia Center, 2020.

Disruptions of Daily Life: Japanese Literary Modernism in the World, by Arthur M. Mitchell.
Cornell University Press, 2020.

Recovering Histories: Life and Labor after Heroin in Reform-Era China, by Nicholas Bartlett.
University of California Press, 2020.

Figures of the World: The Naturalist Novel and Transnational Form, by Christopher Laing Hill.
Northwestern University Press, 2020.

Arbiters of Patriotism: Right Wing Scholars in Imperial Japan, by John Person.
University of Hawaii Press, 2020.

The Chinese Revolution on the Tibetan Frontier, by Benno Weiner.
Cornell University Press, 2020.

Making It Count: Statistics and Statecraft in the Early People's Republic of China,
by Arunabh Ghosh. Princeton University Press, 2020.

Tea War: A History of Capitalism in China and India, by Andrew B. Liu.
Yale University Press, 2020.

Revolution Goes East: Imperial Japan and Soviet Communism, by Tatiana Linkhoeva.
Cornell University Press, 2020.

*Vernacular Industrialism in China: Local Innovation and Translated Technologies in
the Making of a Cosmetics Empire, 1900-1940,* by Eugenia Lean.
Columbia University Press, 2020.

Fighting for Virtue: Justice and Politics in Thailand, by Duncan McCargo.
Cornell University Press, 2020.

Beyond the Steppe Frontier: A History of the Sino-Russian Border, by Sören Urbansky.
Princeton University Press, 2020.

Figure 6.3 Verso of cover painting of Terdak Lingpa, Pema Gyurmé Gyatso, and Lochen Dharmaśrī